The dream state m
adventure as Peter ,
ing dream he experienced in 1989 — long before his legendary involvement with time travel and synchronicity. The dream, the details of which are reviewed in this book, climaxed with a white bat manifesting at Dracula's Citadel. Before his sixth journey to Romania, an annual sojourn Peter Moon has made since 2008 in pursuit of the mysteries presented by Radu Cinamar in the Transylvania book series and summarized again within these pages, Peter realizes that the dream was somehow prophetic and had been pulling him to Romania long before his involvement with time travel, Preston Nichols, Dr. David Anderson or even before he began his public writing career.

Now, upon his arrival in Transylvania in 2013 and twenty-four years after the dream, Peter is spontaneously informed that a white bat had unexpectedly just appeared in a cave sacred to the blue goddess Machandi, a tantric dakini who gave Radu Cinamar a "terma" — a "hidden treasure" in the Tibetan tradition. This terma has unleashed a series of apocalyptic events revealing that there are ancient artifacts and mile long tunnels of pure gold beneath Sarmizegetusa, the ancient capital of Transylvania, all of which has commanded the attention of the world's political and military elite as it holds the keys to the destiny of Mankind.

The appearance of the white bat, identified as a totem of Machandi, reveals a remarkable personal story of how the dream state shapes reality as well as the destiny of an entire nation and its new role in the world.

THE WHITE BAT

By Peter Moon

NEW YORK

The White Bat — The Alchemy of Writing
Copyright © 2014 by Peter Moon
First English language printing, June 2014
International copyright laws apply

Typography by Creative Circle Inc.
Cover art by Solomonari, assisted by Teo Maassen
Published by: Sky Books
　　　　　　　Box 769
　　　　　　　Westbury, New York 11590
　　　　　　　email: *skybooks@yahoo.com*
　　　　　　　website: www.skybooksusa.com
　　　　　　　　　　　www.digitalmontauk.com

Library of Congress Cataloging-in-Publication Data

Moon, Peter
　　　The White Bat
　　　　　　224 pages
　　　　　　ISBN 978-1-937859-15-2 (hard copy format only)
　　　　　　ISBN 978-1-937859-16-9 (for ebook format only)
1. Body, Mind, Spirit: Occultism 2. Body, Mind, Spirit: General
Library of Congress Control Number 2014939996

This book is dedicated to Bica Marinik

CONTENTS

INTRODUCTION

The genesis of this book began with a dream I had circa 1989, a few years before I became a published writer. The imagery and import of the dream were so penetrating to my soul that I immediately wrote down the dream and contoured it into the form of a short story. Although this was simply a creative endeavor based upon a dream of great impact, I would learn decades later, and much to my surprise, that it was a portent of the future.

What happened with this particular story, entitled *The White Bat*, provides a window into the concept that the human mind is a time machine, an idea that I first contemplated as a result of the writings of my friend, Dr. David Anderson, a time control scientist. In order to facilitate a better grasp on this concept and how it might work, I will first describe key events in my life, which happened years apart, and how they eventually impacted my consciousness in a way that precipitated the aforesaid dream and resulting story. As for the story itself, *The White Bat* has a very specific theme. It has to do with transmutation of black into white and/or darkness into light, but it all began with my first encounter with the genre we know as horror movies.

Like most of the kids of my generation, I grew up watching occasional horror movies on television, most of which were produced by Universal Studios. The favorite classics included *Frankenstein, Dracula,* and *The Wolfman.* Personally, I found *Dracula* to be the most frightening as he possessed great strength like the others but also cunning intelligence. He lived eternally and knew many subtle techniques for manipulating the human soul.

Whenever one of these movies would air, word would fly through the kid's grapevine in a way that would certainly affect any young person who heard it. It would begin with the older kids, most of whom had already seen the movie, and would filter down to the little ones, like myself, who would learn about *Dracula* or horror for the first time. If you did not watch it, you were chicken. If you did watch it, you were prepared to be afraid. Looking back, it was certainly one of the psychological challenges of childhood. It was also a great deal of fun.

I heard the whispers circulating about *Frankenstein* and *The Wolfman* well before I would ever learn of *Dracula.* This was perhaps because the latter was less frightening on the outside, and the true horror that he inflicted upon others required a more sophisticated understanding than my young mind possessed. In those days, vampires were not marketed with anywhere near the velocity that they are in today's culture.

9

So it was one day that I sat in our living room on an early Saturday evening when the classic movie *Dracula*, starring Bela Lugosi, came on the television. My father happened to be at home and could not help but notice what I was watching. The first scene in the movie *Dracula* is rather gripping. It shows Dracula's English real estate agent, Mr. Renfield, as he arrives at a peasant village. There are mountain props in the background which are supposed to be the Transylvanian Alps. Even though I was just a young boy, my father gave me a knowing look and said words to the effect of, "Don't you know what that is? It is Transylvania and that is where we all come from."

Although I had no idea what my father meant at that time, a fleeting but distinct discussion occurred at the first commercial break. My grandfather had grown up under the reign of the Austrian-Hungarian Empire, prior to World War I. He was fascinated with history and passed his books as well as his knowledge to my father. While World War I effectively broke up the Austrian-Hungarian Empire, which was its purpose, Transylvania had already been relegated to the newly created country of Romania as a result of the Crimean War. Prior to that, Transylvania was under the territorial domain of Hungary. Our discussion about Transylvania and the Austrian-Hungarian Empire, however, somehow led me to a long enduring misunderstanding that Transylvania was in Hungary as opposed to Romania.

Quite oddly, it was just prior to the writing of *The White Bat* when I happened to read an article in the *New York Times* stating that Transylvania was in Romania, not Hungary. I was rather flabbergasted that I, who did not try to make a habit out of being ignorant about world matters, had been so firmly entrenched with a false datum. Perhaps this revelation of truth regarding Transylvania's territoriality, courtesy of the *New York Times*, is what inspired the dream that led to me writing *The White Bat*. I do not know. It is not always easy to ascertain the precise significance of the hidden aspects of the subconscious. Only years later would I eventually learn some of the true historical significance of our ancestors originating from Transylvania. By "our" I am not referring only to my family but rather to most of the human race and not to any particular nationality, ethnicity or race.

For those of you who have already followed my writing, you already know that Transylvania has deeply influenced my life and soul journey. The events presented here are some of the seeds that precipitated the manifestation of that amazing territory into my life. One of these included the manifestation of one of my greatest childhood fears: Count Dracula.

When I was twelve, I threw up after a little league baseball game and became so ill that I could not consume any beverage or food for a week. During my sleep, I was tortured by either nightmares or the probing of my brain by an exterior source. I cannot tell you which, but it is noteworthy that it occurred at the onset of puberty. It felt like all the data in my head was inherently recorded on old-fashioned tape reels and that someone was ransacking it to download all of it. The reels started and stopped in exactly the same way that old computers used to work. At some point during that week, I awoke to see something in my bedroom closet. The sliding door of the closet was open, and I could see, lurking amongst my hanging clothes, a full visual image of the movie version of Count Dracula as portrayed by Bela Lugosi. My body and mind were both overwhelmed with fear. I screamed out so loud that my father came in to see what was the matter. It was over as quick as it had happened, but I learned to sleep with the closet door shut after that experience. Later, I would attribute this hallucination to a lack of B vitamins compounded by taking in virtually no nutrition during my illness. All in all, this incident suggested that Dracula was one of my greatest fears.

The next key event that precipitated the writing of this story was not unpleasant at all. It occurred while I was reading the novel *2001: A Space Odyssey* by Arthur C. Clarke. This was in July of 1969 during the time of the Apollo 11 moon landing. In that novel, David Bowman has left the mothership in his space pod and is moving through space and into a monolith on Iapetus, a large moon of Saturn. As Bowman approaches the monolith, it manifests as a star gate and he goes through, seeing stars in almost every direction. Then, he experiences what registered in my own mind as something extremely novel and exhilarating. The stars and the sky changed. Instead of seeing white stars in a dark sky, he was witnessing dark stars in a milky white sky. For whatever reason under the sun, this one little incident woke up my entire soul. It was an inversion, a reversal. Although I have never really thought about it until writing these words down at this moment, Bowman goes through a morphogenetic transmutation of the highest order. He is processed, enlightened, put in touch with his most naturally divine aspects, and returned to earth as a star seed. While I was certainly inspired by what happened to David Bowman, most of the exhilaration I experienced while reading that passage occurred at the precise point where the colors of the stars and sky reversed themselves. To this day, I have never forgotten that moment. It was something I have taken with me.

Less than two months later after reading *2001: A Space Odyssey*, I began my initiation as a writer by choosing to take a course in creative writing during my junior year of high school. The first thing we learned in that class, from a very lovely teacher named Hilde Clark, was to keep a journal so as to tap into the stream of consciousness. This represents the collective consciousness, including the unconscious, of life itself. Nowadays, it might be better expressed as the continuous stream of thoughts, data, etc. emanating from the morphogenetic grid. The idea was to tap into the stream with your journal and use that as a springboard for more linear types of writing that might include a short story, poetry or even a novel.

Ms. Clark told me that I was by far the most prolific of any of her students, but it was mostly journal writing that I did in that class. My first, best, and only real complete story was about an inspired leader who was a very wise man who used his knowledge of astrology and a solar eclipse to stun the plebeian folk and thus gain an exalted reputation as a messiah. He was wiser than all of them and had good intentions but found it expedient, as did his colleagues or disciples, to make them think he was far more adept than he actually was. Besides that story, and often written within the contents of the journal itself, there were other attempts at writing different stories, but none of them developed into a completed form or anything that I think is worthy of mention. The class ended after a semester, but I kept the journal and used it sporadically, just not too often.

At some point after finishing the class in creative writing, I read *Dracula* by Bram Stoker. After having seen different movies that borrowed from that book, I wanted to see what the original myth was all about. As far as dramatic fiction goes, it was one of the best books I have ever read as far as creating memorable dramatic suspense that held my attention so much that I still remember it to this day. I recall feeling quite frantic when Van Helsing insists to Lucy's mother that, no matter what, she must not allow Lucy to remove the garland of garlic around her neck. At that point, Lucy had been almost sucked dry of blood from Dracula, and she could not take another attack without becoming a full-fledged vampire herself. After insisting up and down and getting the mother's pledge not to remove the garland, Van Helsing warns her again and musters enough courage to leave Lucy alone. In almost no time at all, Lucy proceeds to talk the inept woman out of doing her duty. The mother's will is easily overcome, the garland is removed, and Lucy is easily overcome by the vampire. I bring this vignette from the book to view because it is so demonstrative of how damaging people's actions can be when they do not recognize the potential for evil.

What was most striking to me about *Dracula*, however, was the beginning of the book when it went into some detail about the vampire's paranormal powers. The range of these was far greater than what I had understood from the movie; and although this was literary fiction, there was something about the vampire's command of life itself, albeit the dark side of life, that rang true on some level of my being. While I had neither particularly believed in or experienced the paranormal to any significant extent in my life up to that point, my consciousness gave it some degree of life. Although I was not seduced by or even desirous of these powers, I had a blinding realization. What if the character in the book, who was as powerful as any creature you might imagine, sought to change his nature and utilize his powers for good instead of evil? It occurred to me that neither he nor most anyone else would have thought about that. I certainly did, and even though the book was fiction, the idea never left me. While the experience of the sky and stars from *2001* was based upon visualization in my imagination, this realization about Dracula had more to do with the properties of just being sentient. *2001* and *Dracula* were two different doorways or approaches to the idea that the darkness could be deliberately changed to light.

After reading *Dracula* and sporadically making entries into my journal, I can recall a particularly poignant moment in my efforts as a writer. An idea entered my mind that was so vibrant that I took a piece of white paper, placed it carefully into my typewriter, and typed out a paragraph, choosing every word very carefully. In a figurative sense, I was writing it in blood. The passage had that much conviction in my mind. It was about a film crew travelling to *Transylvania*, but I believed the country to be Hungary and not Romania. The film crew was out in the boonies and was riding in a large cart of some sort. They were beyond the region where automobile friendly roads might be. For whatever reason, however, I could not get past the first paragraph. The story was never developed or even worked upon. I kept the paper with the neatly typed paragraph for as long as I kept my possessions in that house. Although it was an aborted project, I never forgot the effort or the vision that I tried to convey in that short paragraph.

Nearly two decades later, when I would read the aforementioned article in the *New York Times* about Transylvania being in Romania and not Hungary, I recalled the errant passage in that short paragraph I had written so long ago. I do not like to be wrong. While I do not remember that time period specifically, it was probably that article and the memory of my long ago aborted short story that incited my imagination to generate a dream that would result in *The White Bat*, the story you are about to read. Before you read the story and the magical or mysterious manifestations that seemed to ensue from it, however, I want to share with you that I also intend to use this book as a platform to respond as positively and efficiently as possible to various inquiries that have been made to me, particularly in recent times, with regard to the nature of the method by which I write

There is no question that my writing style is unique. When the topics I am writing about are not necessarily too unique in themselves, my approach to these subjects is often, if not usually, rather unorthodox. The first thing I would tell you with regard to this approach is that it has everything to do with individuality and creativity. When one chooses a path of either creativity or individuality, one is going to distance themselves immediately from the herd and the expected approval mechanisms of society and its institutions. While the preceding statement is true, it is not really an answer that is going to be too helpful beyond the rather obvious nature of what has been stated.

In this book, *The While Bat: The Alchemy of Writing*, I will be examining creativity and writing while at the same time integrating a remarkable story, based upon a dream, that reaches into the paranormal aspects of existence which, at the same time, are linked to the grounded and practical realities of my daily life. For any writing to be effective, it has to have a pragmatic effect on someone. Ideally, the effect will be a positive one for both the author and the reader

While you will get a glimpse into what I term the alchemical process of my own writing style as you read this book, I am also including some very cogent practical advice on how you can utilize the writing process to facilitate your own personal alchemy. By alchemy, I am referring to the process by which base metals (representing lower consciousness) can be transmuted into gold (representing higher consciousness). Accordingly, I would advise you to take notes while reading this book. That begins with a pen, note pad or a computer. Alchemy is about doing and actualization. Reading too often results only in realization. Realization is nice, but it does not necessitate action. I fully realize that many of you reading this book read for enjoyment or curiosity and will not be inclined to put the effort into either writing down your impressions or even getting up to get a pen and paper. That is fine. You can still read the book without doing so, but as you continue reading, you might regret later that you did not do so. In other words, you might later on find yourself compelled to start writing by the nature of what I am describing. This is, after all, a magical text. It is designed so that you might find the magic in yourself, and this involves self-expression: writing.

Writing creates change, both internally and externally, and change is an inherent component in the structure of the universe. You are being invited to embrace it and harness it to your advantage. It is my intention that this book will help you to do just that. And remember, everything written in it was generated by a dream. Accordingly, it might be a good idea to use the paper and pen to note any dreams that you might have while reading these pages. Treat it as the beginning of a journey, your journey into your own mind and beyond.

Peter Moon
Long Island, New York
February 13, 2013

CHAPTER ONE

THE WHITE BAT

Transylvania is an odd place to strangers.

While suffering a bumpy ride on an unpaved road in an old car, I was stunned by the polished beauty of the woods. The dark greens were stimulating yet very forbidding. In the background, the Carpathian Mountains were even more ominous.

As I looked into the forest, it seemed to look back. I found this unsettling to say the least, whereupon I began to miss the comfort of the quaint inn I had stayed in the night before. Instinctively and immediately noticing my discomfort, the driver looked at me directly.

"Ah, you see the forest," he said. "It penetrates the soul does it not? Like a lance piercing a shield. The trick is to take down the shield. Then there is nothing to pierce."

He said nothing more and we remained quiet. Already agitated, I was even more unnerved by his innate comprehension of my uneasiness. Although I am ashamed to admit it, I became afraid. Jumping into a state of mind that was becoming increasingly paranoid, the fear in my mind began to play tricks on me. I began to think of the movie *Dracula* and how the coach driver was Dracula himself. I could not help but think if this was the case with the driver. Of course, this could not be. Although I did not discuss it with him, it was obvious to me that he was a gypsy. I knew for a fact the driver had a regular tourist business and was well known at the hotel. Even so, we were headed toward Poienari Citadel, the fortress that Vlad Tepes effectively used to keep out invaders. Who wouldn't have a tinge of fear at the thought of that and the legends that had been spawned over the centuries? I decided that I could not, however, let my paranoia run any further. Remembering what I had learned in psychology, I took stock of the fact that communication has a tendency to make fears dissipate. I decided to strike up some conversation with this dark-haired, dark-eyed gypsy.

"Tell me, do you come out here often with tourists?" I asked.

"In the day time, yes," he laughed, "but not in the evening."

It was now half an hour before dusk.

"Tell me, why do you really come here?" he asked me.

I began to ask myself the same question, but it was no time to turn back. It was not in my character to prove to myself that I was a chicken, particularly over what I knew was just a little mind-generated fear. I decided to answer the driver.

"I met an old man from your country when I was in New York. He told me I would discover things that I thought were impossible."

The driver looked at me slightly suspiciously.

"What do you want to do with this discovery?" he said.

"I'm a writer," I replied. "I like to discover things and write about them."

"Yes, I see," he said.

As a writer, I consider that it is my first principle to break the truth and report it as I see it. It was my conviction to this that led me to the pursuit of vampires and the grandiose legend erected around Dracula.

Ground-breaking phenomena with UFOs, alien abductions and clairvoyant mediums had already been established. But what of vampires? Too little scientific research had been done in this area. Many stories of medically imbalanced persons craving blood had been documented several times over, but were these people real vampires in the traditional sense? Was there something more sinister and supernatural behind these persons?

I believed not, but I also did not know.

Perhaps it was my destiny one evening when I went to a night club and met an older man who had emigrated from Romania to America. Taverns and bars are an excellent source of fodder for a writer, and this case proved to be no exception.

He was a short man with white hair. I noticed right away that he was from a different land. When he spoke, I asked about his accent and he revealed that he was Romanian. As I had always been a fan of the old *Dracula* movies, I could not help asking him about the legends of Transylvania and what he thought about them. I really did not know what to expect as an answer, but he looked at me very directly.

"A legend?" he questioned. "Yes, I suppose it is a legend."

I found his answer perplexing.

"Please explain," I implored.

"What is a legend but a blend of facts and myth?" he asked rhetorically. "In my culture, the legends of vampires have abounded as long as anyone can remember. As your country is steeped in the tradition of freedom and capitalism, so is my country steeped in the tradition of spirits that thrive on the life blood of others. It runs deep in our blood. My people are an elemental people, close to nature, uncomplicated by technology. A far cry from your world."

I was personally fascinated by his different cultural views, and I knew right away that I wanted to know and understand more of his culture. I still did not take the vampire question too seriously, but I was definitely interested in what he had to say about vampires.

"Does the average person in Transylvania believe in vampires?" I asked. I was incredulous.

"For those who know, it is taken for granted and generally not spoken about," he answered.

"But, if they really believe in this sort of thing, doesn't the fear or excitement generate conversation?"

"No. In the same way you have, time after time, many unsolved murders in the same areas of New York, you do not talk obsessively about them. In fact, reporters cease to report certain routine murders as public outrages. In the same way, my people do not tread where they know they should not. They keep to themselves. And remember this, my friend, to speak of the vampire is to give credence to the vampire. It will also rankle his attention."

"Yes," I replied, "but have you ever seen a vampire?"

"Ah-ha," he laughed. "That is not unlike asking me if I have ever seen a naked woman. To answer your question: only when they wanted me to see them. But, I have no proof for you myself. I only know what I sense. When I have sensed them, I have filled my thoughts with prayer. It is not something I want proof of."

I was genuinely interested in his story, and I was curious if what he was saying could be substantiated, even from just a cultural perspective.

"Do you know where I could perhaps find some proof?" I asked.

"Oh, but there are many stories, both in print and by word of mouth, just like UFOs in your country. It took thousands of reported sightings before most people actually began to believe them, but they are there."

"Do you mean that if I were to go to Transylvania and check the legends and literature that I could find substantiation of what you say and possibly produce tangible evidence?"

I was now incredulous and felt I was holding a very live wire for a good story. I knew the feeling when I had a live wire, and this one was on the mark.

"Yes," he nodded.

"But," I thought out loud, "there are many rich legends of vampires in Transylvania, but I am not talking about the different variations of Hollywood movies. I am talking about indications and evidence suggesting there is truth behind the legends, and if these experiences are so prevalent, or at least mentioned from time to time, why have they not been pursued previously?"

"It is not a comfortable subject," he replied. "Besides, who would believe it? The people there don't care, and the people here won't buy it. Even if you make a headline story, it will tend to be forgotten with the next headline. But I tell you, I must go now. It has been nice talking to you."

When the old man left, I thought about it and wrestled with the idea. I was confident that by travelling to Transylvania, I could come up with a plausible story line even if this man's data was bogus. A fictional format could work just as well. In a worst case scenario, I could "verify" that there was no evidence whatsoever of vampires. Somehow, I doubted this would be the case. I figured that there would at least be a watered-down version to report. There was always the old historical Count Dracula to rehash as well.

Little did I know how unusual things would turn out to be. And one thing I did indeed learn. The more I thought about all this, the more I believed that there was something out there to reconcile with. In my estimation, the legend had some teeth, and I wanted some answers.

As I reflected upon the events and circumstances that had drawn me to this foreign and very remote land, the driver continued on through the woods towards Poeinari Citadel, the fortress in the mountain that had been built by the prisoners of Count Dracula and whom he later impaled. Some say that the spirit of Count Dracula is rumored to dwell at Poeinari Citadel. While the driver was slow and cautious to avoid the bumps, rocks, and holes in the road, I began to sense the emotional devastation and trauma that had taken place in this region so many centuries ago. The only other time I had felt like this was on a battlefield from the Civil War. Whatever the truth of the legends, it was a historical fact that thousands upon thousand of soldiers had died here, many of them being impaled. This was enough horror in itself. I did not need vampires.

The driver eventually parked his car. For a price, I had arranged for him to camp with me at some point near the base of the final ascent to the citadel. It would be a half hour uphill walk to finally reach it. Before long, the final twinkle of dusk had receded and brilliant stars towered in the black sky.

"Twinkles," I thought out loud to myself. "Nothingness but twinkles."

The gypsy made a fire and set up camp. We were not too far away from the castle but not too close either. We ate dried beef and drank a garlic tea which he said would help prevent attacks from evil spirits. As we sat and ate, I began to feel a bit of comfort. The fire warmed me. My comfort, however, was rather short-lived. Once again, the gypsy looked at me very directly. This in itself got my nerves rattling again. His eyes were quite piercing.

"If you go to the fortress at night, you will go alone."

This shocked me even though what he said had already been clearly stated by him at the outset of our journey. His confirmation of our agreement was nevertheless more than I wanted to hear. On another level, I felt lucky that I was at least able to camp close enough so that I could make a midnight ascent to the citadel. The pictures of the citadel I had seen had shown it to be forbidding and in disrepair. For some reason, however, it did not strike the terror in me that walking up through the steep mountain forest did. Even though the gypsy had shocked me with his comment, I still had plenty of reserve and felt that I could break through my current discomfort into a state of mind that was more brave and challenging. I decided to make a jaunt for it and just get the experience over with. Rising to a standing position, I spoke to the gypsy.

"Excuse me now, please. I'm going to get my flashlight and walk towards the citadel."

No sooner had I announced my intentions than the gypsy stood up and grabbed my arm in restraint.

"Wait, my friend. You are much safer in the waning hours of the night. By that time, the hungry spirits will have fed themselves and hunger not for your blood. Wait."

I am not sure whether I was responding to his insistence or his logic, but I heeded his advice. We had some more tea and he entertained me with stories before we slept. Later in the evening, I set the alarm on my digital watch for 4:00 A.M. and tried to get to sleep. Keeping my eyes shut very tight, I blocked out my fears as much as I could. I was soon asleep.

Waking to the sound of light beeps emanating from my digital watch, I let all twenty beeps run their course rather than shutting it off. The sound of civilized noise comforted me somewhat. I was also halfheartedly hoping it would wake the gypsy. At least he was still there and had not gone off to shape-shift into a fabulous monster.

Wanting to get this over with as fast as possible, I grabbed my coat and flashlight and began to walk as fast as I reasonably could up the path to the citadel. The walk was arduous and seemed as if it was never going to end. The forest had a wild feel to it, and I definitely found it intimidating. Eventually, I could see the bright rays of the moon shining on the castle. Although the citadel had a vacant and haunted look to it, it did not strike the terror in me that the wild forest did. Feeling safety in the light, I walked toward it. Finally, upon reaching Poenari Citadel, I turned around to notice that my path back to camp was not at all clear in the dark. A bothersome worry, I contemplated remaining under the moonlight, protected from the wind by the castle wall, until daybreak. Then, I could easily find my way "home" to the camp. It was quite clear that I might get lost if I tried to find my way back in the dark.

Before I could make any further conclusions or plans, I was suddenly struck by fear when I heard a wolf begin to howl in the distance. As soon as I recovered from the shock, another wolf — this one much too close for comfort — howled in return. My fear was now turning into terror. Trying to secure my own safety, I jumped and struggled to climb up to a promenade that circled the castle walls. There were some ancient steps, but they had long since crumbled. As far as wild animals were concerned, I felt a lot safer from this vantage point.

To hell with vampires I thought! The wild is plain scary enough! At this point, I reached a mental calm and what psychologists like to call abnormal perception. I was no longer afraid. I felt incredibly light. I had studied where a high volume of terror can do one of two things. It can shock a person into a permanent or temporary catatonia, or it can knock a person into a state of altered or super-consciousness. This was how I felt.

I then heard a small army of bats fly inward to the citadel. Instead of feeling afraid, I could feel their rhythm. I tried to follow their path, but they were quick and there were too many corridors.

I walked until I heard noises. They were not the kind of noises one would normally hear, but they were the noises of what were similar to the sighs and breaths of a living human being. The sounds were very subtle and almost inaudible. First, I heard the sounds of what would be like normal inhalation and exhalation. Then, the sounds sounded a trifle sensitive and sensuous in nature. Again, I could feel their rhythm. It was not unpleasant. I followed the sounds, trying to find their source. Finding the sounds emanating from a small opening in the citadel, I climbed through and used the flashlight to negotiate some thin corridors. Pursuing these sounds, and before I was too taken in by them, I began to realize that what I was hearing were actually the sounds of seduction. As soon as I thought about this, it occurred to me that these sounds were possibly meant to seduce me into the fold of vampires. Perhaps my increased mental acumen was part of the same trap.

Then it dawned on me! I had tapped into the psychic energy of the vampire by osmosis. I had always been fascinated by the extreme supernatural ability and affected elegance of Dracula in the vampire stories. I always thought that he would be a very grand and powerful character if he would rid himself of his evil agenda. It was now up to me to keep myself from being seduced into this nest of evil. Intuitively, I felt that the energy I was getting from him was opening up my own closed doors of perception.

No sooner had I completed the above thought than I came to an open balcony that overlooked a palace drawing room. Down below was a small throng of female vampires writhing in expectation, hoping to be fulfilled. It reminded me of the feeding frenzy of sharks, only it was much more subdued and intangible. On the whole, the vampires were beautiful and not the motley savage creatures I had seen in some horror movies. All had a transparent ghost-like quality. Some were more sharply defined than others. They all writhed in expectation of fulfillment.

I then thought about the wisdom that the gypsy had shared with me. Go in the morning, he had said. That way they will be fed. He was right as far as I could see. None of them appeared to be hungry for blood, at least for the moment. For all I could tell, I had gone unnoticed. They were all preoccupied with their own ritual.

At this point, a huge bat flew into the room. I could tell without a second thought that it was Count Dracula himself. He transformed into human shape and kept the broad wings of his cape extended. The frenetic writhing of the females now began to pick up in pitch. They began to swim up in the air and around him like ghosts. They appeared much more vaporized and swam under him, around him and through his legs. He stood still. His eyes and his body radiated strong energy. It appeared to be energy that they lived off of. Shrieking sounds of euphoria replaced the panting of desire.

It was no longer a mystery to me. I was watching an orgy of spirits, surrounding a core of very live energy. I did notice at the outskirts of the radiant orb that some of the apparitions were being blocked out, creating a slight turbulence.

Then, one of the spirits on the outside appeared to splice off from the orb. It came straight towards me. As it came closer, its definitions became clearer and much more female. I was now being confronted by a most enticing female apparition. Before I could think or resist, I was overcome by a magnetic force that concentrated on me.

Black hair, red lips and an almost white face. Suspending herself before me, she stood in a gown of gossamer, thrusting it open to reveal pearl-white breasts, pining with desire. I could now feel a pulsating energy enveloping me. But instead of physical contact, the apparition moved toward me like a soft magnet. Feeling sensual urgings, there was no opportunity to respond to them. The apparition began to move through me, very slowly, but convincingly. As she reached midway through me, I began to feel a climaxing sensation, only this was a climaxing sensation of the spirit and not the body. We both began to shake; and almost just as suddenly, she passed through my body and it was over.

I had not lost an ounce of my own consciousness, but I was surprised by what had happened. I looked behind me and saw the apparition soar into the sky. It turned into a bat and flew back through the balcony and back to the spectacle below. As she reached the swirling mass, it began to disperse. Everyone was now calmer and the magnetism was dying down. Dracula, however, looked up in my direction. He did not look like he was happy.

Perhaps I had violated his territory, or perhaps he had read the mind of the apparition and knew where I was. I did not know, but I quickly ran off of the balcony, through the corridors and outside again. Moving quickly down the promenade, it did not take me long to part from the citadel altogether.

Realizing that I could make a fast downhill run back to the camp with the gypsy, I quickly headed in the direction of the forest. Before I could enter, however, I saw the same giant bat that I knew was Dracula. It was waiting for me at the exact point where the forest started, as if he knew my plan of escape. To my good fortune, and before I could think about being afraid, I noticed that it was now daybreak. I felt strong and could hear the screeching of bats flying into the citadel. The giant bat then transformed into a wolf and began to run back towards the castle. I ran after it at full pace. As soon as I could see that it could clearly outrun me and was starting to speed up, I dived, reaching for its hooves. As I grabbed both hooves, they began to disintegrate in my very hands. The wolf had transformed into a purely white bat that began to hover over my prone body. As I began to rise, the white bat transformed once more, only this time it turned into the shape of a man. I could not believe what I was seeing. It was clearly the same character I had identified as Dracula minutes before, only this time he was dressed in a brilliant white suit and cape.

As I stood there stupefied, he looked elegant and bowed gracefully.

"Good morning," he said.

"What has happened?" I asked. "Why are you now dressed in white?"

He laughed and said, "I always dress in white."

"Who are you?"

"I am Dracula, only I am in white."

"Why do you wear white?" I asked.

"I am White Dracula," he replied.

"You're not Count Dracula then?" I wondered.

"Oh, yes. But not the same Dracula you think of. I am the white force within."

I was still confused. Apparently, he could see that and he continued.

"You may have been surprised no doubt to find spirits haunting this citadel. Many people were killed here; but tonight, you have witnessed something that few will either have the chance or nerve to see. You have come out with your life, and this makes you unique."

"So," I stammered, "you have no design to kill me?"

"Of course not," he laughed. "I am a white force. I am good and I congratulate you on last night."

"But many people visit here and come back alive," I responded.

"Yes, but they do not enter the realm where they can see me. This requires an ability that all men possess but do not utilize. It is rare."

"You are teaching me that Dracula is not evil?"

"I mean to say that Dracula is more than a dark force. I am the white faction, and I promote good and limit evil, not unlike a guardian angel. Many of the souls who died here linger, waiting for reconciliation. They were all killed brutally, but it was not an accident that they had this experience. It was in return for something they themselves had done."

"Karma?" I asked.

"Yes," he nodded. "The dark version of who I am savagely killed them, but it was not me. I am here to help them reconcile their fate and to correct their ill-conceived behavior. "

"But why have we not heard of you before?" I asked.

"Because I did not exist until this very moment," he said.

"Where did you come from?"

"I am a reflection of your soul. If you did not make the trip, however, you would never have seen me."

I was a bit confused. Setting out looking to prove whether or not vampires existed, I came out with an experience that was completely different.

"Do you not think," he continued, "that if Dracula was all black and truly a king of the vampires that he would not have consumed the entire Earth and created vast colonies of vampires?"

"I never looked at it that way," I replied. "I wasn't even too sure that vampires existed before tonight. But, I'd always wondered why they could never take over the entire world."

"Checks and balances, my friend," he laughed. "Even the dark and white forces must bow to the will of mother nature, for she is supreme."

Upon completing his sentence, he extended his cape, changed back into a white bat and flew off.

I made my way back to the camp in the early daylight of dawn. As I walked, I thought about what I might write about. As far as what I had experienced thus far, there was no scientific proof I could bring back with me. It did not matter to me, however, for I had experienced something far greater. I had walked into a forbidden territory that virtually no one was allowed to see. That was at least what my so-called "guardian angel" was trying to tell me. This gave me a new authority, but I also realized it was an authority that most people would not recognize. Somehow, and in some way, I would have to reconcile what had happened and choose the best possible method by which to write about it.

When I was most of the way down the mountain from the citadel, I looked at my digital watch and saw that it was 5:45 A.M.. As it had been a short night on sleep, and I was a little tired, I wanted to get as much sleep as possible before the gypsy was going to wake up. When I reached the campsite, I immediately got inside of my sleeping bag and quickly fell asleep.

I soon woke up to the pleasant aroma of bacon cooking in a frying pan. Twisting my neck, I saw the gypsy making breakfast. It was sunny and a beautiful morning. I looked at my watch to find out the time, but it was not on my wrist. Beginning to scavenge, I looked in my bag and looked around the area but could not find it. When the gypsy noticed me, he left his frying pan and approached.

"Looking for this?" he said, smiling as he lifted my watch out of his pocket.

"Yes!" I said. "Why do you have my watch?"

"As soon as you went to bed last night, I took it from your wrist after you fell sound asleep. You are my responsibility on this adventure, and I did not deem it wise for you travel alone at night."

I was confused. Having just looked at my watch before I went to sleep, what he said made no sense. He could not have removed my watch last night.

"Did you dream?" he asked.

His question confused me even more. What was he saying and why was he saying it? I wanted to know how my watch had ended up in his pocket. Then, it came to me as I began to wake up a little more.

"Wait," I said. "I just has an incredible experience. I was headed down the mountain and was looking at my watch. What time is it now?"

"Eight-thirty," he replied.

"If you took my watch off last night and not this morning, then I must have had some incredible dream."

"That is what I hoped would happen," said the gypsy. "The tea we drank last night is particularly good for dreaming."

My mind was now working quickly as I reconciled my current situation from what I had supposedly been dreaming the night before. It all seemed so real. In any event, it did not matter whether it was "real" or not. I knew that I had an experience that I could write about. My story was not only a unique one but was far more than I had hoped to experience. It did not matter whether it was fiction or nonfiction.

"So, you survived the night," the gypsy said, laughing.

"I didn't only survive it. I emerged from it," I replied.

As we ate breakfast, I told him my story and his eyes darted, revealing a sharp interest in what I said. It was clear to me that my experience was equally unique and strange from his perspective. The more I talked, the more I felt a feeling of mutual respect generating from him. The way he responded to me, I began to feel that I was one of very few people who could walk on his ground with authority.

After we finished breakfast, I went to roll up my sleeping bag and gather my belongings. It was time to think about how I would put down my experience on paper.

THE END

CHAPTER TWO

FUNDAMENTALS

During the time you were reading the previous story, *The White Bat*, it is more than likely that you had different impressions. Hopefully, your mind was excited in a creative way. Using your note pad, I invite you to write down the impressions that you had. This is an important step. In Chapter Three, I will discuss how writing down the impressions of my own dream not only transformed into the story you have just read but also served as a platform for a series of experiences that not only evolved into a writing and publishing career but continue to swirl around my life to this day. It should be noted that this process is based upon actually writing down the thoughts that come into your mind whether it be from your dreams, fantasies, or experiences in life.

In writing down your impressions of this story, they could be creative or simply just fact related. Write all of them down. It might have to do with some aspect of history you want to investigate or it might have to do with a story you want to tell or just something that you would like to communicate. You can make your notes either in an abstract form or in as much detail as you like. There are no rules. The point here is to engage and tap into your own creative process. This is the most important step in writing or living. You want to build a conduit to the creative source inside of you. As you develop, it can be cultivated and refined. The first step, however, is to WRITE IT DOWN, even if it is only a rough draft. It does not matter whether you want to be a writer or not. This process creates a bridge between your creative mind or muse and the physical plane. Do not neglect this as it has more implications than just cultivating your own writing skill. I am referring to your own personal psychology. Any writing that you do is an expression of your own inner psychology. Whether you are going to be a writer in any socially significant capacity or not, this activity also serves as a catalyst for the alchemical process which is to transform the base to the noble. Accordingly, we will now examine some key concepts with regards to psychology and the process of writing.

Quite literally, psychology means "the study of the psyche." Any writer should know something about psychology, if only the state of mind of his prospective readers and how they will respond to what he or she has written. It would also behoove a writer to also take one step further and do his best to become as expert as he or she can in the subject of psychology. If becoming an expert in psychology seems intimidating to you, at least make a goal to become fluid and competent with the subject. A good start in this direction is to examine the etymology of the word *psyche*.

> **psyche (n.)** 1640s, "animating spirit," from Latin *psyche*, from Greek *psykhe* "the soul, mind, spirit, breath, life, the invisible animating principle or entity which occupies and directs the

physical body" (personified as Psyke, the lover of Eros), akin to *psykhein* "to blow, cool," from PIE root **bhes*- "to blow" (cf. Sanskrit *bhas-*). The word had extensive sense development in Platonic philosophy and Jewish-influenced theological writing of St. Paul. In English, psychological sense is from 1910.

When we consider that the psyche is the animating spirit of life, it becomes obvious that when a writer is expressing his own personal psychology through whatever literary vehicle he chooses, he is also animating life or at least a particular niche or aspect of life itself. It is self-reflective. A writer is writing about life. If you want to take your journey as a writer one step further and explore the above themes, it is easy to get lost in the various texts that have been written on the subjects of psychology, life, and philosophy. While some of these texts might have some value to you, it is easiest to reduce life and human psychology to their lowest common denominator, and this would be the study of archetypes. Let us first examine the definition.

archetype (n.)
"original pattern from which copies are made," 1540s, from Latin *archetypum*, from Greek *arkhetypon* "pattern, model, figure on a seal," neuter of adjective *arkhetypos* "first-moulded," from *arkhe-* "first" (see *archon*) + *typos* "model, type, blow, mark of a blow" (see *type*). Jungian psychology sense of "pervasive idea or image from the collective unconscious" is from 1919.

Carl Jung was a famous psychologist who dedicated much of his work towards a study of archetypes. You can read his work for further information, much of which was based upon the Tarot and/or Tree of Life. The schematic for the Tree of Life is actually based upon the structure of DNA. Jung also interpreted the Chinese book known as the *I Ching* or *Book of Changes*. This book also consists of archetypes, but it is a different lens than Western versions of the Tarot or Tree of Life. While the *I Ching* is also imitative of DNA, it is also suggestive of computer code in that it deals with a binary system. Whereas a computer code deals with binary digits consisting of *1's* and *0's*, the *I Ching* utilizes lines and broken lines. Whether anyone wants to admit it or not, all religions, philosophies, and mythologies are based upon or are reflexive of the Tree of Life. There is really a very simple reason for this. Religion, philosophy, and mythology are all based upon life, and life, at least that which is physically animated, is based upon DNA; hence, the Tree of Life.

In addition to learning the basics of psychology, it also behooves a writer to grasp and utilize the etymologies of two other words that are the key elements of a writer's stock in trade: *ideas* and *words*.

idea (n.)
late 14c., "archetype of a thing in the mind of God; Platonic 'idea,'" from Latin *idea* "idea," and in Platonic philosophy "archetype," from Greek *idea* "ideal prototype," literally "the look of a thing (as opposed to the reality); form; kind, sort, nature," from *idein* "to see," from PIE *wid-es-ya-*, suffixed form of root *weid-* "to see" (see *vision*). Sense of "result of thinking" first recorded 1640s.

word (n.)
Old English *word* "speech, talk, utterance, word," from Proto-Germanic *wurdan* (cf. Old Saxon, Old Frisian *word*, Dutch *woord*, Old High German, German *wort*, Old Norse *orð*, Gothic *waurd*), from PIE *were-* "speak, say" (see *verb*).

In practical life, words and ideas tend to go hand-in-hand, but experience will tell you that this is not always the case. Everyone has encountered double-speak or instances when words seem to mean one thing but really mean another. This is the realm of deceit such as is witnessed with false advertising or fine print and craftily misleading phrases in legal contracts. When you study the original word meanings of words, it becomes rather obvious that words are patterned after or evolve from ideas, the latter being a purer essence than what is being described.

It is also noteworthy that the word *archetype* has been defined as something emanating from the mind of God. *God* is a very curious word as it is has been used in language, and this curiosity has not gone unnoticed by religions who pretty much unilaterally state that whatever word is used to describe God is not really an accurate one. While *God* always refers to the Creator of universal reality, modern definitions of the word all clearly state or directly imply that either a condition of worship or rulership applies. In other words, it is not enough that God created the world, but He must also be revered and worshipped for this act. If you are not willing to buckle under to that, you have to at least acknowledge his rulership or authority. There is no question that the word *God* has been defined in such a way that the observer is pigeon-holed with regard to how he should view God. If God is viewed through this construct, we are but agents working upon his easel if we are not the pigment and brushes themselves.

None of this is meant to suggest that a writer should become immersed in theology. What is important, however, is that one realize that one is embarking on a creative enterprise. Whereas God is deemed to be the Creator of the Universe, an author is the creator of the world that they write about whether it is fiction or non-fiction. The word *author* derives from the Latin *auctorem* which means "enlarger, founder, master, leader," literally "one who causes to grow." This not only means creating the world you write about but also includes seeding your audience and contouring your writing so that it has application in the real world. While this is not an absolute requisite, it is important if you want people to pay attention to your work. It is also quite suitable to write for your own selfish purposes if that is your particular desire.

First and foremost, a writer is going to concern himself with words and ideas. While an idea by its very nature is pure or absolute, a word is always going to be a deviation from such. When a word is at its best, it is a clear approximation of a particular idea. In such a case, the difference between the word and the idea is negligible. Words, however, can also create havoc. If you study the etymology and history of the words *word* and *weird*, you will find they have a common denominator in the way they were both once spelled: *wyrd*. Weirdness is a deviation of what is expected. Once again, words distort the actuality of what they are describing. This very principle is really just a shadow aspect of what makes up words: spelling. Here we have the concept of conjuring and casting spells through the subtle art of spelling words or creating *grammar* as in *grammaton* which gives rise to words such as *tetragrammaton, pentagrammaton* and *hexagrammaton*. This obviously goes further back in history to the more esoteric ancestral aspects of our modern language, but every writer should know as much as possible about the tools of his trade or art. With the concept of *wyrd* and conjuring in mind, let us now examine the definition of the word *weird*.

> **weird (n.)**
> Old English *wyrd* (n.) "fate, destiny," literally "that which comes," from Proto-Germanic **wurthis* (cf. Old Saxon *wurd*, Old High German *wurt* "fate," Old Norse *urðr* "fate, one of the three Norns"), from PIE **wert-* "to turn, wind," (cf. German *werden*, Old English *weorðan* "to become"), from root **wer-* "to turn, bend" (see *versus*). For sense development from "turning" to "becoming," cf. phrase turn into "become." The modern sense of *weird* developed from Middle English use of weird sisters for the three fates or Norns (in Germanic mythology), the goddesses who controlled human destiny. They were portrayed as odd or frightening in appearance.

While the identification of the word *weird* with fate or destiny takes us in a certain direction, I would like to focus on the relationship of *weird* to *wert* or "to turn, wind or bend." If we consider an absolute state of perfection in the of "mind of God" as is alluded to in the aforementioned etymology of *idea*, the words *weird* and *word* both suggest a twisting or aberration. If we consider the undisturbed entirety of the electromagnetic spectrum to be representative of the absolute, we gain an insight into the plausibility of how the universe evolved into what it is. This is especially so when we consider that the Old English definition for *wer* was related to "becoming" or "turning" as in the sense of "turning into" (something). This is akin to the very concept of birthing and creation itself.

Once again, theological implications resurface when we consider the old phrase: *In the beginning was the Word, and the Word was (with) God.* While you can readily make your own conclusions, the Word in this sense was specifically defined as the Logos. Let us look at that etymology now.

> **Logos (n.)**
> "the divine Word, second person of the Christian Trinity," from Greek *logos* "word, speech, discourse," also "reason," from PIE root **leg-* "to collect" (with derivatives meaning "to speak," on notion of "to pick out words;" see *lecture* (n.)); used by Neo-Platonists in various metaphysical and theological senses and picked up by New Testament writers. Other English formations from *logos* include *logolatry* "worship of words, unreasonable regard for words or verbal truth" (1810 in Coleridge); *logomania* (1870); *logophobia* (1923).

It is noteworthy to view the words that are related phonetically to *Logos* which include *lecture, logic, logistics,* and *legitimate.* Note the etymologies of *logic* and *lecture.*

> **logic (n.)**
> mid-14c., "branch of philosophy that treats of forms of thinking," from Old French *logique* (13c.), from Latin (ars) *logica,* from Greek *logike* (*techne*) "reasoning (art)," from fem. of *logikos* "pertaining to speaking or reasoning," from *logos* "reason, idea, word" (see *logos*). Meaning "logical argumentation" is from c.1600.

> **lecture (n.)**
> late 14c., "action of reading, that which is read," from Medieval Latin *lectura* "a reading, lecture," from Latin *lectus,* past participle of *legere* "to read," originally "to gather, collect, pick out, choose" (cf. election), from PIE **leg-* "to pick together, gather, collect" (cf. Greek *legein* "to say, tell, speak, declare," originally, in Homer, "to pick out, select, collect, enumerate;" *lexis* "speech, diction;" *logos* "word, speech, thought,

account;" Latin *lignum* "wood, firewood," literally "that which is gathered").

From the above etymologies, you can see that the very concept of the Logos has everything to do with "tying things together." Whether it be the application of logic, an invocation of the Logos, or administering a lecture, one is trying to synchronize elements of an ideal that is of an absolute nature. While that is an over-simplification of the Logos, it is a very useful and expository over-simplification. For a writer, he or she must pick out what he is going to communicate and decide how to communicate it. Words are not only key, they mimic and employ the birthing or creative process itself. What you communicate and how you do it is not only up to you, it is a reflection of who you are. To be more specific, it refers to your psyche.

Before we conclude our very cursory look at the subject of psychology, it is important to harken back to the etymology of the word *psyche* and take note that the Greek goddess Psyke was the lover of Eros or Cupid. Such relationships were never accidentally depicted by mythographers, and this particular relationship is not only intriguing, it offers a vital principle to any writer who wants to get his work known and consumed by the masses. It is a little complex to explain so I will try to keep it as simple as possible.

The idea that Psyke and Eros are inextricably intertwined together not only explains why Freud, the so-called father of modern psychology, was so fascinated with the sexual impulse but also gives some credence to his idea that sex is the underlying fundamental issue with regard to all human psychological problems. This idea, in a more general manner, is also exposited in Aleister Crowley's *The Book of the Law* where the primary mandate is *Do What Thou Wilt Shalt Be the Whole of the Law; Love Under Will*. In the latter, the Will compares to the psyche while Love is equatable to Eros. While the relationship of Psyke and Eros can be viewed as the underlying principle of psychology, it can also be viewed as the underlying foundation of Western occultism. It is important to point out, in both respects, that love does not necessarily have to translate into sexual lust or desire. There are long traditions of ascetic practices that involve the non-sexual aspects of Eros. While these might seem more high-minded, they are too often filled with the vampiric traps that also accompany the Left Hand Path of physical tantra. In any event, contemplating the relationship of Psyke and Eros in an archetypal sense will most definitely feed your muse as a writer, and this applies whether you are going to write about romance or the ascetic practices of a pious lama.

Psyke and Eros were archetypal entities long before the Greeks renamed and contoured them, but the latter did so in an intriguing and particular fashion. Instead of just writing about them as they might any other myth, Psyke and Erose were included in a work known as *The Golden Ass* in a way that subsequent artisans would refer to as *mise en abyme*, a French phrase that literally means "placed into abyss". Most often, *mise en abyme* refers to the "barbershop mirror-effect" or the visual experience you have when you stand between two mirrors and see a virtually infinite reproduction of one's image. *Mise en abyme*, however, has other meanings in literature and the creative arts. More specifically, it refers to an image which contains a smaller copy of itself, the sequence appearing to recur infinitely. In literature, it refers to a vignette within a story or a story within a story. The myth of Psyke and Eros appears within a bigger work in a somewhat similar manner, but the implications are far more subtle than in a visual work. It is particularly appropriate for Psyke and Eros to appear this way because these two archetypal forces are the very essence of reproduction, and *mise en abyme* is the epitome of reproduction.

Whether or not a writer chooses to utilize *mise en abyme* as a literary technique, it is very wise for them to not only grasp the principle itself but to also study it and integrate it into their own writing. Why? The so-called infinite mirror effect described above is representative of how a literary work becomes known. In other words, it is the principle of fame or creating a meme. The word *meme* is based upon *mime* and specifically refers to "an idea, behavior or style that spreads from person to person within a culture." A meme is how ideas are circulated into a culture and it includes the transmission of one mind to another via symbols, writing, speech, gestures, rituals or any other phenomena that can be imitated. In a cultural context, memes are sometimes regarded as being parallel to how genes work in an organism because they self-replicate, mutate and adjust to the environment. While a writer cannot only influence the culture by eliciting and circulating memes, he or she is dependent upon such to get his work digested by the masses.

Another important aspect of *mise en abyme* is that any literature that is released into the world is going to serve as an infinite reflection of the author. It would therefore be very wise to deeply consider the totality of what one is writing and the karmic effects it will produce for yourself and others.

In 1991, I wrote *The Montauk Project: Experiments in Time* with Preston Nichols and published it the following year. This book most definitely had a *mise en abyme* effect that reverberated throughout the entirety of the morphogenetic grid. At the time I am writing these words, it is what I am mostly known for even though it is not my story. My name is attached to it because I served as the ghost writer. The Montauk Project is a psychologically "heavy" subject to be identified with because it primarily deals with two psychological archetypes: Uranus and Pluto. In astrology, Uranus rules electromagnetism and super technology. Besides that, Uranus represents unfettered and compulsive creation without discrimination. It was for this reason that Saturn/Cronos, in mythology, castrated his father, Uranus, with his scythe and established an orderly arrangement to the universe, and this included the constructs of time itself. Pluto/Hades, on the outer rim of the solar system, represents psychic faculties as well as all the accoutrements of the underworld. Pluto puts a pitchfork to your chest and makes you confront all of your crimes and misdeeds in order to purge them from your soul; hence, the word purgatory. When this is finally accomplished, and it could take eons, you are released to the Elysian Fields whereupon you can frolic in the sun.

At this stage of my career, just over twenty years since *The Montauk Project* was published, the effect that this book has had on humanity has resulted in many people becoming aware of the sludge inside of them as well as the sludge that is within the collective consciousness. This includes an admixture of mind-control programming with psychic awareness, if not abilities, and a consciousness of deep emotional wounds that have had a tendency to escalate the more they are brought to view and discussed. This has resulted in a certain and not insignificant portion of the population rallying around this phenomena and seeking to make themselves poster boys or girls for such. While the desirability of one wanting to become a poster boy/girl for mind-control phenomena is highly questionable if not downright insane in itself, what these people are resonating with is the *mis en abyme* of their own consciousness. The horrors of such trauma have to be acknowledged and discharged before they can move on with their lives. Becoming a poster boy/girl only continues and reinforces the trauma-based thought forms. Discharging such emotional trauma can be very challenging, but it all begins with the realization that one is ultimately responsible for one's karma, particularly as it relates to their future life. This requires accessing the creative aspects of one's consciousness and will complement any therapeutic techniques. It can even serve as the senior therapy if one can learn to be agile with their mind.

With regard to myself, the dream that inspired the story you have read in this book, *The White Bat*, all occurred prior to my knowledge of the material that is written in *The Montauk Project: Experiments in Time*. In this regard, it is the a priori factor which has set the tone for so much that has happened in my writing career. The dream itself was playing off of the original inspiration and cognition I had experienced when reading the novel *Dracula* as I realized the potential, if not the plausibility, of such a powerful character using his powers for good instead of evil. This struck a chord inside of me that resonated throughout the entirety of my being. It was not, however, something I thought too much about as I recognized the story to be fiction. It did, however, stir up the archetypes residing in my own psyche. Without getting too complicated, I had made the decision that if I had been confronted with such powers, I would choose to transmute the negative into the positive. For some reason that reached well beyond my own ordinary day-to-day thinking processes, this theme was reenergized and displayed itself to me in a penetrating dream two decades later. Essentially, I was being initiated into the primary principle of alchemy: to turn the base into the noble, i.e. to turn base metal into gold.

With all of this in mind, I once again invite you to write down your own impressions and creative ideas. While the so-called "movie" of my life has proven itself to be of interest to others, the process I am inviting you to engage in (and mentioned at the beginning of this chapter) is about *your* movie. These writing exercises can enable you to detect and identify key ingredients in your own personality or consciousness that can bridge the gaps between yourself and the physical universe. In the Tarot, this archetypal experience that I am suggesting to you is actually represented by the Major Arcana card known as the Last Judgment. In the *Thoth Deck*, Aleister Crowley identified this card as *The Aeon* where he had a baby Horus depicted as the Babe in the Abyss. The Hebrew letter *shin* is attributed to this path which is highly significant as it represents the full and complete integration of the left brain with the right brain. In ancient times, these two functions were known as the Left Eye of Horus and the Right Eye of Horus. Horus, the son of Osiris, represents the manifestation of the Divine in the Age of Aquarius, the astrological age we are now in. By doing the writing exercise I have suggested — just writing down your impressions and ideas — you are taking the first step towards becoming the director of your own movie.

I will now share what happened in my life as a result of writing down the dream I had about the white bat.

CHAPTER THREE

AFTERMATH

As soon as I finished writing *The White Bat*, I shared it with my wife and she was very impressed. There was definitely something special about the story, and I attributed that to the natural influence of it having come from a rather extraordinary dream. When I told some friends of mine, they got excited about the story without having even read it. They immediately encouraged me to submit it to a literary agent that they knew and had done some work for in the past. These two friends were a couple and were big science fiction fans who knew many if not most of the classic science fiction authors.

Due to their enthusiasm and prodding, I submitted the story to this particular agent but soon received a form letter back in the mail. His agency had grown to great proportions since they had last worked with him, and he now wanted a fee of $200 to review any story. Both of my friends were surprised and put off by that response. Even so, due to the momentum that had been generated by the story and against my better judgment, I resubmitted the story with the fee requested. I could easily afford the fee at the time so the money issue did not bother me. The principle of it, however, did not give me a good feeling. I soon received a very well thought out rejection letter that was very well typed by one of the agent's assistants. Essentially, the story was praised beyond belief, but it was rejected because it was not like the work of Stephen King. It was obvious that this agent was using his considerable reputation in the literary field to make an ancillary income off of fledgling authors. To say something was not worthy of the market because it was not like Stephen King, however, was ludicrous. It is important, however, to realize that Stephen King was the best selling author of that era. He was the guiding standard of the industry, at least as far as commercial sales. While this might be considered wrong or unjust, it is a very important lesson for anyone aspiring to commercial writing. The industry wants what it wants and hungry readers determine the market. Name recognition is not only very important, it is even more than very important. My friends even explained to me the reason that some or much of Ray Bradbury's published writing was poor. Once he had made a name for himself and was a sellable author, the publisher would solicit his old material, stories that had failed to sell previously or that the author was not happy with in the first place, and slap his name onto it and sell it. Such is the adoration for certain authors that this despicable practice did not really hurt their fan base. Instead, it left a deeper hunger for the vintage Bradbury or whatever author this applied to.

With regard to Stephen King, he even became a victim of the aforesaid principle even after his incredible commercial success. He published a series of novels under a pseudonym, Richard Bachman, and had nowhere near the success he enjoyed under his given name. Had he submitted those novels without any track record, it is extremely likely that they would have been minimized and probably not accepted at all.

As I am a very pragmatic person, I did not pursue this any further. My wife and I had a thriving advertising and design business at the time, and this excursion into creative writing was a side activity I could leave alone, at least for a while. This had been my first attempt to try and get my own writing published, and it was not a lost cause in the long run. My pragmatism told me that if I wanted to sell anything, I would have to have a market of ready readers who were interested in a particular subject. Accordingly, I mused over subjects that would interest people. As I was primarily interested in writing about the spiritual or metaphysical aspects of life, particularly from a scientific reference frame, I ended up focusing on Atlantis. As a matter of fact, I had never been particularly interested in Atlantis up to that point. When that subject came up in my reading, I was always more interested in Lemuria, a culture that was much more obscure and advanced. What I noticed about Atlantis, however, was that our culture has been obsessed with Atlantis ever since the stories of it found their way into literature. People like to debate about it, wax romantic or to engage in psychological drama concerning how it is playing out in society today.

I also realized that hundreds of manuscripts have been published on the subject of Atlantis since at least the time of Plato. No matter how many works had already been printed, there was no danger of this subject becoming outdated. People want to read about Atlantis. Although it might not be the biggest potential audience, it was at least an audience and a rather sizable one. And while Atlantis was not my favorite subject, it did present some intrigue to me as the prospect offered both the scientific aspects of technology as well as the spiritual aspects of existence, all combined with ancient and mysterious history. Even though the potential market for this was nowhere near the horror suspense genre of Stephen King, Atlantis was far more palatable to my inclinations. It was a compromise but an acceptable and pragmatic one. At the time, however, I had no idea how pragmatic my inclinations were. I was just following my desire to be a writer that I had harbored since my teens.

Thus it was that I wrote a manuscript that began with the last days of Atlantis that was primarily right out of my imagination. I cannot locate the manuscript at this time, and although it was never completed, I had gotten at least one-quarter into the story, maybe even a little more. The story was written a while after *The White Bat*, and one of the more intriguing aspects of the story to me included a crystal clear pyramid located in the Atlas Mountains of Northern Africa in or near today's Morocco. It was not a huge pyramid like the Great Pyramid but was rather small and exuded many different colors in a holographic manner. The pyramid was accompanied by the sudden and inexplicable appearance and disappearance of various creatures or characters.

Another aspect of the story included a cylinder artifact with obscure markings that sent out beams into space when activated. It beamed out to either a space ship or to Mars. I do not quite remember, but the activation of this cylinder resulted in a visit from Martians who were humanoid as opposed to being little green men or the like. All of this is interesting to me because it came right out of my imagination. I had yet to learn of the ancient and esoteric histories or theories of the Elder Race or Blue Race who had come from Mars. Holograms and pyramids were just interesting fodder for a story. At the time, I had no idea that so much of my future writing, if not all of it, would embrace or run parallel to these various themes.

Although I had no idea of it at the time, my chance meeting with Preston Nichols and collaboration with him in writing *The Montauk Project: Experiments in Time* was thrusting me further into the Atlantean theme. In the book *Pyramids of Montauk,* I discovered theories, legends, and historical indications that Montauk itself was tied to the Lost Continent. Montauk, which is really an underwater mountain and geologically distinct from the rest of Long Island, was cited as the top of an ancient Atlantean mountain top. The royal tribe of the Long Island Native Americans were the Montauk Pharoahs who, according to some of the tribe, were originally from Egypt. According to legend and some historical sources, Egypt was a remnant of the last Atlantean culture. The correspondences, however, did not end here.

Through a very remarkable and mysterious process of synchronicity, I would meet Olive Pharoah, the matriarch of the Montauk Indians. When I called her to see if she had received a revised edition of *The Pyramids of Montauk,* I learned from her sister that she got the book that very day but could not look at it as she just left in an ambulance due to a bleeding gall bladder. Immediately after that, I went back to work and the next document I picked up concerned an old Atlantean healing technique for healing the gall bladder through the use of olive oil. Only then did I realize Olive Pharoah's name of *Olive* was serving as a fulcrum of synchronicity. Due to circumstances explained in great detail in *The Montauk Book of the Living,* I was investigating all possible connections and synchronicities with olives and the Mount of Olives due to a mysterious "quantum relic" given to me by my friend Kenn Arthur. Although Kenn was very snide about Preston's Montauk Project stories, he was the first one to point out to me the Atlantean connection to Montauk. He also told me that Atlantis used the designation of Pharoah just as Egypt had.

The so-called quantum relic was a 1909 playbill from *The New Montauk Theatre* which featured the Ziegfield Follies. Years later, I would discover that two pictures of Christ on Mount Olive had been hidden within the cardboard backing of the framed playbill. The pictures of Christ actually fell out as I handed them to Duncan Cameron, the main psychic from the

Montauk Project who, according to the readings of himself and Preston, had been trained to become the Antichrist. My extensive research into the olive theme is described in *The Montauk Book of the Living*, but it ended up with the discovery that the original archetypal character who gave the olive to Mankind was Antinea, the blue queen of Atlantis, also known as a Kahena, who settled in an area in the Ahaggar Mountains of present day Algeria. The Greeks adopted her and transliterated her name into Athena.

All of the above revelations have transpired like a slow time-release discovery that has extended over the duration of my writing career with a tendency to unravel in the manner of how one pieces together a jigsaw puzzle. When one looks at and assesses the finished puzzle, at least at this juncture, it points to a mysterious and ancient Elder Race or Blue Race that either lived or lives within the Inner Earth and colonized this planet long before the Atlantean civilization. It is also of interest that Queen Antinea, who is most definitely identified with the Blue Race, and her descendants were recognized to have copper-based Rh-negative blood. So far, scientists have not been able to determine that Rh-negative blood is indigenous to this planet. Many years later, when I was facilitating the publishing of Romanian author, Radu Cinamar, I learned of his encounter with Machandi, a blue goddess he encountered in both Tibet and Transylvania, who possesses virtually the same characteristics as Antinea except that she comes from a different tradition.

While I will revisit this thread with the Elder Race later on, it is important to highlight the fact that I stumbled into and acquired all of this information as a natural consequence of executing my desire to write a creative fictional story about Atlantis. The dream that inspired *The White Bat* was actually the a priori factor in the drama that was unfolding. As will be demonstrated, both stories were feeding off of each other in the way things evolved in my life and writing.

To me, *The White Bat* was just a story based upon a dream. While it was also a *mis en abyme* of how I chose to view the world, I had no great aspirations for it to manifest as far as it has. As you will read in this book, the theme of this "innocent dream or story" has reached a remarkable degree of manifestation in my life and work. It is important to emphasize that creativity is the gateway to manifestation. Do not underestimate your own ability in this regard. I will now relate some of the key factors that occurred which demonstrate that the dream I had was prophetic if not a suggestion of the human mind being a time machine.

My story about Atlantis was essentially interrupted by my encounter with Preston Nichols and the subsequent interest I acquired in investigating the Montauk Project. As interesting as the Montauk Project investigation was, the endeavor was wrought with problematic and negative energies. There was no doubt in my own mind, however, that I was seeking to find the white in the darkness of Montauk. It was what I wanted to do. As I actually wrote the manuscript, I was visited by Men In Black in my dreams but never in person. There was also an actual agent of some agency who tried stalking my house, but he did not bother me. This was due to the reason that I had absolutely no fear of him. During this period, at very specific times, I sometimes witnessed unmarked black military helicopters appearing. Every time it occurred, it was always at the precise moment when I was thinking about key aspects of the Montauk Project. It was as if these helicopters were phantoms that would appear whenever particularly sensitive issues came up.

There are also a couple of other factors I should mention that influenced my Montauk investigation as well as the theme that is brought forth in *The White Bat*. One was a procedure I read about when I studied Scientology in 1971. In a book, which was really a pamphlet at the time that cost 80 cents, entitled *Scientology 8-80*, it stated that one could rehabilitate or fix any condition in an individual by having the person view black spots in his own energetic field and then turn them white. What I have said is a paraphrase based upon memory, but it was referred to as black and white processing. In regular Scientology counseling as practiced by the Church of Scientology, it was almost never done. It was, however, considered a valid and powerful process. The book even stated that it could raise the dead. Although it really amounted to an anecdotal part of the discovery process of Scientology when it came to day-to-day matters, I never forgot it.

The second factor which reinforced this theme occurred over a year later after I had made my way to L. Ron Hubbard's yacht, the *Apollo*, which had become my new home. My father wrote to me and asked if there was anything he could get for me. Yes, I told him. There was a book I had begun reading entitled *Lords of Light* by Roger Zelazny. It was popular amongst the local Scientologists and had been passed around a lot. It was about a colonized planet, a monkey named Siddartha and featured psychotronic devices which were called prayer machines. I cannot tell you much about the book beyond that as I never did finish reading it. My father did his best to find the book, but he could not locate a copy. Instead, he sent me another book by Zelazny entitled *Jack of Shadows*. My father had assumed, quite incorrectly, that I was a Zelazny fan. I was not but was merely interested in that one book. Nevertheless, I read the book. Although the book did not particularly appeal to me, it had a strange resonance with me. Much of it had to do with the fact that my father had tried his best to do something for me, and it was a gift from him. He thought I would like it so he sent it to me. The next thing I knew, I was reading the book and was deeply entrenched in the mind-set presented which would become a major theme of my life.

Jack of Shadows is a story that takes place on a planet that does not rotate. Like the moon, one side of the planet is in darkness while the other remains in light. In the world of light, science rules the day. In the world of night, magic is the ruler. In the day world, the protagonist is a university professor and is nobody too special. In the darkness, however, he is known as Shadowjack, and he possesses a very peculiar and special ability. While the magical people of the night world derive their power from a specific fixed location, he is different as his power derives from shadow. When faced with either complete darkness or complete light, he is lost or powerless, but give him a bit of shadow and his potency is unmatched.

In the strangest way, this book gripped me. If I examine not only why it gripped me but why it became a major operating theme in my life, I can offer myself a rather precise answer. At the same time that the book took me into a world that was dark and hellacious beyond belief, it presented a psychological reference frame with how to survive it. Many people have asked me how I survived the crazy world of Scientology and came out unscathed from the experience. I really cannot attribute it all to the reading of *Jack of Shadows*, but it certainly did help me to navigate through the shadow world of that organization. More importantly, however, it enabled and encouraged me to navigate my way through the extensive shadow world of Montauk and its occult connections.

Looking back, the entire experience is a classic case of asking for the light and receiving the dark. It is an old saw that if you seek the dark, you will find the light and vice versa. I find it ironic that this book not only passed through the hands of my father, but that he was actually the point of origin. He cared for me very deeply and was not happy at all with my life decision to become a full-time Scientologist. Although he was not a religious man, I can imagine that he prayed for me, at least in his own way. Although he had no idea how much he contributed to my life in this regard, he gave me a gift which would forever influence my life in a positive way. The expression of love in a gift can create amazing results at times.

With the book *Jack of Shadows* in my arsenal, I not only learned how to navigate the shadow world but to create shadows as well. I worked in the shadow of L. Ron Hubbard, a man who definitely operated in the shadows. As a member of his personal office, I was privy to all sorts of information that the rank and file of Scientology were completely unaware of. I would eventually learn, however, that he was operating over the undercurrent of someone who cast a much larger shadow: Aleister Crowley.

Discovering the magical connections between these two celebrated characters required a lot of shadow-jacking on my part. It was in the wake of this that I was led to the Montauk Project, a scheme which cast a shadow that reached beyond the circles of time itself.

CHAPTER FOUR

SHADOW SCRYING

Before we go any further, it is advisable to review the meaning of the word shadow. The definition is quite simple. A shadow simply refers to the dark area or shape resulting from an object between a source of light and a surface. The etymologies of *shade* and *shadow* follow.

shadow (n.)
Old English *sceadwe, sceaduwe*, oblique cases of *sceadu* (see shade).

shadow (v.)
late Old English *sceadwian* "to protect as with covering wings" (cf. also overshadow), from the root of *shadow* (n.). Meaning "to follow like a shadow" is from c.1600 in an isolated instance; not attested again until 1872.

shade (n.)
Old English *sceadu* "shade, shadow, darkness," also "shady place, protection from glare or heat," from Proto-Germanic **skadwo* (cf. Old Saxon *skado*, Middle Dutch *scade,* Dutch *schaduw*, Old High German *scato*, German *Schatten*, Gothic *skadus*), from PIE **skotwa*, from root **skot-* "dark, shade" (cf. Greek *skotos* "darkness," Albanian *kot* "darkness," Old Irish *scath*, Old Welsh *scod*, Breton *squeut* "darkness"). Meaning "grade of color" first recorded 1680s (cf. French nuance, from *nue* "cloud"). Meaning "ghost" is from 1610s.

It is interesting to note that root words or phonemes like *kot, scato, skot,* and *scatos* are equivalent to the word *cat.* As the cat represents the feminine energy, this tells us something very significant about the nature of the shadow. In particular, it tells us that the concept of shadow is fundamental to the function of creation. Creation, if visualized in the form of the monochord or in the pure and unadulterated aspect of the electromagnetic spectrum, only occurs when the pure form (such as pure light) is blocked, obfuscated, or otherwise played around with or manipulated. After that takes place, you have creation in all of its myriad forms.

Much ado has been made about holy vessels such as the Ark of the Covenant or the Holy Grail, both of which shut out light and are metaphors for the womb which is itself the cauldron of creation and is designed to host an operation that occurs in darkness. Every individual comes into this world through the womb. In the birthing process, there is an inextricable relationship between the principle of the shadow and the barbershop mirror effect known as *mise en abyme*. What actually manifests as a human being is a reflection or shadow of many different factors with the personality acting as the front man or representative.

As a human being, you yourself have a shadow. It represents all of the hidden aspects of your consciousness, some of which you are aware of and others which you are not. While your shadow might contain negativity, it also contains far more and that includes the positive. The shadow not only contains your hidden potential but also the potentiality of the entire known and unknown universe(s) which might or might not be able to manifest some day. As this book is meant to be a work book on writing, I am trying to put you in touch with your own shadow. It is your own womb of creation. While virtually everyone has shallow or petty thoughts, there is also a deep reservoir inside of yourself that can be tapped. That is why I have encouraged you to note down your thoughts as you read this book. I want you to tap the mother lode if possible. One of the most efficient ways that you can tap this mother lode is by writing, a practice which has been employed for millennia.

Not everyone is going to be a commercial author, but that is not the point. In our current culture, most everyone has a website or other means of expression. A business card would represent the irreducible minimum with regard to the necessity of writing. While you might not be writing books, most people want a resume or synopsis that represents their vocation or role in society. A resume or profile is how you express yourself to the world. The implications of what I am suggesting here, however, go way beyond one's vocation. It also has everything to do with your personal psychology.

In ancient Egyptian myth, the goddess Isis had a dark twin sister named Nephtys. She represents the shadow. The Hebrews have Lilith. There is also the concept of the devil, a word which is expressed in Latin as *diabolus* and in Spanish as *diabolo*, both words referring to "double" and alluding to the shadow self. You can study further about all these shadow archetypes if you want to. It is certainly not a new idea.

It is important to realize that you have different characteristics which embody your regular-world self. This is what the world sees you as. It includes your job, your family, your adventures, your financial status and just about everything else anyone might be able to see if they had a spy camera on you. There are also those aspects which remain without manifestation. These would also include choices and options you wanted to make but did not. They could be both positive or negative. While this includes fears and inhibitions, it could also be dreams or ideals that you never lived up to. Beyond the obvious fears and unrealized dreams, however, there is a vast potential which I have already alluded to above. In the infinite knowledge embedded within your DNA, and it reaches out to the deepest aspects of creation.

At this point, I will not elaborate on the shadow any further. You might want to read a little or a lot about it on your own. The only thing else I will say for the time being is that it is your personal reservoir and it is a very powerful resource to tap. It is that which remains within you, without manifestation, and is the womb of creation. As this book is partially a work book, I will now give you some exercises to tap your shadow.

Exercise 1 — The Dark Room

Step 0 — Find yourself a dark room, and by that is meant a room that is completely dark. All cracks or leaks of light must be covered with a towel, dark tape or whatever. An army blanket sometimes works for larger windows. A walk in closet can be ideal, but you can use a pantry, a closet, a hallway or even a bathroom. This first step of finding a dark room can be very challenging to many people. The inertia you have to overcome to find a dark place is a great task master in itself. It is an obstacle to overcoming your own shadow side and getting it to work for you.

Step 1 — Go inside the dark room for fifteen minutes a day. You can stand or sit in a chair if you like. Relax. Sit up straight and elongate your neck at the shoulders so that you have correct posture. Using your imagination, scan downward from the crown of your head down to your toes. Always scan downwards, and as you do, clear away all your mental, emotional, and physical blockages or disabilities. This is a very powerful exercise, but most people will not get this far. Do this two or three times a day, but only do it for fifteen minutes at a time. Do not do it for fourteen or sixteen minutes. Set an alarm. This step is to be done for one week.

Step 2 — For the second week, continue to go into the dark room two or three times a day (again, fifteen minutes at a time), but be completely still. Do this also for one week.

Step 3 — For the third week, do joint manipulation in the dark room. This means that you are moving your body in whatever way it wants to move. You are getting the kinks out of your system. It is important to breathe in, as slowly as possible, through your nose and exhale equally slowly through your mouth. Do this for one week for fifteen minutes at a time two or three times a day.

Step 4 — For the fourth week, do anything you want to in complete darkness. Once again, it is done two or three times a day for fifteen minutes at a time.

Step 5 — Most people will not get this far. If you do, however, you are a possible candidate for Chi Gong training and have demonstrated that you can tap the mother lode. This dark room exercise, if you continue it, will enable you to do incredible things, particularly if you do further training. If you get this far, write to me while you are on step 4, and I will prepare you for step 5.

At this writing, I have been a diligent practitioner of Taoist Chi Gong for over six years under the tutelage of Grand Master Roosevelt Gainey of Brooklyn, New York. For the purposes of this book on writing, I have included the dark room exercise because it will help you tap your own potential through the medium of writing. So that you understand its power, I will point out how important this step of the dark room is.

When I started Chi Gong class in May of 2007, there were many students. They were very advanced, but not too many of them are around anymore. In particular was one lady who practiced very hard and could do remarkable things. She could overcome masters and even levitated off of a table once. Although I did not see this nor did I attempt to chronicle her accomplishments, she was an inspiration to us all for what she had achieved. Despite her skills, she had never done the dark room despite the dictates and encouragement of our teacher. In the end, she could not handle her abilities nor further instructions. She is no longer with us. My teacher said her mind had gone. According to what she had told me personally, she had never done the spiritual work I had done. The dark room would have fixed her.

Many of my fellow students do not do the dark room. It makes you take a look at yourself at a deep level. You might not like what you see. The response, however, is to overcome your attitudes and not be pushed around by them or what others might think of you. The dark room will definitely put you in touch with your shadow self and also the better part of you.

The next exercise can be done in conjunction with the dark room or by itself and completely separately. It involves the process of writing and connects both of the hemispheres of your brain.

Exercise 2 — The Waterfall

Step 1 — Write your name exactly as you did when you first learned to write it (when you were in the first grade or whenever) and do this as slowly as possible. After you write your name, think of a time when you were hurt. As you think of the time when you were hurt, visualize that you are now under a waterfall and change the problem of the past that caused this to happen. Dissolve all the charge. Repeat this step three times and do it for an entire week.

Step 2 — The second week, write something nice about yourself. Visualize yourself going to a waterfall and tell yourself that you will now do everything in a like manner. In other words, you are going to carry that nice quality with yourself forever. Repeat this step three times and do it every day for one week.

Step 3 — For the third week, write (using printing as opposed to cursive writing) down as slowly as possible, "I FORGIVE ALL THOSE WHO HAVE EVER HURT ME." Think of an instance where you were hurt, go to an imaginary waterfall and dissolve all the emotional charge connected with it. Repeat this step three times and do it every day for one week.

Step 4 — For the fourth week, write (using printing as opposed to cursive writing) down as slowly as possible, "I FORGIVE MYSELF FOR ALL THE THINGS I HAVE EVER DONE WRONG." Think of an instance where you did something wrong, go to an imaginary waterfall and dissolve all the emotional charge connected with it. Repeat this step three times and do it every day for one week.

Step 5 — Write whatever you want. This might include whatever you want to accomplish. Repeat any of the above steps if you feel it is necessary.

If you actually do the above exercises, they will change your life substantially and get you in touch with your own *mise en abyme* factor. While it is expected that you might not like either some or much of what you see in yourself, this gives you the opportunity to change. It is also a route to creating internal happiness. Your future is determined by YOU.

I realize that the majority of people who read my books do so because it either excites or entertains their mind in a unique way. It often enables one to recognize portions of the life stream or consciousness that are an integral part of themselves but have been previously relegated to an unfamiliar status for a plethora of different reasons. One of the key components of intelligent life is recognition. These processes facilitate the process of internal recognition. If you can go into complete darkness and create, you are not only emulating the Creator, you are getting in touch with the deepest aspect of who you truly are. This is the smithy of an artist whether you are a graphic artist, a writer, a martial artist or pretty much anything else.

The sky is the limit.

CHAPTER FIVE

DESTINY

At the time I originally wrote *The White Bat* short story, Romania was still under communism. I had neither the desire nor expectation to ever visit there. If it were not for my involvement in writing *The Montauk Project*, I never would have made it to Romania in the first place. After I had actually travelled to Romania five times, I felt it behooved me to review my life in order better understand exactly how things came into play.

As I found and dusted off the original manuscript for *The White Bat* and looked it over, I had a stunning realization that my many trips to Romania were actually preceded and precipitated by an entire series of stunning syn-chronicities. The only reason I even travelled to Romania at all was a result of my association with Dr. David Anderson, the time control scientist. As a result of his research into time, he collected an entire library on the subject. This included *The Montauk Project: Experiments in Time* which, he said, woke him up spiritually. Consequently, he took a further interest in the subject and became a subscriber to the *Montauk Pulse* newsletter. In 1999, he was in Germany when he was asked to speak in Romania. This was to be at Atlantykron, an annual conference of writers, artists and scientists who meet on an island in the Danube adjacent to the ancient ruins of Capidava. David was deeply moved by what he experienced there, particularly the highly intel-ligent people he met. Upon returning to his Time Travel Research Center on Long Island, one of his first orders of business was to attend *Montauk Night*, a monthly meeting that was hosted by Preston Nichols and myself. This is how I met David, and we went to lunch soon afterwards. David talked a lot about Atlantykron and how he wanted me to meet certain people. He was also quite passionate about creating a charitable foundation for Romanian artists, writers, and scientists. His dedication towards helping Romanian youth as well as youth in general eventually resulted in the establishment of the World Genesis Foundation, a charitable organization which he founded and is registered in the state of New Mexico. Getting me to Romania, how-ever, was not so easy. Although I met David in 1999, he was not able to get me to Romania until 2008. Just as my adventures with him have had a lot of unexpected twists and turns, so have there been other events in my life which enabled all of this to happen. What I would emphasize at this point, however, is that my dream was either a beckoning for me to come to Romania or a subconscious recognition of the future.

How David actually arrived at Montauk Night is a little sketchy and strange to say the least. According to a friend of mine who attended the meet-ings, he found out about our meetings through her in a chat room where the Montauk Project was the topic of discussion. This friend, who I will refer to as Debbie, said that she engaged him about coming to the meetings. I then received an e-mail from him asking about them and if it was all right to attend. According to Debbie, David would not admit to having been the one in the chat room although it was rather obvious to her. Debbie is a psychic astrologer whose business is often focused around putting soul mates together. She had a lot of contact with David in the dream state before ever encountering him in the chat room or in person. I mention this as it suggests if not outright demonstrates a strong connection between David Anderson and the R.E.M. realm. It is important to keep the R.E.M. realm in mind because this entire book is based upon a dream. In that regard, I will also advise you to integrate the dream world into your own writing, art or creativity. By advising you, I mean that I intend to share specific techniques to assist you in this process, but that will be done in the subsequent chapter.

From the outside, it might seem that the only reason I made it to Romania is due to my connection to David Anderson and our mutual interest in time travel and the Montauk Project. At first glance, I thought it was that simple myself until I began to look further into the actual dynamics of everything that has happened. That not only includes my adventures in Romania but also the events that precipitated my involvement in *The Montauk Project*. The Montauk Project did not fall into my lap by accident. It was based upon a series of life events and explorations of consciousness that were precipitated by all sorts of studies. These included the Tree of Life but also the themes we have already visited thus far in this book. While some of these aspects have been discussed in previous books, I will share some aspects of these which I have never particularly written about. It has everything to do with the study of archetypes.

For those of you who are not already familiar with my previous books, I was deeply involved in Scientology from 1972-1983 and worked in the Personal Office of L. Ron Hubbard. I wrote about my general experiences in *The Montauk Book of the Dead*, published in 2005. Scientology is a controversial subject as well as a double-edged sword in many respects. What was good about it, if you were lucky enough to enjoy the circumstances by which you could avail yourself of it, was the quiet time it allowed for you to go deep inside of your body-mind-soul complex and explore the hidden depths. I spent literally hundreds upon hundreds of hours deeply exploring the caverns of my own body-mind-soul interface. This was virtually "alone time" with no one telling me what to think or believe about myself. Ultimately, it is up to you to make your own conclusions. How well you interface with the physical universe afterwards is a testament to how well you did the work. I mention this because people often explain dismay, wrath, or condemnation that they were not helped by Scientology. Under the circumstances, I can certainly understand why they were upset, but I will share a few secrets with you. Neither Scientology or any other system under the sun is going to help you. This can only be done by you exploring and excavating the caverns of your own soul yourself. A system is only a protocol towards this end.

In the case of Dianetics and Scientology, that system was a theory based upon clearing the dysfunction of your own mind, not unlike clearing a hard drive in a computer that has viruses, faulty indexes and bad blocks. Hubbard used the metaphor of an adding machine with held down sevens. In other words, no matter what numbers you would add up, an extra seven or more would always work its way into the final sum and give a wrong answer. By suggesting a computer, I have used a more modern analogy to give a more embracing concept for modern times. Any system, Scientology or not, that is designed to clear up the mind is not unlike a disk utility program for a computer. There are different utility programs for repairing a hard drive, but you are the one who has to choose the utility program and do the work. The ultimate test is whether or not you are able to interface with your environment in a functional manner and without the pitfalls of held down sevens or any other analogy you might want to use to describe this principle.

After one clears out their own mental debris, one is not free from the paradigm of dysfunction. Theoretically, one re-emerges into a world where most everyone, to put it politely, has a less than ideally functioning mind. Unfortunately, the world is not so constructed that a jolly functional man can step out into the world without any cares and have everyone slap him on the back and greet him in a brotherhood of solidarity. If one has truly cleared out one's mental debris, there is a definite vulnerability. If one emits a positive charge into a sea of negative charges, one has the potential to be an attractor of negative energy or to be consumed by it. It is like being a bright flame in the darkness that attract moths. The upper levels of Scientology were dedicated to banishing the moths.

If you have ever had occasion to read scandals or claims of fraud about the upper levels of Scientology, you will read that Scientologists believe in an evil alien war lord named Xenu. This, quite understandably, makes Scientology sound like a candidate for being the nuttiest thing on the planet. I would be quick to counter this claim, however, because I think that the political system of this planet, which is often dedicated towards destroying life, is far nuttier. In any event, it is not quite accurate to say that Scientologists believe in Xenu. Personally, I never heard the term Xenu until I was in Scientology for eight years. After that, I do not think I ever heard the term iterated by anyone; perhaps once or twice at most. As the name Xenu only appeared in highly confidential material, it remained or remains unknown to most Scientologists as even a concept. On a personal level, I never paid but scant attention to Xenu. In order for you to have a more inside understanding of what was actually at work in this scenario, I will first explain some trade secrets about L. Ron Hubbard, his clearing techniques and what was at work in the equation.

L. Ron Hubbard based much of Scientology upon his imagination, but let me first share a couple of quotes from Albert Einstein on the subject.

"Imagination is more important than knowledge. For knowledge is limited to all we now know and understand, while imagination embraces the entire world, and all there ever will be to know and understand. — *Albert Einstein*

"To know is nothing at all; to imagine is everything." — *Albert Einstein*

Einstein is often lauded for his endorsement of the process of imagination. Hubbard, who was a more prolific practitioner and advocate of utilizing the faculty of imagination, is usually castigated for his indulgences in this regard. Einstein, of course, did not create a cult and all of the subsequent fallout accompanied with it. Nevertheless, I want to stress the potential power and usefulness of imagination, particularly as I was able to use it within my own Scientology experiences.

The entire criterion of being declared "Clear" in Scientology was based upon one's ability to imagine. Many ex-Scientologists are disabused when they discover the truth about the "clear cognition" as it was called. In Scientology, preclears were only allowed to attest and be declared Clear if they stated words to the effect that they realized that they were the creators of their own reactive mind. Such aforementioned people get upset because they felt that they should have been told that in the first place. It would have saved them the money and effort. Such people, however, obviously received no benefit or they would not be complaining. In actuality, most people are not up to creating what is going on in their own mind. If they were, they would not be seeking out solutions that would help them in this sphere of operation. The entire trick or secret here is to examine what is in your mind that makes you tick and to eradicate what needs to be eradicated and to enhance what needs to be enhanced. If you are so insightful to see that you were imagining or creating your own past mental trauma or debris by not being fully aware of what you were doing, you are in a position to take back your own power. What you create mentally is now the faculty of your own domain.

Hubbard went so far as to say that a clear was capable of creating his or her own universe. This was a highly imaginative state, and he most certainly exhibited that type of thinking, all of which was part and parcel of his assertion that Xenu was the evil leader of the Galactic Confederacy and had engaged in the mass implanting of spirits which resulted in virtually all of humanity being possessed with body thetans. In Scientology, a thetan is the word for spirit. Body thetans were considered to be attached to the body or ganglia with independent minds of their own that could cause illness, unwanted mental patterns or otherwise wreak havoc upon an individual.

When I was introduced to this confidential level, in a separate and cloistered course room that was off limits to most, the story about Xenu was really a background story that was designed to give you a reference frame for dealing with the phenomena you were about to deal with. It was obviously based upon Hubbard's own interpretation of the history of the universe. Like most everything Hubbard said about history, it was highly imaginative. From what I was told by a friend of mine who was involved with Hubbard, the basic template for this information originated in the early 1960s when it appeared in many separate auditing sessions. In other words, it was drudged up from the buried debris in several different preclears who were not comparing notes or incidents from each other.

In any event, if you were properly trained and prepared, the object of the upper level procedures was not to believe in Xenu. To me, Xenu was an abstract concept at best who might or might not have some tangibility to ordinary reality. What you were supposed to do was to go trolling, with the help of a biofeedback device known as the e-meter, for disembodied spirits, entities, unit of consciousness or whatever you want to call them. The body itself was usually the strongest indicator of such phenomena. For example, you might feel a pain or sensation in the body that was accompanied by a discharge on the e-meter. This is like a fish biting. You pursue it and you just might find the meter reading again with a spirit manifesting itself, either in your own mind or in an etheric frame of reference. What manifested could be ordinary or quite bizarre. It could be a clown from Elizabethan days, a repressed nun from the Crusades or a warrior who worked for Xenu and is upset about having been slaughtered. In such a scenario, the sky is the limit. When one reaches this realm, however, you are not just dealing with your personal imagination. You are, in fact, dealing with the imagination of the universe itself. We are talking about the collective unconscious and beyond.

When one engages a spirit under such a circumstance, one has to counsel or help the spirit in order to come to a reconciliation. If it was attached to you or in your sphere of influence, there was a reason. Under the best of circumstances, one releases the spirit which would be accompanied by a discharge on the e-meter and emotional relief of both parties. Much of this communication could or would occur telepathically.

As you might readily understand, a person could go crazy doing this if they were not properly prepared or in the right frame of mind. There are also a number of people who have bemoaned or disparaged this procedure because they felt no significant change in their life. While some faked it at the time they did it for status reasons, there are others who caught no significant "fish" for whatever reason. The value of such a procedure, whether

51

a Scientology procedure per se or not, is whether or not you were able to accomplish anything. The ultimate test of the procedure's value is if one can take their experience and then integrate it in a meaningful or useful way into their own personal life. If you are adept it at, you can even considerably change the moods and attitudes of people around you in a positive way. The reason for this is that spirits often contaminate an entire office or area of people.

While this level met with varying degrees of success or failure with various individuals, the stated objective of the entire procedure was to arrive at a point where one was a completely self-determined individual without influence from other-determined entities. You might find this an absurd proposition if you consider how suggestible or other-determined certain Scientologists and ex-Scientologists have demonstrated themselves to be.

Beyond this level, the upper levels of Scientology were originally designed to extrovert one from the restrictions and fixated introversions that accompany living in the physical universe and eventually being able to exteriorize (travel outside of one's body). While these objectives were met with either varying or perhaps limited degrees of success in different individuals, and I want to be considerate and careful not to minimize what certain people might or did achieve, the entire process was short circuited. The reason for this is that there were hidden booby traps that remained unseen. I will touch on this a bit more later, but there was a second factor which curtailed any further potential progress in using the upper levels of Scientology. It had to do with a development that was designed to enhance the identification and vanquishing of body thetans. It was called New Era Dianetics for OTs (the acronym for such being NOTS) and was basically the refinement of processes that were developed and utilized to save Hubbard's life. Independent of Hubbard, these procedures were corrupted and the proof is in the pudding. If you take what I have said here at face value and without being judgmental, it is clear that body thetans are parasitic on the individual. If you study the history of Scientology and the level known as NOTS, you will see that every individual who ever did it had an even bigger parasite connected to it: the Church itself. It has taken some people ten, twenty or even thirty years to realize that the only significant parasite inside of them was the Church of Scientology.

Due to all of the knowledge I had acquired in over a decade, I left Scientology forever in 1983. It was very clear to me that none of this was going to come to a very good end. I even ran into direct and personal conflict with one of the facilitators of these incorrect procedures. He ended up in "The Hole," a prison that many former Scientology executives have been relegated to. It consists of two huge trailers that are closed to the outside with prison bars on the doors and windows. There are indeed consequences for one's actions. This person I am referring to did what he did for prestige and money, severely compromising his integrity in the process.

52

Besides my own integrity and common sense, another reason I did not fall prey to any of this nonsense had to do with my own personal discovery of phenomena that came up in my own auditing experiences. They showed up on the e-meter, too. I saw that there were similar spirits or thetans within the structure of the physical universe itself, and these had to be addressed as well. Scientologists consider that the physical universe is comprised of Matter, Energy, Space and Time. Consequently, I referred to these as MEST thetans. I readily recognized these to be similar to the nature spirits said to reside in inanimate objects in the Shinto religion of Japan. These could be further broken down into Matter Thetans, Energy Thetans, Space Thetans and Time Thetans. You are now beginning to get a rough idea of how I stumbled upon Preston Nichols, Duncan Cameron, David Anderson and other interesting characters. There is considerably more to the equation, but I have to be very simple in this narrative so as not to get lost in what might prove to be a very intriguing distraction.

I am quick to point out that an ardent student of theology can find correlations with what I have termed MEST thetans. This realm is under the influence of what theologians sometimes refer to as the Demiurge. The Demiurge has different semantic nuances, but it basically refers to the Creator and his agents. Sometimes the Creator of physical reality is distinguished from the a priori Higher Essence. In some theologies, the Creator is even positioned as being evil, having fallen from the Higher Essence. The agents of the Demiurge, not all of which are evil, are identified in Christianity as Principalities and by the Greeks as Archons. There are different names as well. The qualities of good and evil are attributed through the lens of the theologian or experiencer.

Any religious system, including Scientology, fits into a master template which is really symbolic of all the possible permutations of life, all of which is actually imbedded in a DNA molecule. If I did not already clearly state or imply it, the Tree of Life is a symbolic rendering of DNA. Actually, a Tree of Life rendering is really nothing more than a schematic of life trying to understand itself. A book is really not much different except that it is usually focused on only a narrow aspect of the Tree. The best sort of book is one that operates through or reflects the principle of *mis en abyme* so that you will witness the infinite reflection of life and be able to relate yourself to it.

If you are so lucky as to be able to clear yourself of all such entities as I have alluded to, whether they are real or imaginary, you may have peeled off more of the onion, but you are still in a new predicament. You are not quite like the flame attracting moths because you can repel the moths and other determinisms away from you. You are, however, under the influence of the Demiurge. This not only refers to the agents of creation as stated above but the resultant creation itself. These spirits/agents have a history and agenda that is as old as the concepts of heaven and hell themselves. Basic theology will tell you that a spirit cannot possibly overcome the restrictions of the MEST or physical universe without any limitations without dealing with the agents of the Demiurge, jinn or whatever you want to call them. This is noteworthy with regards to Hubbard's Scientology schematic because he always said that Scientology did not intrude upon the Eighth Dynamic which, in Scientology parlance, refers to the realm of the Creator. In my estimation, and to put it mildly, this was a rather extreme oversight on his part.

While Hubbard had arguably created a first step towards either a potential reconciliation with or overcoming of the Demiurge, he certainly ended up with far less than such. Nevertheless, he was far from clueless with regards to either the subject or scenario at hand. His early work with Jack Parsons was, amongst other things, an attempt to emulate the magical work of John Dee and Edward Kelly who invoked Enochian angels. Dee and his angels claimed that these angels were, in fact, the same forces or jinn that King Solomon had worked with. Bringing King Solomon into this paradigm is important because he is considered noteworthy for having been unique in his ability to command the jinn as well as to heal. He did this through a secret word, *shin*, which has not only been adopted by Freemasonry but is the keystone upon which all of creation rests. Originally, *shin* referred to the moon and was used to name the capital city of Babylon which was known as Shinar, and it is where we get the word *shine*. The Hebrews adopted it because their totem, the wild boar, had teeth that were shaped like a crescent moon. To this day, *shin* means "tooth" in Hebrew, but it is also recognized to mean "spirit" or "change" in esoteric Judaism. In the Age of Pisces, *shin* was co-opted to convey the name Yeshua (Jesus) which is actually a transliteration of the Hebrew letters *yod he shin vau he*. This concept was utilized by the creators of Christianity to name the savior or solvent to the predicament of Mankind. The earlier matriarchal traditions of this planet, however, also utilized this principle and symbol- ized it with the pentagram, each point of the star representing one of the five letters and standing for Fire, Water, Spirit, Earth and Air. The pentagram is also symbolic of life because virtually all molecular structures in biochemistry are pentagonal in nature whereas molecular structures in ordinary (non-life based) chemistry are six-sided.

While I have dedicated an entire book to the meaning of *shin* (entitled *Synchronicity and the Seventh Seal*) and have further expounded upon it in the epilogue of *Mystery of Egypt*, I have included it here for at least three specific reasons. First, *shin* does represent the cornerstone of all life processes as well as the occult matrix of all magical processes. Second, it's role in the Solomonic analogy needs to be viewed in relation to my experiences with Hubbard and Scientology. More on this will be said later on. Third, the original definition for *shin* referred to the moon and its reflective quality which is akin to the principle of *mis en abyme* I explained earlier in this book. This also fits in with the principle used by Shadow Jack as explained earlier. One uses the mirror in the same way that he used a shadow. Give him just a little bit of shadow and he will quench the darkness. When you shine the truth in someone's face, it is like the reflection of a mirror. It can have a powerful effect.

I was not in a position to quell the shadows that cast their darkness over the environment I was in during my last days in Scientology. I took what I had learned and moved forward. Rather than shining a mirror or casting a shadow on anything, I grounded myself in the business world. Four years later, I would discover the depths of L. Ron Hubbard's fascination with Aleister Crowley and the occult and decided to seriously study these subjects myself. During these studies, however, I was always attempting to transmute any negative elements I discovered to a higher level. People who study this work are usually obsessed to selfishly use whatever they discover to their own immediate advantage. While this is understandable, it cuts off the elements and fruits of higher learning. When I read Aleister Crowley's *Book of Thoth*, I realized their was something missing from the Scientology paradigm. I am referring to positive spiritual entities in and about the universe. Accordingly, I began to invoke positive entities. I soon realized from my occult studies that most of this could, would or should have to do with the concept of the Goddess. It was during this period when the dream of the white bat came to me. Positive characters, all of whom were in the realm of operating spirits, began to appear. I have written about them in my many books, but I am quick to add that their positive qualities are only a part of their entire make-up. Characters like Preston Nichols and David Anderson have only so much to offer, and we can neither expect nor depend upon them to explain everything. In both cases, they have been agents of a positive force which has sought to help Mankind understand the intricacies of as well as the predicament of time.

If there is anything unfortunate about invocation or prayers, it is that they do not always get answered in a timely manner. As far as solving the entire predicament of the unified field, it is like living in the dark world of Shadow Jack where the only light is from the continued burning of slow lava eruptions. This world is analogous to a pit where gargoyles on the outer edges guard the passage way in and out. You pray to the Higher Essence for a futuristic search light made of lasers that will also enable you to burn your way through the mountains. Instead of a more dramatic response, the gargoyles at the outer edges of the pit shit small pocket flashlights out of their asses in what appears to be a flimsy answer to your request. Occasionally, they will also shit a small but somewhat effective pistol-sized hand laser. It is just enough to keep you going and to let you know that your communication had a powerful impact on some level. There are many ways to look at it, but what I want to emphasize is that my invocation for positive entities was a meaningful but somewhat limited response. The dream of the white bat was all the universe could provide at that particular time for whatever reasons.

Stumbling upon the time projects was actually a result and/or extension of my occult studies which were an extension of my effort to reconcile my experiences with Scientology and L. Ron Hubbard. I was actually holding up a virtual mirror when I met with Preston Nichols, and the first words to come out of his mouth featured the story about Aleister Crowley and the Wilson Brothers.* These were reflected back at me with abundant instances of synchronicity, all of which resonated like windows across time.

While the runway to get me to Romania was a long and slow wind-up process, most of my recent research has involved that country. I will recount how all of that transpired later on; but first, I want to once again emphasize that *shin* was the underlying principle at work. I am referring to the reflective quality of *shin* when it is meant to represent the moon. This is, once again, *mis en abyme*.

When you write anything, whether it is a novel, a poem, a resume or a website, what you write is a *mis en abyme* of yourself. What you write is like a beacon of yourself resonating across time and space. Do not underestimate this idea and keep it in mind when you compose anything, whether it is art, literature or even when you carry out a small task in life.

In my case, and in the tradition of Shadowjack, I was sending out a mirror effect that was resonating with time projects. Even though the results are a little slower than all of us might prefer, I cannot really complain. Eventually, I would learn that my results would be far more grandiose and far-reaching than I had ever imagined. These results, however, would literally take decades to manifest.

---

* The book *Montauk Revisited: Adventures in Synchronicity* by Preston B. Nichols and Peter Moon reveals the occult circumstances behind the Montauk Project which circle around the legendary Wilson Brothers, Preston and Marcus Wilson, the first manufacturers of scientific instruments in Great Britain who are believed to be the earlier incarnations of Preston Nichols and Duncan Cameron. When Peter Moon began to investigate the Montauk Project, he discovered a high degree of synchronicity concerning the names Wilson and Cameron, all of which led him to having a face to face meeting with Marjorie Cameron whose real last name was Wilson. Marjorie Cameron is well known as the wife of Jet Propulsion Laboratory founder Jack Parsons. Together they participated in the Babalon Working with L. Ron Hubbard in 1946. The Babalon Working has been heralded as the greatest magical experiment of the 20th Century and sought to overthrow the patriarchal tyranny that has ruled the earth for many millennia.

CHAPTER SIX

INTEGRATION OF THE DREAM

As the entirety of this book is based upon a dream, it is important that I address this topic and particularly from a pragmatic standpoint. If you have not already acted upon my suggestion to utilize a note pad while reading this book, I hope that the last chapter will change your mind and that you will start writing down your own impressions, ideas, and creative thoughts. Writing not only engages your creative mind with your linear mind, it synthesizes your experiences. If you do this wisely, it creates harmony. There is no limit to how deep you can go; but even if you do not wish to go deeply, you can at least utilize it at the more obvious and practical levels of your existence.

When you dream, you are accessing a part of your mind-brain-complex that is not only tied to your deeper emotions and archetypes but is also tied to what Jung called the collective unconscious. In other words, all beings share a common thread of consciousness of the ecosystem that is reflected in the brain which is acting like an antenna. That is where the equation becomes extremely interesting to an astute observer. When spirits from various factions seek to influence various individuals, it is this aforesaid part of the brain apparatus that is being used in order to make their inroads. Different individuals attract different spirits from various places.

One individual who experienced a rather over-the-top connection to this part of the mind-brain-body complex was Phil Dick, a popular science fiction writer. He did not, however, make this connection through a dream as we would typically think of it. It happened as a result of him mistakenly altering the directions for Linus Pauling's avant-garde Vitamin C therapy which consists primarily of taking mega doses of Vitamin C in a prescribed regimen. Exceeding the mega doses by leaps and bounds, Dick began to have out-of-this-world paranormal experiences which he attributed to his unintentional misuse of the therapy. According to Dick, he theorized that the Vitamin C had burned a hole through his corpus callosum with a resulting interface of the two cranial hemispheres that was unprecedented, at least in regards to most people. This created more than an ordinary dream state. According to Dick, the time period of 70 A.D. in Jerusalem was superimposed upon his real life in Orange County, California during the 1970s. It had to do with the "evil empire" of the Romans sacking of the Second Temple and all the drama that went with it. What he described however was not typical history we have all heard before but rather a hidden history of King Felix (which the Christ in the *Bible* was patterned after) and how it was all centered around the concept of *Yod-He-Shin-Vau-He*. He describes this in his book *VALIS*.

Dick's own conclusions, all based upon his rather wild experiences, led him to equate *shin* as being representative of the corpus callosum of the human brain. Scientifically, the corpus callosum is the primary but not exclusive region of the brain that allows communication and coordination to take place between the two hemisphere of the brain. Understand that I am not encouraging you to do what Phil Dick did but rather to grasp the role of *shin* as it relates to the integration of opposites. In this case, we are talking about the two parts of the brain which represent the linear and non-linear aspects of reality. As far as writing goes, you are simply trying to integrate the creative portion of your brain with the linear aspect. This is you activating your own microcosmic orbit. In the bigger scheme, *shin* represents the path of the Tarot known as either the *Last Judgment* or the *New Aeon* which is where the spirit of all Mankind reunites with the Creator. It is akin to reconciling the earth realm with that of heaven. It is *mis en abyme* all the way. The "Mirror of God" is now coming into a clearer view if not a full view. In this respect, it is the Creator finding itself by way of reconciling the shards of the lens that were separated. Any work of art features divine inspiration, but everything depends upon how much mirror you can or choose to reflect.

It could be readily argued that the ultimate book would bring everyone back to the Creator and reconcile all unresolved issues. One can, of course, consider the *Bible* and question how that work fits into the equation. Rather than commenting on the book itself, I would rather you just consider how people have utilized the *Bible* to wreak havoc. What they are doing, however, is holding up a mirror of themselves. The "God" such people seek to unleash upon the masses is an equal reflection of them. One can also use the *Bible* in a positive direction. As the *Bible* is not foolproof from being misused, so does it tell us that its authors were far from perfect. The fact that *shin* does not manifest itself in the *Bible* other than in the most hidden context also suggests something about the nature of the Creator itself. There are aspects that are hidden or occulted.

These hidden or intangible aspects of *shin* also fit into the realm of dreams. Just as dreams are an effort of the organism to reconcile its linear experiences in life so is *shin* a principle by which Mankind can reconcile with the Creator. This correspondence, however, suggests that *shin* equates to an effort on one's part, just as a dream employs effort to reconcile a situation in life. It should be noted in respect to this that the symbol for *shin*, long before it ever became a Hebrew letter, evolved out of the three-pronged trident which is identified with Poseiden or Neptune. This is an important correspondence because, in astrology, Neptune is considered to be the ruler of dreams.

To give a little more perspective on the archetype of Neptune and its role in the realm of dreams, it is also considered to represent the higher octave of Venus as well as recognized to be the ruler of all spirituality, illusion and deception. It is very easy to see how this works if you see someone who is frustrated by Venus. In order to satisfy their longing, they will daydream about someone as if they are unconsciously or consciously appealing to

Neptune, the ruler of the dream world. The connection between Neptune and Venus reflects back to the archetypes of Cupid and Psyke which we examined earlier in Chapter 2. Love, represented by Cupid, and the individual will, represented by Psyche, are not only bound to each other archetypally, they represent the essential ingredients of the created world. The Hindus refer to the created world as maya and it is illusionary. Illusions, once again, are the realm of Neptune. Nevertheless, the duality inspired story of Cupid and Psyke was deliberately portrayed through the principle of *mis en abyme* in a written fashion that was a story within a story. Whether a person's world is delusional or a construct of the reality-based illusion called maya, it is not an accident that creation revolves around the yin and yang of relationships. The creation of DNA is a *mis en abyme* of the prior or older DNA that precipitated it. All DNA is a *mis en abyme* of all other DNA with sex being the engaging or mirroring of two separate mirrors to create a third mirror.

When we consider *shin* in relation to dreams, it is the bridge between worlds, only one of which is the connection between the incarnated world with the unincarnated world. Dreams, as a part of *shin*, represent the bridge between the world that is awake and the world that is asleep. As the gateway between worlds, *shin* was a closely guarded secret during the Age of Pisces, representing the secret formula by which the universe is created and changed. It is a creative process. As a part of this creative process, dreaming is not only an excellent opportunity to harness creativity, it is also an integral part of how your mind works. What you are trying to do either as an artist or as a liver of life is to tie the worlds together. *Shin* and/or *mis en abyme* is the integration point, and it is wise to contemplate it and put your focus upon it.

It will also help your understanding if you consider that the human mind can be likened to a time machine. If you imagine yourself walking down Main Street, the non-linear functions of the brain receive perceptions indiscriminately and without respect to linear functionality. This means that time is not necessarily processed with regards to all the perceptions that are taken in. One readily sees this aspect with hallucinogenic drugs and other altered states of consciousness, both of which are sometimes cited or utilized in brain experiments. In this respect, all the stores on Main Street can be rearranged in any way you might imagine. The linear functions of the brain, however, provide an index of a time line where most everything makes sense. There are, however, other indexes that operate without respect to time and that includes the smells you smell and everything you think, feel, see, hear and so on. If you do the Dark Room exercises I suggested earlier in this book, you are opening the door to non-linear perception. The Dark Room is an unlimited gateway, and it should not be underestimated. How successful you will be is only restricted by the limitations you yourself impose upon your own imagination.

The linear functions of the brain reduce a myriad of perceptions to ordinary experience. When an artist indulges in abstract thinking, he takes the opportunity to reiterate experiences or perceptions without regard to linear logic. If one is clever and fortunate, one can even create a threshold to other realms of existence that have a meaningful and practical interface with ordinary linear reality. When there is no feedback or tie-in to one's ordinary reality, however, the value of dreaming is questionable. The trick here is to seek out and build such a tie-in. This requires study, experience, and practice. Such study should include lucid dreaming, the ultimate experience in dreaming. This means to "wake up" during your dream to the point where you are self-aware and know that you are dreaming. Such instances present opportunities that one generally does not have during their normal waking state. If you can visualize thoughts in complete simulated reality, you can also work out real life problems. To help you with lucid dreaming, I will give you two separate exercises that will encourage lucid dreaming.

Dream Exercise 1 — Details

Step 0 — Get yourself a dream journal and write down your dreams.

Step 1 — During your regular day to day activity, make a practice of noticing particular details in the environment. Such details could include anything. Notice such details at least thirty times a day.

Step 2 — When you become lucid (self-aware that you are dreaming) in a dream, seek to maintain the lucidity and begin to breathe deeply with long slow breaths. Inhale through the nose and exhale through the mouth.

Step 3 — As you continue to breathe, do a chi gong exercise. This will help you maintain your lucid state. If you do not know any chi gong, learn some. Use a book or the internet.

Step 4 — Enter your experiences in your dream journal.

Dream Exercise 2 — Flying

Step 1 — Every time you see a clock or time piece during the day, ask yourself the following three questions: 1) What time is it? 2) Is this a dream? 3) Can I fly?

Step 2 — When you become lucid, repeat Step 2 from Dream Exercise 1. Once again, you are seeking to maintain the lucidity by breathing deeply with long slow breaths. Inhale through the nose and exhale through the mouth.

Step 3 — As you continue to breathe, do a chi gong exercise. This will help you maintain your lucid state. If you do not know any chi gong, learn some.

Step 4 — Enter your experiences in your dream journal.

While these exercises will help you, never consider that you should be a slave to your dreams. They are a window into the past, present, future and also to other worlds. What you do in life is more dependent upon you than anyone else or any system. Dreams are a reflection of yourself, your environment, and the collective unconscious.

When you are dreaming, it is very important to understand that you are experiencing a stimulation of the visual cortex. Interestingly, there is a visual cortex on the left side of the brain which receives input from the right and a visual cortex on the right side which receives input from the left. Essentially, the visual cortex receives input from the retina. It also, however, receives input from other sources, particularly when you are dreaming. While I will not elaborate on that here, you can easily realize what is being alluded to.

With regard to dreaming, creativity, and general living, it is important to understand another aspect concerning the visual cortex. Words or illustrations on paper also stimulate the visual cortex. This is what writing and art are all about. The *Bible* is an excellent example. Everyone who has ever read it has had their own visual cortex stimulated. Obviously, everyone's visual cortex is stimulated in a different way although there will often be commonalities that many would agree upon. When an evangelist or a minister preaches about the Second Coming or Revelation, he is stimulating the visual cortex of his congregation based upon what has been stimulated in himself.

One of the biggest dichotomies in Christianity, to make an example of just one religion, is that there is a rather large disparity of opinions. Those who can stimulate the visual cortex in a more persuasive way, depending upon the prejudices of a particular audience, will certainly attract more adherents. The *Bible* itself is all about stimulation of the visual cortex. Whoever wrote, collated and edited the *Bible* were stimulating the visual cortex. Often referred to as the divinely inspired word of God, the *Bible* is clearly an example of writing from faith, sometimes interspersing it with what passes as a semblance of history to some historians. There is no question that it aspires to integrate Mankind with the Divinity. How good a job it does depends upon the opinion and experience of the observer. For it to even register in someone's mind, however, the visual cortex has to be stimulated in a way that is considered meaningful. The success of such an endeavor as writing a holy book depends upon how successfully it can stick to reality and explain circumstances by which the Divinity can or does interface with the earthly world. Adherents will, however, go out of their way and create their own lenses as to convince you that such a book is Divine. In any case, this is all about stimulation of the visual cortex. The biggest problem with religious stimulation of the visual cortex, in a practical sense, is that people can become very ungrounded over such matters and this might include giving away their possessions and common sense. The is simply the dark side of *mis en abyme*.

With regard to the visual cortex, it is necessary or advisable to stimulate it and enhance the stimulation. I highly recommend the dark room because it is free and it makes you your own intermediary with the archetypal forces of creation. Willful lucid dreaming does the same thing.

If you do such exercises, you will sooner or later encounter phenomena that is out of the ordinary. If you do this and suddenly find yourself with an overwhelming need to tell someone about your experiences, you had best learn how to ground yourself. In Chi Gong, we do a stance referred to as Equilibrium. One does this by holding one's arms around a large but imaginary beach ball. While one is holding this imaginary beach ball, one also sits on a large imaginary beach ball. The coccyx rests on the top of the imaginary ball. The knees are slightly bent, and the neck is elongated at the shoulders. The chin moves back so that the head is directly in alignment with the spine. One is in effect putting one's body in what is called natural alignment. It takes a lot of practice. This stance can be done in five minute increments for a total of twenty minutes a day (optimal). It grounds one to the earth and also does wonders for the entire body in terms of circulation as well as many other "mysterious" processes that will escape the traditional Western mind.

The visual cortex is also the realm of remote viewing, a term which has created considerable excitement as well as opportunities for unscrupulous people in the seminar business. It has accordingly acquired a very dubious if not outright bad name. The field of remote viewing has produced all sorts of claims and a lot of bragging but very little meaningful tangibility. The armed services have utilized countless people in this endeavor. Tibetan sects have also practiced such techniques for millennia. One has to ask oneself: Has the use of these techniques bettered the world or done otherwise? I will leave you to be the judge. If remote viewing worked and was being used with good intent, you would not see all the problems we have in the world.

In any case, remote viewing does stimulate the visual cortex, even when it is downright wrong. There are, of course, wars being waged to control, stimulate and steer your visual cortex. There are dream wars, ELF wave wars, and a host of other technologies designed to limit or otherwise compromise your own ability to "see." Ultimately, you are the only one who can shut off the noise that might get in your way. This is best done via the Dark Room.

There is another key component as to why these aforesaid remote viewing procedures do not ultimately work in a meaningful or tangible way. This is due to the fact that they are not integrated into and through the heart. Endeavors seeking to utilize remote viewing are usually done for greed and power. This cuts off the circulation, not only for the individual but for the planet as well. This is why mass protests such as Occupy Wall Street do not ultimately work. The people participating might be well intended, but they are not really operating from their own heart. Even though they might think they are operating with their heart, they are being manipulated into thinking they are solving something when they really are not. Solving the world situation begins by reconciling your own heart and then allowing that to reverberate through your own mental, spiritual, emotional and physical bodies and into the environment. Only then can the world's problems be solved.

Keep in mind that the Chinese word for heart is *shin*. As *shin*, the heart is the ultimate point of integration for your dreams and creative work. If you want to make your dream come true, put your heart into your dream. Do not be discouraged if it does not happen overnight. Some things take time and you have to integrate time into your heart as well. In Chi Gong, anything that is of value takes time.

CHAPTER SEVEN

THE TIME REACTOR

As I said earlier, there were never any particular desires or realistic expectations on my part to ever visit Romania. The first time it was ever even considered was when Dr. David Anderson suggested it rather passionately upon our first meeting. Even so, it was neither a firm invitation nor something I thought would necessarily take place. He was new to Romania himself at that point. My main interest in David Anderson at that juncture was primarily with regard to his time control technology. Even so, it took me a while before I could consider him too seriously as having any sort of meaningful role in my life. While it was obvious he was very well connected in government circles, his technology was seemingly in a stage of infancy. I say seemingly because the past, present and future are all intricately connected when you arrive at the more esoteric and fundamental aspects of time research. Yesterday can soon turn into tomorrow and vice versa. In my estimation, to make a statement of finality about his early research is unwise.

At our first meeting, David discussed his time reactor technology. As I have already discussed this in some depth in other books, I will only give a brief summary here. At that time period, in 1999, he owned a company called the Time Travel Research Center located in an industrial park in Hauppauge, Long Island, New York.

The history of the time reactor, which is essentially a device to control or facilitate manipulation of time, began while David was serving in the United States Air Force. At that time, the military was experiencing a major problem with their satellites in orbit. As satellites drift several meters every year if left to their regular orbiting path, it compromises their usefulness. Asked if he could help resolve this issue, David's approach to this problem was more than a little unique and quite brilliant. He created a space-time module based upon Einstein's Theory of Special Relativity. It was very advanced stuff, but he actually worked out a paradigm whereby space-time could literally be warped so as to maintain the orbits of satellites.

Upon leaving the Air Force, David patented the necessary algorithms for accomplishing this manipulation of space-time. He then parlayed this into the creation of the Time Travel Research Center which licensed this advanced technology to the Government and to industry for the specific purpose of maintaining the orbit of their satellites. Besides the facility on Long Island, there was a theoretical research center in Romania and a larger lab, which still exists to this day, in northwestern New Mexico.

Extrapolating upon what he had learned with satellite applications, David's subsequent research utilized laser beams to create a self-contained field, approximately the size of a soccer ball, in which time could be slowed down or speeded up. This was and is of great interest to the medical field because it means that transplantable organs can have a much longer shelf life. The Time Travel Research Center was taken very seriously and attracted considerable investment dollars from investors in the medical sector.

The construction of a time reactor begins with utilizing an antenna to induce a high speed rotational electromagnetic field. A special environment is then created by emitting a chemical reagent in the form of a gas into the core of the field and then contouring it with twelve high energy lasers that in turn induce a time warp field. Control of this field is facilitated through multiple sensors (over forty) in each laser which enables the field to be maintained. The exact tangential or curved positioning of the lasers is a key component in maintaining the special environment. This begets the boundary layer which not only produces a Doppler Effect, but it was a key challenge in the early research of the time reactor. The Doppler Effect refers to the change in frequency of a wave for an observer moving relative to its source. A prime example is the sound of a siren as an ambulance moves towards you and then away from you. The Doppler Effect creates a virtual "bubble" wherein the rate of time begins to either slow down or speed up compared to the outside of the virtual bubble. The boundary layer was a critical issue, at least in the early stages of development, because plants that traversed it melted in a very unpleasant fashion. This is reminiscent of although not exactly identical to the fallout suffered by sailors in the Philadelphia Experiment.

As the time reactor went through its various stages of development, a rather astonishing side benefit was noticed. The twisting of spacetime results in a tremendous amount of stored potential energy that is separated by the different regions of twisted or curved spacetime. This observation is in alignment with Einstein's theory of general relativity which predicted that rotating bodies drag space-time around themselves in a phenomenon known as frame-dragging. In what amounts to a rough metaphor, imagine the air swirling around a tornado that displaces dust and air that moves around it. So does the actual fabric of space- time move when a planet rotates but very slightly. Although the twisting of spacetime is very small, a huge rotating body like the earth contains enormous levels of potential energy by reason of the tension in the fabric of spacetime that is caused by inertial frame-dragging.

A time reactor is clean and inexpensive compared to current systems in use and there are no dangerous by-products. A time reactor not only generates high levels of clean power but also containable and controllable time-warped fields and closed time-like curves and is able to utilize the stored potential energy across any region of curved spacetime or hyperspace. This includes any area of curved spacetime, whether naturally or artificially created. A time reactor is the only system of its kind that will generate such power and a time-warped field. Accordingly, the device has been patented, and you can view these documents on the following pages.

This Acknowledgement Receipt evidences receipt on the noted date by the USPTO of the indicated documents, characterized by the applicant, and including page counts, where applicable. It serves as evidence of receipt similar to a Post Card, as described in MPEP 503.

New Applications Under 35 U.S.C. 111

If a new application is being filed and the application includes the necessary components for a filing date (see 37 CFR 1.53(b)-(d) and MPEP 506), a Filing Receipt (37 CFR 1.54) will be issued in due course and the date shown on this Acknowledgement Receipt will establish the filing date of the application.

National Stage of an International Application under 35 U.S.C. 371

If a timely submission to enter the national stage of an international application is compliant with the conditions of 35 U.S.C. 371 and other applicable requirements a Form PCT/DO/EO/903 indicating acceptance of the application as a national stage submission under 35 U.S.C. 371 will be issued in addition to the Filing Receipt, in due course.

New International Application Filed with the USPTO as a Receiving Office

If a new international application is being filed and the international application includes the necessary components for an international filing date (see PCT Article 11 and MPEP 1810), a Notification of the International Application Number and of the International Filing Date (Form PCT/RO/105) will be issued in due course, subject to prescriptions concerning national security, and the date shown on this Acknowledgement Receipt will establish the international filing date of the application.

Electronic Acknowledgement Receipt

EFS ID:	6627843
Application Number:	61286110
International Application Number:	
Confirmation Number:	2469
Title of Invention:	A system accessing and applying stored potential energy within regions of curved space-time or hyperspace.
First Named Inventor/Applicant Name:	David Anderson
Correspondence Address:	David Anderson 620 Park Avenue # 308 Rochester　　　　　　　　　NY　　　　14607 US　　　585 747-9541 David.Anderson@AndersonMultinational.com
Filer:	Adam Thomas/Jo Ann Valino
Filer Authorized By:	Adam Thomas
Attorney Docket Number:	
Receipt Date:	14-DEC-2009
Filing Date:	
Time Stamp:	14:12:58

RAM confirmation Number	499	
Deposit Account	502617	
Authorized User		

File Listing:

Document Number	Document Description	File Name	File Size(Bytes)/ Message Digest	Multi Part /.zip	Pages (if appl.)
1	Provisional Cover Sheet (SB16)	6647339_ProvisionalSB.pdf	782218 25c445bf610ae0bb28a108fe48cf088262b640de	no	3
Warnings:					
Information:					
2	Specification	6647339ABX-desc.pdf	43415 b2d686e7ec8986348c2102e5fc9519595b914a88	no	4
Warnings:					
Information:					
3	Claims	6647339ABX-clms.pdf	24301 e4e084a36dda7d0284ee380623551b06b80f208a	no	1
Warnings:					
Information:					
4	Abstract	6647339ABX-abst.pdf	18950 90b7b6062be28b3b1a750eb1ba1af15ea0456338	no	1
Warnings:					
Information:					
5	Drawings-only black and white line drawings	6647339ABX-draw.pdf	140430 43c98baf60a01bc5a48479592c0ebaf84a498424	no	2
Warnings:					
Information:					
6	Fee Worksheet (PTO-875)	fee-info.pdf	28653 d9c396b7dcf588933336c9e5b0Bd85742c30e4b4	no	2
Warnings:					
Information:					
		Total Files Size (in bytes):	1037967		

A system accessing and applying stored potential energy within regions of curved space-time or hyperspace.

DESCRIPTION

[Para 1] The present invention relates to a system accessing and applying stored potential energy within regions of curved space-time or hyperspace.

[Para 2] The product is comprised of the following components:

o The environment 1 is any region between and including two or more separated points in between which is a region of manmade or naturally-occurring curved space-time or hyperspace.

o The Reactor Emitter 2 is an assembly, located at any of a set of multiple points in space that are separated across a region of curved space-time or hyperspace, which produces an information and energy beam when activated. The form of the beam may include but is not limited to thermal, chemical, electrical, radiant, nuclear, magnetic, elastic, sound, mechanical, space-time-generated or any other form of information and energy known in the art that has the ability to enable the coupling and discharge of the space-time-motive force stored within regions of curved space-time or hyperspace.

o The Reactor Power Collector 3 is an assembly, located at any of a set of multiple points that are separated across a region of curved space-time or hyperspace, which captures the energy within the space-time-motive force when it is coupled and discharged between the points. The form of the energy captured by a reactor power collector 3 may include but is not limited to thermal, chemical, electrical, radiant, nuclear, magnetic, elastic, sound, mechanical, space-time-generated or any other form of energy known in the art that may be generated when space-time-motive force is coupled and discharged across regions of curved space-time or through hyperspace.

o The Energy storage device 4 is an assembly that receives, stores, and releases energy created by the operation of the time reactor. The forms of the energy stored, processed and released by the energy storage device 4 may include but are not limited to thermal, chemical, electrical, radiant, nuclear, magnetic, elastic, sound, mechanical and space-time-generated energy. The energy storage device 4 may consist of other types of energy storage devices know in the art, including but not limited to batteries and fuel cells.

o The Power Conduit 5 comprises energy.

[Para 3] Necessary elements of the time reactor include at least one reactor emitter 2, one reactor power collector 3, one power conduit 5 and a control system 6 operating in the aforementioned environment 1. If generated power is not immediately consumed then an energy storage device 4 may be included. If the application of generated fields is desired then a reactor field chamber 7 may be added. The system could include additional reactor emitters 2, reactor power collectors 3, and power conduits 5. (Not shown.) In addition, multiple complete time reactor systems of any size may be used to increase the total power generation capability or to create additional and different types generated fields, within or near the reactor location, for different application (Not shown.).

[Para 4] The embodiment shown in the drawing example includes single reactor emitter 2 and two reactor power collectors 3 connected via power conduits 5 to an energy storage device 4 at a single location (A) in a curved space-time environment 1. A control system 6 with bi-directional communication to each component is also shown in addition to a reactor field chamber 7 in close proximity to the reactor power collectors 3 and the energy storage device 4. Further, the drawing is a diagram only, and one embodiment of the time reactor may include these components located differently with respect to each other. In one variation there may be just a single reactor emitter 2 and single reactor power collector 3. In another variation the reactor power collector 3 could instead be an array of reactor power collectors 3. In yet another variation there could be multiple reactor emitters 2 and reactor power collectors 3 at the same or at multiple different points that are separated from each other across curved space-time or hyperspace. The time reactor system may be configured in many different ways and scales.

[Para 5] In operation all components of the time reactor are in an off state in which no components are powered or activated. When all components are powered and the reactor emitter 2 is activated, a multi-path information and energy beam is directed between two points (A and B) separated across curved space-time or hyperspace. The resulting effect of the multi-path beam is to couple and create a discharge path for the space-time-motive force stored in the curved space-time between the two points or across hyperspace. The discharge of the space-time motive force is coupled into the reactor power collectors 3 then conducted through the power conduits 5 into the energy storage device 4. The reactor control system 6 manages the entire operation including the balancing and conditioning of the energy in the energy storage device 4 and controlling the fields in the reactor field chamber 7 that are created by the space-time-motive force and energy delivered through the power conduits 5 into the energy storage device 4.

[Para 6] The design of each component will vary significantly based upon application. The size of the time reactor could vary from a micro-level to a much larger application covering a large area on the surface of a planet, other surface, or may cover multiple surfaces at different points. The design characteristics of each individual component and part will vary greatly based upon many application design criteria. These design criteria include the time reactor operational environment, its physical size, the number of reactor emitters 2 and reactor power collectors 3, the paths and medium through which the coupling and discharge of space-time-motive force occurs, the generated power levels, and the relative positioning of all components and parts.

[Para 7] The elements of the time reactor may be reconfigured in many different ways to produce the same results. A single time reactor may include some parts and components at a single point or at two or more points that are separated across a region of curved space-time or hyperspace. Additionally, multiple complete time reactors may be used to increase power generation capacity or generate different formations of time-warped fields and closed time-like curves.

[Para 8] Because one benefit of this invention is power generation, and the physical scale of the invention can range from micro to large-scale applications, the applications are vast. In most applications to use the time reactor all components and parts would be activated and the control system 6 would be used to generate the conditions necessary to initiate the coupling, discharging and collecting of the energy in the space-time motive force stored in the curved space-time or hyperspace in the time reactors operating environment 1. The control system 6 would manage all feedback and control, balancing and conditioning all individual parts, components and the overall system to ensure efficient and effective operation during activation, operation and shutdown. This includes all aspects of field generation, control and application in the reactor field chamber 7.

[Para 9] The invention is not limited to power generation. For example the fields generated by the coupling of space-time-motive force may be concentrated and controlled in or near the reactor field chamber 7 producing time-warped fields including closed time-like curves permitting relative time acceleration and deceleration within the reactor field chamber 7 that can be used for multiple applications. In addition, the operation of the time reactor may create carrier waveforms in the structure of space-time that may permit modulation and accelerated long distance communication through space-time or hyperspace. It may also be possible to use the characteristics of the coupled space-time motive force and the time reactor to create fields providing force-at-a-distance through space-time. In addition, the invention creates conditions that may be valuable for multi-dimensional computing and many applications in research and development in the area of space-time physics and high-energy systems.

What is claimed is:

[Claim 1] A system accessing and applying stored potential energy within regions of curved space-time or hyperspace.

ABSTRACT

This world lacks a source of plentiful and clean energy. Present power generation systems are inefficient, expensive and create harmful byproducts of operation. Also, there is not presently a reliable source of time-warped fields and closed time-like curves for use in spacetime research and applications. This invention generates both high levels of clean power and time-warped fields, including closed time-like curves. This invention accesses and harvests the potential energy between points separated by regions of twisted or curved space-time or hyperspace. This can include curved space-time that is caused by inertial frame dragging around the earth, any rotating body, or other natural or artificially created effect on a large or micro scale. When the system is activated the space-time-motive force stored in the tension of curved space-time or across hyperspace is coupled and discharged providing an abundant source of clean energy and time-warped fields, including closed time-like curves.

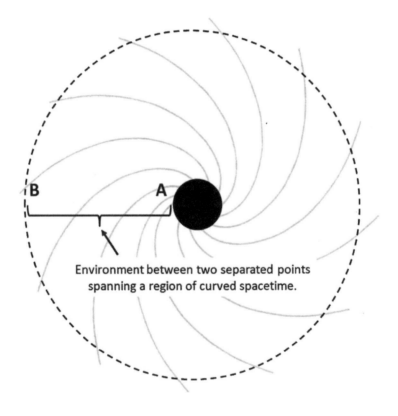

Environment between two separated points
spanning a region of curved spacetime.

1 Environment
2 Reactor Emitter
3 Reactor Power Collector
4 Energy Storage Device
5 Power Conduits
6 Control System
7 Reactor Field Chamber

←‑‑→ Feedback and Control
∞∞∞∞ Information and Energy Beam
⋛ Coupled Spacetime-motive Force

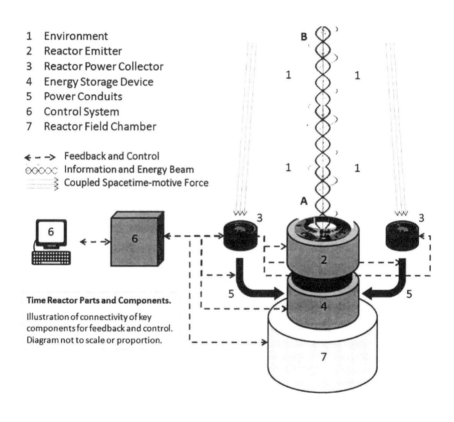

Time Reactor Parts and Components.

Illustration of connectivity of key components for feedback and control. Diagram not to scale or proportion.

I have included David's patent filing for at least a couple of reasons. First, it substantiates what I have just written about the time reactor; and second, it was reportedly removed from the U.S. patent rolls. I was not able to find it on Google Patents. There are also several patents that David has filed, but I do not have further information upon them.

When one patents technology that is crucial to the defense of the United States, the Defense Department often establishes a partnership with the inventor. This is the case with David. Regular procedures do not necessarily apply. At one point, where the patent application for the time reactor might still remain, it was filed in the public domain. This was once the subject of a very mysterious coded post card I once received from David that was sent from Bethlehem in Palestine. He had been involved in some sort of high level conference and perceived the eventuality that perhaps he would not survive and that his inventions might be lost to humanity. As a potential precaution, he gave me a coded message on where to find them in the public domain.

You can read more about the time reactor in my books and newsletters as well as David's latest website which is *www.andersoninstitute.com*. There is, however, another reason why I included this data about the time reactor. If you go back to Chapter One of this book and review the story about the white bat, you will see that it features a circumstance which is reminiscent of a time reactor. Of particular note is the disturbance around the boundary layer.

> "At this point, a huge bat flew into the room. I could tell without a second thought that it was Count Dracula himself. He transformed into human shape and kept the broad wings of his cape extended. The frenetic writhing of the females now began to pick up in pitch. They began to swim up in the air and around him like ghosts. They appeared much more vaporized and swam under him, around him and through his legs. He stood still. His eyes and his body radiated strong energy. It appeared to be energy that they lived off of. Shrieking sounds of euphoria replaced the panting of desire.
>
> It was no longer a mystery to me. I was watching an orgy of spirits, surrounding a core of very live energy. I did notice at the outskirts of the radiant orb that some of the apparitions were being blocked out, creating a slight turbulence.
>
> Then, one of the spirits on the outside appeared to splice off from the orb. It came straight towards me. As it came closer its definitions became clearer and much more female. I was now being confronted by a most enticing female apparition. Before I could think or resist, I was overcome by a magnetic force that concentrated on me."

It is also noteworthy that the female spirit spliced off of the orb on a tangent, not unlike the tangential factors of the time bubble created by the time reactor. In certain key respects, my dream was mimicking certain aspects of the time reactor. This might be a worthy coincidence in and of itself, but it takes on a deeper significance when you consider that it was David Anderson who brought me to Romania.

There are, however, other aspects of this scenario in this dream that at first glance do not appear to have anything to do with the time reactor. I am referring to the observation that it is Dracula himself that generates the entire ensemble through his magic; and further, this seems to be part and parcel of the magnetic attraction he possesses over his brides. While David's approach is through science and engineering, Dracula's approach is through will and magic, and his sphere is laden with beings. All of this begs us to ask different questions. Is there a great power or being that is working behind the scenes of David's research? Is there a force that is working in concert between the two of us? Any thoughts you might have on this topic are best noted in your own journal. There are many different pathways to explore.

It is interesting to note that during my first meeting with David, he told me an interesting anecdote about his first trip to Romania. He had visited Bran Castle, a tourist attraction that is incorrectly billed as Dracula's Castle. In reality, Vlad Tepes might have spent about fourteen days there, but he never occupied it in any capacity of rulership or even as a home dwelling. Nevertheless, the place does a steady business and has all sorts of history strewn about to convince people of its authenticity. In any event, David told me about a rather unnerving experience he had there when he was, as I recall, walking down a stairwell. He saw a portrait of a young man who looked exactly like he did as a young man. The resemblance was too much for him. The portrait featured no particular description of who this person was.

As you will learn in the rest of this book, there is a very rich current beneath the Romanian culture than most anyone has ever imagined. This not only includes ancient history and the antecedents of religion but modern and future science. It also includes exotic subjects such as alchemy and the realms of the Inner Earth. The more I have learned about Romania, the less strange it is that I would have been brought to that remarkable country by a scientist who has been successful with time control technology. My story, dictated by my dream, was giving me a taste of the time reactor, a device that was not actually invented yet. This is just one example of the human mind, via the R.E.M. realm, being a time machine.

For those of you who are familiar with the archetypes of the Cabala, it is interesting to contemplate where the time reactor or any time machine fits into the equation of consciousness. If you are not familiar with the Cabala or its terms, it is an excellent study in archetypes, and I encourage you to do so. Accordingly, I have written a rather brief primer on it in Appendix A for those who are new to it.

The most obvious cabalistic identification for the time reactor would seem to be the pathway known as The Chariot. In *The Book of Thoth*, The Chariot is the path of the throne energies (also known as the supernals or upper triad) beginning their first stage of manifestation. It is essentially the first or primal efforts of the Creator making a home for itself. For this reason, it is assigned to Cancer which represents the hearth and is ruled by the moon. This card also represents the beginning of emotions in the Tree of Life. As the moon equates to *shin*, we have the principle of *mis en abyme* showing itself once again. This is the "first" reflection of the Creator or Shekinah.

In cabalistic terms, The Chariot emanates from Binah, the sepiroth of Understanding, and flows to Geburah, the sepiroth of Severity. Binah is ruled by Saturn, and this represents both time and structure. Geburah is ruled by Mars and this implies all the excruciating circumstances of raw survival. This is the raw effort of a creature trying to survive in a challenging world and all the emotions that go with it. Mars is a fighter and conqueror, and this path includes the aspects of eating, being eaten and all the martial drama that goes with that.

The Chariot is characterized as conquest through hard work, conviction and overcoming a great struggle. It represents overcoming opposing forces, enemies and obstacles, sometimes referring to your own demons. Most of all, it is sheer will power. It requires control to bring together opposing forces and quarreling emotions.

These opposing forces are given a symbolic rendition in the *Rider-Waite Tarot* where there are two sphinxes with headdresses. Both the sphinxes and the headdresses are black and white inversions of each other. This not only represents the push-pull of duality but suggests that there are two aspects to the sphinx which arise out of duality. The Charioteer, however, uses reins to harness them and move forward. In this respect, the Charioteer not only can steer the sphinx, he can answer its riddles. In this respect, the Charioteer is carrying out a divine edict or energy and is not unlike a pharaoh leading an army into battle while driving a chariot in what amounts to a conquest of the physical realm.

Traditionally, the Chariot is considered to be a perplexing card to define. It is both warfare and reconciliation in the name of transmutation, and this includes the transmutation of the elements. In the *Thoth Tarot*, the sphinxes are depicted as the four cherubs which are depicted as the fixed signs of the Zodiac: the lion (Leo), the eagle (Scorpio), the water bearer (Aquarius), and the bull (Taurus). In the *Rider-Waite Tarot*, we have a black sphinx and a white sphinx , both with the headdress of a pharaoh. The reconciliation of these two opposing renditions is not only rather easy, it is particularly intriguing. The sphinx itself is an evolution of the Cherubs which represent the four elements of tetragrammaton: fire, water, air and earth. In Freemasonry, the paw of the sphinx is the key as it represents *shin* due to a paw having five toes and this represents the pentagram. This is the spirit being injected into the four elements but also demonstrating will over the elements. It was the Lion's Paw that King Solomon used to resurrect Hiram Abiff from the dead.

The Charioteer is therefore the driving force of the Shekinah or Divine Will. He is driving the elements and forcing them or forging them into an existence by his will which is an expression of divinity. It is especially interesting to consider that this metaphorical expression would include the paws of the sphinxes hitting the ground. This, in a sense, is an archetypal representation of *shin* as pentacles hitting or touching the ground and forging themselves through the sepiroth of severity (Geburah) and eventually falling down to the sepiroth of Hesod, the ruler of which is Mercury, the god of commerce and hermetic wisdom. The path from Geburah to Hesod is The Hanged Man who cares nothing about money at all for he is unattached to materiality. From Hesod/Mercury, these metaphorical coins fall down to the Earth (Malkuth) via the path card known as The Last Judgmemt or New Aeon which is, according to the attributes of the *Thoth Tarot*, ruled by *shin*. Pentacles are depicted as coins with a pentagram on them in the *Rider-Waite Tarot*, and they are referred to as coins in the *Thoth Tarot*. Thus it is that *shin* is the coin of the realm. The fact that a coin is double-sided is also not an accident.

One aspect I would like to add to the concept of The Last Judgment is that people often view this in a questionable if not outright wrong fashion. It is typical for most people, even if they are not Judaic-Christian, to view the concept of a Last Judgement as something they have to prepare for in what will eventually amount to a reconciling of a karmic balance sheet. While it is highly advisable to remain accountable for one's actions and to not dismiss such a notion, the path of The Last Judgment also applies in the past tense. In other words, you ended up on the earth plane (Malkuth) by reason of the fact that you were already judged and assigned a place in the world. It is your life — your movie. The pentacles (coins) you have or do not have are a direct result of this judgment. I am quick to point out, however, that pentacles are not just currency in the monetary sense but also currency in the spiritual sense. Having abundant wealth can be a test for various individual who have it. What is important is that you have been rendered a life by a higher power, and it is your task to live it. As this is a highly personal subject, I will not comment further. Working with the Tree of Life is called path work, and it will put you right into your element. It is also great for inspiring creativity.

I have discussed these aspects of the Tree as it gives some archetypal insight into the province of David Anderson and how he fits into the scheme of my own "movie," particularly in regards to his facilitating my first trip to

Romania. Before that had happened, however, *The Montauk Project* had been published in the Romanian language. As David had a presence in Romania, I asked the publisher to dedicate the Romanian version to him. Independent of this request, my publisher had an opportunity to meet David. I eventually confused the circumstances and incorrectly thought that David had arranged for the publication of *The Montauk Project* in Romanian. What had actually happened was that a man by the name of Sorin Hurmuz was working as an editor in a Romanian publishing house and was asked by his boss to review *The Montauk Project* and to assess whether or not they should publish it. After reading it, his response was an affirmative yes, but the publisher declined to take the advice. Sorin then negotiated with me for the Romanian language rights and created his own publishing company, Daksha Publishing, with *The Montauk Project* as his lead-in to the business. Shortly after the book was published in Romanian, he received an email from Radu Cinamar who asked him if he would like to publish his work. This was a manuscript for what is now titled in English as *Transylvanian Sunrise*. After Sorin agreed to publish Radu's book, he had it translated into English and sent it to me to see if I would publish it in America. Although I found the book interesting, I could not finish reading it due to other pressing commitments and issues. It stayed at the bottom of a pile on my desk for four years.

In the meantime, there had been a lot of drama surrounding the Time Travel Research Center. I will not recount it in this book, but the upshot was that David had to shut it down in 2003 due to pressures put upon him. He went to work at Bosch Industries in Rochester, New York and began to work in high security laser systems which included the most advanced technology in biosensory devices. Some of his work during this time was in India.

Not long after David moved to Rochester, he called me and asked if I would take the remaining library and archives of the Time Travel Research Center. His plans for utilizing these as part of a time travel museum had changed, and he had no need or place to store these belongings. Accordingly, I went to Rochester with Preston Nichols and we loaded all of David's materials into Preston's van and moved it to Sky Books. At that meeting, David told me that he would not be able to work with me again for five years. That was the last I heard from him except for an occasional post card, and there was at least one phone call. One post card was from China where he had studied Tibetan monks and their concepts about time.

Over the years, Radu Cinamar's manuscript remained at the bottom of my desk. In 2007, a friend was staying with me and I asked him to read the manuscript. He loved it and encouraged me to publish it. After finally reading the manuscript, I began negotiations which lasted for several months and concluded with an agreement in March of 2008. Shortly after that agreement, and it struck me as a timed response, I received my first email from David in a long long time. It was now five years later, and he asked if I would like an all-expenses paid trip to Romania in order to visit Atlantykron and also enjoy a three day cultural tour of the country. Personally, I was a little flabbergasted that he was so punctual with regard to the five years.

So it was that, in April of 2008, it was arranged for me to visit Romania at the end of July. As David arranged my travel personally, we had a few discussions. Part of these included just personal chatting. In one of these conversations, I asked if he knew about Radu Cinamar's work. It took David a while to realize who I was talking about. After all, Radu is not his real name. When he did realize who I meant, David specifically stated that he knew who I was talking about but that he did not want to discuss it on the phone. This gave me the definite impression that David knew much or at least something significant about Radu's writings. So that you understand what I was anticipating to learn from David and all the excitement that this prospect generated, I will now give you a brief summary of what Radu Cinamar's first book, *Transylvanian Sunrise*, is about.

The main character in *Transylvanian Sunrise* is Cezar Brad, the head of Romania's most secretive intelligence department, known as DZ or Department Zero. He hand-picked Radu to reveal the various secrets that are stated in the book. Cezar himself came to the attention of the Romanian secret service on the day he was born. When the doctor was not able to cut his incredibly thick and strong umbilical cord, he duly reported this, just as he would any other anomaly, to the government authorities. Cezar's parents were subsequently visited by state security and a financial arrangement was made whereby they would report any unusual behavior emanating from or associated with the child. As Cezar began to demonstrate extra sensitive or psychic behavior, he was brought under the tutelage of a mysterious man who, quite literally, set up Department Zero while on loan to Romania on behalf of the Chinese government as part of a cultural exchange program between the two communist countries. Known as Dr. Xien, he examined and trained Cezar in many disciplines, particularly psychic ones, before hand-picking him to eventually become the head of Department Zero. As you will soon learn, this paved the way for an incredible ground-breaking discovery to take place beneath the Romanian Sphinx in the Bucegi Mountains of Romania. While Dr. Xien is an intriguing and very mysterious character, who ostensibly knew what he was doing with regard to enabling the discovery to take place, we find out very little else about him in *Transylvanian Sunrise*.

It was while running the "X Files" department of the Romanian government that Cezar was approached by a man who would change the destiny of Romania forever. This was Signore Massini, one of the highest ranking members of Italian Freemasonry who also claimed to be a high ranking member of the Bilderbergers. Massini explained that the satellite radar technology of the

Pentagon revealed that there was a hidden chamber beneath the Romanian Sphinx. He offered Cezar, who had considerable autonomy when it came to conducting secret investigations, many false promises if he would cooperate in letting his people excavate in order to reach this chamber.

Although he did not trust Massini one bit, Cezar knew that, if he resisted this request, he would soon be replaced in Department Zero. As the Romanian President and the head of security were the only ones outside of Department Zero to know of its existence, Cezar realized that Massini must have very special connections indeed for him to even know who Cezar was. Accordingly, he felt the smartest thing to do was to play along.

Eventually, through its strange affiliation with Italian Freemasonry, the Pentagon sent in American troops to do the tunneling and excavation required to access the hidden chamber. It took high-powered atomic laser technology to get the job done and there were many difficulties. After many trials and tribulations, success was achieved. The hidden chamber was unsealed and it revealed far more than one might ever imagine. This included technology whereby one could place their hand on a table and see their own DNA in microscopic form in three-dimensional holograms. Other devices on the table enabled one to see the DNA of alien species from other planets with accompanying star renderings so that one could see where they actually came from. By placing two hands on different parts of the table, one could also "mix" the DNA of two species so as to see how they might look if hybridized. As the tables themselves were six feet high, it seemed the creatures who built them, perhaps 50,000 years ago, were gigantic compared to humans of today.

This remarkable chamber also included a "Projection Hall" whereby one could see a holographic rendition of the history of Earth that was tailored to the individuality of whoever might be viewing it. This history, however, abruptly cuts off in about the Fifth Century A.D., perhaps because it required some sort of software update. One of the more intriguing aspects of the Projection Hall is that it also contains three mysterious tunnels that lead into the bowels of the Earth and similar facilitates in Iraq, Mongolia, Tibet and also beneath the Giza Plateau in Egypt. One of the tunnels leads, quite enigmatically, into the Inner Earth itself.

Although this was the most remarkable discovery ever made in the history of archeology, the politics around the situation became highly strained with the Romanians, the Americans and the Italian Freemasonry all vying for control. Despite the extreme political tension, Cezar Brad arranged for Radu Cinamar to visit the hidden chamber and the projection hall itself in order that he could write about it. This resulted in the book *Transylvanian Sunrise*.

Political tensions reached a climax when American soldiers stationed in Iraq caught on to what was happening in Romania. A similar chamber with holographic technology had already been previously discovered near

Baghdad during the Persian Gulf War. As American soldiers were watching over this mysterious chamber in Iraq, a sudden and unexpected holographic projection emerged and revealed that a similar device in Romania had been discovered. Their report to their superiors resulted in a rather furious investigation which eventually revealed that the Pentagon, unknown to the President by reason of regular command channels, had forces in Romania. Ultimately, the American president called the Romanian president in an effort to find out what was going on. Considerable diplomatic chaos and tensions arose between the Americans and Romanians, but after many heated negotiations, unprecedented diplomatic relations were established between Romania and the United States with the former becoming a member of NATO. A benefit of all the diplomatic furor was that the Italian Freemason was forced to abandon the scene for his own self-preservation.

Transylvanian Sunrise ends with Radu Cinamar being allowed to have a short visit to the holographic chamber beneath the Sphinx. At that point, the chamber had only been under investigation for about a month. While some of the technology had been figured out, the entire potential of what they had discovered remained virtually untapped.

At the time I accepted David Anderson's gracious offer to visit Romania, I was only one of a couple of Americans who had read the manuscript for *Transylvanian Sunrise*. The Romanian language version of this book, however, had been in print for about four years under the title *Vitor cu cap de mort* which translates as "Death Head's Future." Traveling to Romania was nowhere near as exciting as the prospect that David was going to be able to give me a briefing on what this was all about and how his technology might fit into this rather wild and adventurous scenario. As David had also extended me the courtesy of allowing me to have a guest, I invited Tantra Bensko to help me with taking video footage.

Instead of receiving any sort of information of any kind, we were thrown into very chaotic circumstances that made the trip rather challenging to say the least. It started with our flight being delayed which resulted in the hotel cancelling our reservations. We had no place to stay our first night and the guide for our scheduled cultural tour never showed up due to the mix-ups. Despite knowing nothing of the Romanian language, however, I was able to figure out how to ride a local bus from Sinaia to Bușteni and then take the breathtaking cable car ride to the Romanian Sphinx.

Going to the Sphinx in the Bucegi Mountains was most definitely the highlight of the entire 2008 trip. It is located above the treeline and is surrounded by spacious views of beautiful mountain scenery. The general energy of the area was peaceful, and it gave me a sense of forever. The Sphinx has suffered wind erosion since its formation, allegedly some 50,000 years ago. Although it has no obvious paws, I made my way to the area in front of the

Sphinx which would serve as being between its paws. As is apropos for a meeting with a sphinx, I asked a question: "What is the connection between David Anderson and Radu Cinamar?"

When I finally got to Atlantykron, three days after our arrival in Romania, David was not about to provide any sort of answer. He was under security silence. I would eventually get out of him that one of his Romanian colleagues once told him that he met Radu under a different name. David also told me that he would be going back into the time travel business but that no news would be officially released until winter.

Although David's plight was very disappointing, Radu had an audio CD delivered to me via Sorin Hurmuz, our Romanian publisher. In the CD, Radu stated that he would like to meet David Anderson. According to him, which was later substantiated in letters to me, the two had never met.

As the years have gone by and after at least five additional trips to Romania, I would eventually figure out what the connection is between Radu Cinamar and the time travel technology of David Anderson. It is the person who is writing these words: myself. Through the mysterious vehicle of the white bat, I was being pulled to Romania by forces that were beyond any ordinary explanation. They first showed themselves in the magical dream that is relayed in the first chapter of this book. As you will learn later on in this book, magical forces were working through mysterious channels to precipitate my arrival at a particular locale in Romania at a future date in 2014. David initiated my presence in Romania by providing the first invitation and plane ticket in 2008. Radu and his guides provided me with an intriguing story and a rather exotic paradigm to explore. There have also been various other people who have helped me and guided me to understand and explore this utterly remarkable country and some of its most potent esoteric secrets. It would, however, take a long time and several trips for that mysterious country to open up and share the secret of the white bat.

CHAPTER EIGHT

ARCHETYPES

Whether or not you have heeded my advice to note down your impressions on paper as you read this book, you are at least noting them in your mind. The impressions are there whether or not you write them down. Even if you do not particularly agree with what has been written, the visual cortex and the creative/intuitive part of your brain is being stimulated. When you write it down, however, it is a synthesizing process that grounds the experience.

As this book deals with so many elements which are either new or exotic to most of the reading audience, I would advise you to compare and evaluate the more novel aspects of what you read with archetypes; in particular, those which are depicted in the Cabalistic Tree of Life. I have already given a rather involved example with David Anderson's time reactor, and this can serve as an introduction to thinking in such a manner. You might find other correspondences that I either missed or did not mention.

Let us now evaluate the archetypal nature of what was presented in the last chapter with regard to the holographic chamber beneath the Romanian Sphinx. In my estimation, this fits into what is depicted in the Tarot as The Magician, a path which travels from the throne energies of Kether, ruled by Pluto, to the structural blueprint room of Binah (ruled by Saturn). Saturn is also identified as Mother Mary and the blossoming of the Shekinah which later passes through The Chariot as discussed in Chapter Six.

On the outside, The Magician represents the stage magician, the master of illusion and deception. Even if you do not accept the loftier ideas presented by Radu, his story fits into the archetype of The Magician.

The esoteric aspect of The Magician expresses the ability to bridge the gap between heaven and earth. This was the designed role of the Pharaoh, but it degenerated considerably over millennia The infinity sign over the magician's head symbolizes a divine presence through accessibility of the infinite mind. This is the same as tapping one's full potential.

The Magician follows The Fool who has learned just enough about the world to make himself dangerous. This is an aspirant who thinks of himself as a powerful force in the world. The Magician guides The Fool out of the cave and into the light of the sun and is bringing darkness into the light. Embracing and embodying the doctrine of "as above, so below," The Magician teaches that mastery in one realm may bring mastery in another. While The Magician also symbolizes unification of all planes of existence, he warns that it is dangerous to apply the lessons from one realm to another. Above all, The Magician transcends duality as a result of having learned the fundamental elements of the universe which are represented in the four suits of the Tarot.

It is for the above reasons that you will see the trace of The Magician on other pathways of the Tree, only two of which are The Sun and Alchemy (also known as Art) as well as the cards of the Minor Arcana. When consulting the Tree, it is always wise to remember that The Magician is at the inception of the Tree itself and is always present, either as a resource or as an adverse component.

In the case of the Bucegi chamber, we have a rather exotic representation of The Magician, and it includes the blueprint for all possible renditions of DNA. This is also the energy of Bast and Pan.

It is important to reiterate that the Tarot is a *mis en abyme* of DNA. It is a mirror into the circumstances of the soul. In this respect, The Magician is the mercurial fluid or quicksilver that not only represents the creational component of DNA but that which is within the entire circulatory system. With the Bucegi chamber, we have a look into The Magician's laboratory. The three tunnels within it remind us that Pluto, the god of the underworld, is the planetary ruler of Kether, the sephiroth from which The Magician emanates. Associated with the crown chakra, Kether refers to that which is beyond the mind's abilities to comprehend. The very proposition of the Bucegi chamber most definitely alludes to such. Pluto, however, is also recognized as the ruler of the underworld and is often associated with Hades. This, however, is different than the Christian idea of hell. Pluto sees that one's misdeeds or sins are purged so that he or she can transmute their negative characteristics into a blossoming of transcendence to a higher place. All of this, at least as far as Radu's story goes, suggests that either "higher beings" or the supreme force that is connected with the Inner Earth.

Whether you are writing, investigating or just plain living, it is always advisable to recognize The Magician archetype and use it to your benefit. There is, however, a word of warning I should give you about using any of these archetypes or those of any other system. There is also a dark side to the Cabala, and this is known as the Q'lipoth. There are different versions of what this is and how it fits in to the scheme of life, but it is simple and easy to view it as the natural and negative correspondent to the sephiroth of the Tree of Life. It has been said that any emanation of the divinity through the sephiroth results in either a negative reaction or flow which seeks to stop such. These are sometimes said to form a shell or external region around a sephirothic element, sometimes as a veneer of protection. The main danger in dealing with the Q'lipoth is that as soon as people either recognize or study it, they too often polarize and become consumed by it. This is why there is a negative fascination with the Hollywood version of Dracula or vampires in general.

Learned scholars over millennia have given great warnings to those who would aspire to reach the divine realm of Kether. One is advised to keep one's thoughts pure, display no hardness, always turn one's ears so that one should hear good, and to distance one's eyes from looking at evil. This, however, should not be misinterpreted to suggest that one should not face up to evil situations when one is confronted with them in life, particularly when it is one's path to face and deal with such. Rather, it is advisable to seek out, augment, and promote goodness. This dissipates the negative. This is one of the trickiest aspects of UFOlogy. People think they are uncovering secrets and "the truth" when they are really leading themselves down a black hole, all the way encouraged by Q'lipothic entities. This is a technique whereby a mystery is created so as to attract moths to a flame. There is currently in our culture an endless marketing of conspiracies and New Age mysteries. While it is not impossible for these to be benign or instructive, it is mostly an endless game that leads nowhere. In the case of UFOlogy and abductions, it perpetuates a mind-set that is degenerative without any redeemable or transmutative experiences. The answer is to reach above the foray and aspire to the consciousness of infinity, or what we call the infinite mind in Chi Gong. From this perspective, you can forge your own magic wand and go about the business of creating your life in the image you would choose.

Anyone can reach outward or inward and make contact with the most divine aspects of their own soul. For some, it can be a fountain of miraculous and inexhaustible energy that emanates through them. For others, it might be a more subtle inspiration that one chooses to bring to mind whenever one chooses. However it manifests for an individual, this is the realm of the magician and you should recognize it in yourself. There are many names for it and some, correctly or incorrectly, would be identified as the Lord, Jesus, Kundalini, the Divine Ray, or a host of other names. Many people are inspired for many different reasons and through many different systems of interpretation. Such experiences, however, are not unique to any particular spiritual system.

Earlier, I made a suggestion that one should not be too enthusiastic about sharing one's greater enlightenments with others. I am reiterating this now. The more enlightenment you experience, the less others around you are able to understand. Even a so-called "supportive" spiritual group can come down on you when you make a big breakthrough. A true breakthrough does not require a validation by another human. There are some who might understand and who might even give you further insights, but do not expect this as a general rule. The more you can be your own judge and jury, at least with regard to the internal aspects of your own psychology, the better off you will be. This is, of course, providing that you are not creating a cacophony of chaos to those in your environment. Discretion is always a good idea.

Working with archetypes is not only fun, it can be very instructive with regard to situations and the general drama of your own life. When we take on more grandiose circumstances, such as the tales of Radu Cinamar, archetypes give us invaluable insight, particularly in regards to not going off of the deep end.

CHAPTER NINE

SACRED JOURNEY

Although my cultural tour on my first trip to Romania was short-circuited, I was introduced to some key features of the Romanian culture. This occurred at Atlantykron where I met different professors and other key people who were kind enough to teach me about their ancient heritage.

Throughout history, Romanian culture and history has been very poorly understood. Sometimes, this has been a deliberate attempt by those who have a vested interested in restricting knowledge for political reasons. There are many different names for the ancient people who occupied the land that is now called Romania. These include but are not limited to the Dacians, Dracians, Thracians, proto-Thracians, Gettae, Goths, Scythians, and Hyperboreans. The most exalted god of the ancient Dacians, at least in terms of popularity, was Zalmoxis. When the Greek historian, Herodotus, visited the Scythians, he learned about Zalmoxis and was told that he had been a disciple of Pythagoras who had transformed himself into a god. Quite correctly, Herodotus concluded that the relationship between Zalmoxis and Pythagoras might have been the other way around. Pythagoras learned his esoteric knowledge in Egypt who learned it from Zalmoxis. This is an ancient tradition that goes back at least to the Age of Gemini (8,000-6,000 B.C.) as Gemini is the hidden esoteric name or synonym for Zalmoxis. In the Tree of Life schematic, Zalmoxis fits very nicely into the path known as The Lovers, sometimes also referred to as the Twins or Gemini.

For many reasons, Zalmoxis is a very important archetype for understanding the phenomena that is associated with this book. This will become clearer as you continue but do pay it due attention. If you want to understand the culture of Romania and all of its undercurrents, you need to become familiar with Zalmoxis.

To many, the etymology of *Zalmoxis* is either unknown or debatable. The most commonly accepted version to scholars is that it means "leaping god" because he is said to have transformed himself into a god from the human state. One can see this phonetically with *zal* equating to *sal* which means "leap" as in the word *salmon*, a word that also tied to *Solomon*. *Moxis* is essentially the same word as *Moses* which means "messiah" or "deliverer." Having been said to have taught the Egyptians, Zalmoxis was associated with Egypt long before Moses came along. The name *Moses* or *Tutmosis*, the latter used by several pharaohs, is clearly associated with the name *Zalmoxis*. I have also been informed that Zalmoxis in Romanian is *Zamolxes* which means *A Zamisli*, "to conceive." Notice the correlation between The Lovers and the conceiving and delivering of a baby. This suggests that the role of a messiah has to do with birthing. We see this concept in the virgin birth of Jesus, baptism and also the Christian idea of being "born again."

With regard to Zalmoxis teaching the Egyptians, it is widely recognized that a pharaoh by the name of Tutmosis III sponsored a hermetic mystery school in Egypt. If you carefully break down the phonetics and etymology of *Tutmosis*, there is a very interesting correspondence with the tradition that it was Zalmoxis, or someone of that name, who taught the Egyptians. Tutmosis I was carrying on in the tradition of his earlier ancestors of the same name. The first association is that the name *Thutmosis* = *Thoth* + *mosis/moses*. The second is a little more obscure but the name *Thoth* was also known as Valom. This was pointed out to me on a recent journey when I was visiting Ialomita Cave, just down the mountain from the Romanian Sphinx. Ialomita is pronounced similar to *Yao-lo-mita*. The *v* in Valom is convertible to a *y* if you consider a *y* to be a *v* with a tail. Repeating the earlier steps just covered, one can see the following phonetic and etymological correspondences:

Thutmosis = Thoth + mosis/moses
Thoth = Valom = Ialom as in Ialomita
valom = ialom = xalom (x being silent) + mosis = zalomosis = zalmoxis

There are hundreds of books on Zalmoxis in the Romanian language, and I have read none of them. While these feature many diverse opinions, legends, history and truth, I can only offer what unique understanding I have been able to acquire through my own discussions with very special Romanians and the subsequent filtering of my own internal processes which is based, at least in part, upon the Tree of Life schematic.

Although commonly recognized either as a god or human who transformed into a god, Zalmoxis is also viewed as an ancient principle for the astrological sign of Gemini, a word which stems from "germinate" and refers to the twins. In this respect, Zalmoxis is positioned with the genus of DNA, and it is at this very point where we can identify with the idea of animating matter. This is virtually the same as *shin*. The symbol of Zalmoxis or Gemini is really the swastika as rendered below (on the left) where you can visualize it as being made up of two numeral 2's. This association with the number 2 is not accidental as the original symbolism referred to pairs or twins and the fact that Zalmoxis represents two very important twins that were native to ancient Dacia (the land we know today as Romania and which the Greeks referred to as Hyperborea): Apollo and Artemis (or Diana). There were several other sets of twins who embodied this archetype as well.

If you look at the swastika on the right (at the bottom of the previous page), you will see that it can be construed as 666. Specifically, when the swastika is turned around and whorled ("whorl" is one of the meanings of swastika) or whirled, it reveals "6" as it moves from one position to another. 666 refers to our carbon-based material universe for the simple reason that the carbon atom has 6 protons, 6 neutrons and 6 electrons.

When we go back to the swastika on the left, we can see that it can be construed to represent two numeral "2's" or the number 22, a master number in numerology. 22 represents the life path of a "master builder." This is not only a Masonic reference, but 22 is highlighted by the fact that the Tarot features 22 major arcana which are the pathways connecting the sephiroth (or spheres) of the Tree of Life.

While the swastika represents 22, we can also see the numeral 5 in its construction (on the right) along with the 6 already referred to. 5+6 represent 11 (designated as the number of Abrahadabra by Aleister Crowley) or the hexagram over the pentagram (see *The Montauk Book of the Living* for a detailed diagram) which reveals the pattern of the Cabalistic Tree of Life which, when turned or twisted, represents the mobius strip of DNA. Two of these strands equals 11 + 11 or 22. These two strands of DNA represent, once again, Gemini, which means germinate.

In such a construct as Gemini or The Lovers, Zalmoxis represents both the principle and the process by which life germinates. In the deeper aspect, this is the principle that is represented and elucidated in archetypes. In the actual process of the gestation of life and its many permutations, it is the biological animation which could lead up to and possibly include remarkable characters that were either named Zalmoxis or lived up to this archetypal representation. When we reach such an exalted state of creation, however, this leads us to the sephiroth of Tipareth because The Lovers takes us there from Binah, and it is known as pathway number 6.

Tipareth, designated as beauty, could be referred to as the crowning glory of manifestation. This is the realm assigned to Christ or the ultimate harmony and reconciliation, and this includes the reconciliation of opposites, whether they be black or white. This emphasis on black and white in Tipareth is mentioned in classic interpretations, and I am choosing to emphasize it a bit as this is a central theme of this book. This embracing of one's opposite nature is the key to transcendence. In the archetype of Zalmoxis, we have transcendence from a man to a god.

Although I have shared much with you, I did not learn so much about Zalmoxis during my first journey to Atlantykron. At that time, all I understood was that he was the patron deity of the Dacians and was said to have transformed into a god after retreating to the Inner Earth via a cave and emerging four years later. To understand the Romanian culture, however, I was told I would have to understand Zalmoxis and the religious capital of ancient Dacia in what is now known as Transylvania: Sarmizegetusa.

On the surface, besides being the legendary home of Zalmoxis, Sarmizegetusa is an assortment of ruins that are a partial reconstruction of carefully crafted wooden posts and stone temples and monuments that were originally constructed so as to align with the movement of the celestial bodies in the sky. An archeologist could easily dedicate an entire career to understanding the mysteries of this ancient civilization. Above and beyond what I have just described, however, the entire area is swarming with ruins that extend to at least five kilometers surrounding the center. These, in turn, are built upon layers and layers of ancient civilizations that existed long before what is considered to be recorded history. Some of these feature pyramids and tunnels of pure gold. There are many remarkable tales that have been told about this area, and they are taken very seriously by Romanians, particularly the politicians and also treasure hunters. There is considerable history and information that will corroborate if not prove many of these tales. The Roman Empire looted the area for hundreds of tons of pure gold, and they barely scratched the surface.

It has never been nor is it my intention to approach this area as an archeologist. While there is unlimited archeological opportunity in this area, I will leave that to others, many of whom might well be predisposed towards missing the forest for the trees or to otherwise deliberately obfuscate the truth. Ground-penetrating radar (by the British) has revealed that there are also pyramids beneath the ground. In any case, I was strongly encouraged to visit this area to get a grasp of the undercurrent of the true Romanian or Dacian culture. Told that I could expect to have remarkable experiences of a spiritual nature, I was advised to visit Sarmizegetusa in the form of a sacred journey to the spiritual capital of ancient Dacia.

Before I returned to Romania for my second visit, in 2009, I prepared myself to go to Sarmizegetusa either before or after attending Atlantykron. This proved to be a very difficult if not impossible task. I could find no cooperation whatsoever. Although many Romanians speak English and it is their second language, it can be very challenging to travel through this country without having a Romanian by your side. I do not recommend travelling alone or without a native Romanian. The Ministry of Tourism was of no help, and I was not able to get anywhere until I wrote to Nicole Vasilcovschi, a young Romanian woman who befriended me as soon as I had arrived at Atlantykron in 2008. Nicole is an Orthodox Christian who recognized my spirit on sight and gave me a big hug. More importantly, she volunteered to personally escort me to Sarmizegetusa, a place she had never been to but recognized as a part of her own sacred heritage as a native Romanian. Nicole made all the major logistical challenges vanish.

My second trip to Romania began at Atlantykron where I would meet up with Nicole. When I arrived, David Anderson was giving lectures on the actual science of time travel, much of it focused on the Invariance of the Space-Time Interval which demonstrates mathematically that the phenomena we know as time is convertible to distance and can therefore be computed (past, present or future) with algebraic geometry. I have given the details of this in both the *Montauk Pulse* as well as *Transylvanian Moonrise*. This was exciting because David had not spoken publicly in over six years, and he was even kind enough to patiently and privately tutor me on this concept. We also did some tag-team lectures where he would talk about the scientific feasibility of time travel, and I would intersperse what he was saying with tales of the Montauk Project and Radu Cinamar. Most of the people at Atlantykron had not read any of Radu's books although some had heard about them.

Nicole and I also met with other people who gave us further information and tips about Sarmizegetusa. Besides being told that it was a sacred journey, we were told that fifty percent of the experience is in the journey itself. Most importantly, we were told by two important esoteric sources that one should spend three days at Sarmizegetusa in order to have the full experience. Unfortunately, this last bit of news came too late for us to change our planning. We were only scheduled to spend one day at Sarmizegetusa. Although I took this advice to heart, it would actually be four years before I could spend a full three days in the area.

On our early morning departure from Atlantykron, we acquired another partner on our sacred journey. This was Nicole's friend, Cristina Balan, who shares the same home town, Suceava, a large city in northern Romania. Cristina did not want to travel home alone on the train so she asked if she could join us on the sacred journey. Afterwards, they would go home to Suceava, and I would travel alone on the train to Bucharest.

Even though it was a last minute and unexpected arrangement, Cristina became a very important part of the journey, and I began to notice this right away. After we departed the island by boat, we walked to a nearby modern bus which would take us to Cernavoda where everyone would catch a train to return home. We ended up waiting in the bus for almost two hours. As Nicole attended to other matters, I ended up alone with Cristina and discovered that she was utterly brilliant. She had also spent a year in America and speaks very good English. Cristina began to educate me on ancient Romanian history. Amongst many other things, she told me that the ancient Dacians and Gettae were essentially the same people. Historians, correctly or incorrectly, sometimes make distinctions, but the Gettae are generally recognized as being the antecedents or source of the Celtic culture who migrated both eastward, southward and westward. The Gettae are very important to any study of Romania because there is an important aspect of this culture which has remained obscured to history by reason of deliberate omission. I am talking about the Gothic culture or the Goths. If you look at the word *Goth* and *Gettae*, you will see that they are phonetic equivalents. They are actually the same people. If you choose to study conventional history, you will learn that most historical accounts about the Goths are from a mid-6th century bureaucrat named Joradanes who wrote an admitted work of fiction entitled *Getica*. He did, however, acknowledge that Zalmoxis was the god of the Goths. The more you study about the history of Eastern Europe, the more you will learn that there were political reasons to obscure the true heritage and culture of the area.

As Cristina shared her personal knowledge with me, we were joined in our conversation by Bica Marinik, a very special man and professor who was the resident astronomer of Atlantykron. An expert on the archeology of Sarmizegetusa, he had lectured on it a few nights earlier. As his lecture was in Romanian, I was unable to retain any of it. In the bus, however, he spoke extensively about the area to me and particularly about the ancient history of the Dacians. Although he speaks decent English, he chose to speak in his native Romanian and have Cristina translate his words into English. Bica was always generous with his knowledge and was very popular with the students. As his life came to a dramatic end in conjunction with my third sacred journey to Sarmizegetusa in 2013, I have chosen to dedicate this book to him. I will explain that later on in the book, but it turned out to be more than a little ironic that he was positioned as a gatekeeper on my first sacred journey.

When Nicole finally returned to the bus and everyone was aboard, we took the short bus ride to Cernavoda. Once there, we had to wait some six hours before the train to Bucharest would arrive. This exhaustive waiting was only the first challenge on our journey. Remember, we were told that half of the experience is in the journey itself. As Nicole did not have the foresight to buy our tickets early so that we would not have to change seats, we had many more adventures. This included changing trains in the middle of the night, jumping from the train itself onto huge chunks of gravel and running to the next platform before the next train would leave. This included carrying sizable luggage in relative if not pure darkness.

With only a couple hours of sleep for myself, we finally reached our first destination in Orăştie, a city in Hunedoara County. Located in southwestern Transylvania, Orăştie is within an hour of Sarmizegetusa. Nicole had arranged for us to stay in the local monastery of the Old Orthodox Church. It was here where I experienced a rather remarkable synchronicity. After we had settled in and slept, a monk was showing us the grounds and vegetable garden. He explained that the first stone for this monastery had been laid on the day of a solar eclipse, August 11, 1999. I was amazed because I knew very well that this was the day that Dr. David Anderson had walked into my life in order to

SOLAR CALENDAR WHEEL AT SARMIZEGETUSA

attend a Montauk Night lecture on Long Island. The August 11 date not only fits precisely into the time period of the annual biorhythm upon which the Philadelphia Experiment and Montauk Project were based (which is August 10th through the 14th), August 11, 2009 was the actual day we would travel and explore Sarmizegetusa. If you break down the numerology of August 11, 2009, it equates to 8-11-2009 or 8-11-11. This can be readily interpreted as 8 equating to infinity with 11-11 representing the two mobius strips of DNA. 11-11, of course, also equates to 22, the number of Zalmoxis or Gemini as discussed above. There are also 22 letters in the original Hebrew alphabet which have been chosen to designate the 22 pathways of the Tarot.

If this sacred journey I was taking was indeed to the spiritual home of Zalmoxis, Sarmizegetusa, there was no question that all of my cumulative adventures of synchronicity had led me to this ancient locale. As time would tell, there was more mystery here for me to explore than I could easily imagine, but it would choose to unveil itself over a period of years.

We arrived at Sarmizegetusa at 7:00 o'clock in the morning, and it was rather breathtaking to arrive at dawn with virtually no one there. Much of my attention was on taking video of the area as well as just taking in the energy of the spot. After a while, I saw a woman standing alone in the solar wheel. Despite her extremely limited English, we were able to

CALCAR — REMNANTS OF ANCIENT COLUMNS

become friends, and we are now friends for life. Her husband joined us, and I took them both to Nicole and Cristina so that an unfettered translation could occur. Lenutz and her husband Mihai took us on a long uphill hike to Fete Alba (which means White Faces in Romanian), a citadel atop a mountain that is said to be the last stronghold of the Dacian empire before the Roman conquest. According to accepted tradition, Fete Alba got its name as a result of the female Dacian warriors who came out to fight. As they did not have beards, the Roman legions referred to them as "white faces." The accepted tradition tells us that this Roman legion that was set out to conquer the last stronghold of the Dacians was a legion of Moors who had joined the Roman Empire. An additional and perhaps more authentic account that has been told to me is that Fete Alba was actually the last stronghold of the Moors.

I have gone into more details of this journey in *Transylvania Moonrise*. In retrospect, the most important part of the journey was actually taking it and being exposed to the energy of the area. Only later would I realize the mechanics of why the energy was so special. Essentially, a grappling hook was attached between me and Sarmizegetusa. It has not only not loosened over the years, the attachment has grown much stronger.

The only other part of the journey I will mention is a lucid dream I had while I slept during the early morning of August 12, 2008. In the dream, I

SOLAR DISK AT SARMIZEGETUSA

was completely outside of my body. There was a bright blue sky and I could look over the entirety of Romania. Suddenly, I saw ominous black helicopters approaching a tall edifice which represented the central government or a similarly related institution. There was a huge dark cloud over this building that clearly represented a very dark cloud over Romania. These were not my conclusions, but it is simply how the information was presented to me in the dream. It was extremely dramatic and spoke of the truth. At least that was the context I was given. While experiencing the great freedom of an out-of-body experience, I was suddenly confronted with the opposite: mind control operations and worse in the archetypal form of a black helicopter. In the same vein, a flash of truth went through my mind that told me I was not connected to this dark cloud in any way. In other words, there was no danger. The cloud, however, was still a part of the landscape.

After a day-long but pleasant train ride back to Bucharest, I flew home the following day. I would await a meeting with David Anderson that was supposed to take place some two months later. He was very happy with my participation at Atlantykron and hoped I would continue in the future.

CHAPTER TEN

THE MUSE

Everything that a writer writes stems from his or her muse. This statement is true whether we are writing fiction or non-fiction. While one could write a whole book on the subject of the muse, I will keep it as simple and practical as possible. What follows is the etymology and definition of the word *muse*. I have put the important part of the etymology in bold type.

> **The Muses** (Ancient Greek: *Μοῦσαι, moūsai*: perhaps from the o-grade* of the Proto-Indo-European root **men-* "**think**") in Greek mythology, poetry and literature, are the goddesses of the inspiration of literature, science and the arts. They were considered the source of the knowledge, related orally for centuries in the ancient culture that was contained in poetic lyrics and myths.

The key to utilizing this definition of *muse* is the root *men* being equated to "think." Let us now take a quick look at the etymology of the word *think*. Again, I have put the important part of the etymology in bold type.

> **think** (v.) Old English *þencan* "**conceive in the mind, think, consider, intend**" (past tense *þohte*, p.p. *geþoht*), probably originally "**cause to appear to oneself,**" from Proto-Germanic **thankjan* (cf. Old Frisian *thinka*, Old Saxon thenkian, Old High German *denchen*, German *denken*, Old Norse *þekkja*, Gothic *þagkjan*); Old English *þencan* is the causative form of the distinct Old English verb *þyncan* "**to seem or appear**" (past tense *þuhte*, past participle *geþuht*), from Proto-Germanic **thunkjan* (cf. German *dünken*, *däuchte*). Both are from PIE **tong-* "**to think, feel**" which also is the root of *thought* and *thank*. The two meanings converged in Middle English and *þyncan* "**to seem**" was absorbed, except for archaic *methinks* "it seems to me." Jocular past participle *thunk* (not historical, but by analogy of drink, sink, etc.) is recorded from 1876.

When we reduce the idea of the muse to simply thinking or causing to appear to oneself, we have to look no further than the concept of the barber shop mirror effect that we call *mis en abyme*. It is simply a reflection of what you are perceiving. This is what the Dark Room exercise I previously gave

---

* The term zero grade is from linguistics and refers to vowel alteration that is used for different words. When different forms of a word root or word elements appear with a vowel (as in sing, sang, sung, song), it is called full grade. When no vowel is used, it is called zero grade.

to you is all about. It will put you in touch with your muse and stimulate it as will most every suggestion I have thus far given you in this book.

Traditionally, the muses have been depicted as the embodiments of metrical speech called *mousike* which is where we get the word *music*. Mousike, however, was just one of the muses. The others included Science, Geography, Mathematics, Philosophy, Art, Drama, and inspiration. Although the muses have been dressed up to accommodate the accoutrements of civilization, there were originally only three Muses, all daughters of Plusia with either Zeus or Uranus. The important aspect of the muse, whether it is personified or not, is that is refers to the primordial aspect of your mind. In Chi Gong we call this the primordial mind. Accordingly, I will give you another exercise which will not only help you to access your muse but will also help you in more ways than you might imagine.

Primordial Mind Exercise

Step 1 — Put your attention on the primordial mind. This is the exact spot on your head near the cowlick of your hair except that it is in the center of the head. Another way of describing it is in the exact center of where a Jewish person would wear a yarmulke.

Step 2 — Once you have your attention fully on your primordial mind, now move it slowly to the frontal lobe or the area which is sometimes called the Third Eye. As you move your attention, notice where your mind goes. Pay attention to your thinking processes.

Step 3 — When you are in the frontal lobe, now go back to the primordial mind and pay attention once again to where your mind goes, paying attention to your thinking processes.

Step 4 — Repeat this fifty times daily. Never stop for the rest of your life.

This exercise might seem innocuous at first glance. It is, however, extremely powerful. There is far too little written about the primordial mind, but it is a stronger and more primal part of you that is not complicated. The frontal lobe or processor is filled with all sorts of figure-figure and is where complex equations or thinking is accomplished. Both have their uses, and going back and forth will give you the best of both worlds. If you ever have occasion to muscle-test yourself, you will find that you are much stronger when your attention is on your primordial mind. Most importantly, this will also put you in touch with your own muse. Done in conjunction with the Dark Room exercise, you will have even more access to your muse.

The whole idea of moving your attention from one part of the brain to another will increase your alertness and also make you smarter as you will be paying far more attention to what you are thinking as well as the way you are thinking. There are no limits to this exercise and it can be expanded upon. If you wish, you can follow up on this angle of the primordial mind by reading about primordial essence in the Tibetan Bön tradition where Dzogchen is referred to as the primordial state or natural condition. One seeks enlightenment through accessing this primordial state. Dzogchen is one's ultimate nature and is pure and all-compassing primordial clarity. It is timeless. In Dzogchen, one's nature is viewed as a mirror which reflects with complete openness but is not effected by the reflections, not unlike a crystal ball. When one actualizes this mirror-like clarity, one achieves rigpa or knowledge. Once again, we have the principle of *mis en abyme*. A primordial freedom comes from grasping one's mind. The opposite is ignorance.

The main idea here is for you to access your primordial mind in order to stimulate your muse. You can read all about it if you want, but you must exercise it in practice. In ancient Greece, there was the Valley of the Muses. It featured activities and competitions to promote the muse, but the most important aspect was that of creating a sacred space. Every writer or artist best writes from a sacred space. The word *sacred* refers to that which is holy, pure and is integrated or "whole." You can contour this concept any way you want, but there is really nothing more pure and unadulterated than the Dark Room itself and the essence of your own unadulterated reflection. One can also cultivate the Inner Smile and have it radiate outwards as you smile into all your conflicts and problems. As you write, keep an energetic connection to your own sacred space. It is also important to note at this juncture that it is the heart that integrates the higher functions of the mind with the worldly aspects of existence.

Before I leave you to cultivate your connection to your own muse, I would like to point out that the ancients viewed the poetic voice as kingship. In other words, only the king would have enough breadth of vision to write a poem that would be worthy of describing the cosmic paradigm that everyone lived by. There were even competitions for such. He who could see or grasp the situation the best would be the most worthy to rule. This is how the Mystery Schools such as the Eleusinian Mysteries originated. It began with people explaining and dramatizing various metaphors for existence.

The problem with such a contest as vying for kingship through writing has everything to do with game theory as offered by Dr. John von Neumann. Applying game theory to such intractable subjects as the weather and the stock market, von Neuman indicated that the only thing you can reliably count on in any game is that someone is going to cheat. When you apply this concept to religion, you see that there are certain texts that are revered beyond all others. While some of these may or may not make reasonably decent attempts to explain the cosmic paradigm, you will definitely find that many of them have been reinforced with mental manipulation or threat of violence. This is, in effect, the same as cheating. In other words, they are not good enough to stand on their own. Whether or not such texts have merit or not is really beside the point. In its own way, life will use its own processes to write and rewrite its experience in seeking to explain the cosmic paradigm. This is why so many ancient texts, some of them being discovered only recently, are being reexamined and reinterpreted.

This should be your impetus as you do your own writing. By that, I mean that you should look at who you are and what you either reflect or represent by looking into the magic mirror or *mis en abyme* of your own soul. What you thought in the past or what you think today is certainly subject to modification and rewriting at any given moment in the future, but it is you who will choose it. If society at large is rewriting their own history, there is no reason why you cannot rewrite your own history or at least the paradigm by which you live by, if only towards your own advantage.

While you might not be so bold so to attempt to supplant various religious texts, you should at least try to explain what you are writing about in a way that is superior to what anyone else might have said about the particular subject or facet of existence that you are explaining. By superior, I am referring to the proposition that you should make your writing as clear and entertaining as possible so that it holds the interest of your audience. This involves assessing your public's attention span as well as other characteristics that they might possess.

Before you read further, I would first invite you to note down your thoughts and also pay some attention to your own muse. Listen to what it tells you. If you are lucky, it will be talking up a storm by now. Even so, one can make the most progress by qualifying and refining what you hear. That is what quiet time and the Dark Room are for. Silence is golden.

With regard to my own adventures in Romania, I have found myself on a path where forces independent of myself seem to be rewriting history in a way that other authors have not thought of, let alone experienced. If it were not for me accessing my own muse and writing *The White Bat*, I would never have discovered that path.

CHAPTER ELEVEN

SYNTHESIS

After returning from Romania in 2009, I was visited by Dr. David Anderson in October. The purpose of the meeting was social, but it was also to do a "wrap-up" on Atlantykron business for that year. Every year, I have a "wrap-up" meeting, usually by telephone, with the president of the World Genesis Foundation to assess how things went at Atlantykron and what might be done for the future. In those days, David was the president of the foundation and the meetings were with him. As I said, this was an in-person visit.

This was the first opportunity I had to show David the video footage I had taken at Atlantykron as well as Sarmizegetusa. He was very interested. Additionally, I had him listen to the audio CD from Radu Cinamar. Afterwards, he said that he was impressed at how much Radu had trusted me. He also told me the story of how he had tried to go to bat for me with the Romanian government and get me an audience with Radu. In the end, they all referred him back to Sorin Hurmuz, my Romanian publisher who had personally hand delivered the audio CD to me. From this meeting, I soon concluded that David had never met Radu. Eventually, however, I realized that if David was privy to any of the secrets about the Bucegi Mountains that it might be at a higher level of command channels than Radu operated on, at least at that time. I wondered if David possibly knew the lama, Repa Sundhi. My e-mail requests to David on this point have remained unanswered.

The most exciting aspect of the meeting with David was when he said that he would publicly release the information that he had lectured and shared with me at Atlantykron that year. In addition to that, he told me that he would soon be releasing other information, all of which you already have been exposed to in Chapter Seven (with regard to the time reactor). That winter, David revealed further information about the time reactor, including the fact that it had now been developed to the point where humans could be placed within the self-contained field and thereby experience either the slowing down or speeding up of time. To those in the field, however, the experience would seem like a normal passing of time. It would only appear to be speeded up or slowed down to those on the outside. Besides commenting that India was the most advanced country in time technology, there was also a discussion of something called a Time Tremor Detector. His research into time alteration was such that he had developed instrumentation that would detect when someone was engaging in experiments that manipulate time. This evolved into a device called a TTD or Time Tremor Detector. While all of his developments are very interesting, what I know of them has already been discussed in other books and *The Montauk Pulse*. This was a very interesting time with many new revelations from David, many of them conveyed in radio broadcasts with myself as well as with others.

While all of this was going on, there was another development taking place. An event was being planned for the Montauk Medicine Man, Artie Crippen, also known as Red Medicine, to return to Montauk for the first time in thirty years. The whole effort attracted a lot of challenges and problems. This included various people attacking the event as well as the potential venues for the event.

By January, I was almost ready to suggest that the event be scrapped. My inclination changed, however, during a visit to two psychic friends of mine in New Jersey. Telling one of them all about my interaction with the Medicine Man and how he had changed my life (by introducing me to Taoist Chi Gong) but also emphasizing what his medicine represented to Montauk, I had a stunning realization. The real purpose of this event was not to make it a success with regard to any conventional standards of success but rather to simply get the Medicine Man back to Montauk, even if it were only for a day or two. It did not matter if one other person came. It had been thirty years since the Medicine Man had even been at Montauk, and this was going to be a reunification with his ancestral land. That was all that mattered. We would see what magic might precipitate from that. There was, however, another magical factor at work.

When we originally planned this event, I had suggested to the event coordinator that we hold it during the anniversary of the transmission of *The Book of the Law* which occurred in Cairo from April 8-10 in 1904. The event coordinator was amenable, and I cannot underestimate what role these dates played in getting everything to synchronize together. Many people consider that *The Book of the Law* is a satanic book or something of the like, but it is actually a coded message which, quite admittedly, can be viewed as a complete horror show to those who are ignorant of the code. While it is understandable that people can be confused by this, it is a matter of *mis en abyme* all the way. Be careful what you project. Accordingly, I have included a more involved explanation of *The Book of the Law* in Appendix B if you are not already familiar with my earlier writings on this subject.

A short time before the event, I had a dream where I found myself walking through the balcony or mezzanine level of a hotel looking for David Anderson. I soon saw a well-dressed woman who said she was his wife, but she walked away to take care of her own business. I then looked down to the lobby and saw a man who said David would arrive soon. This man said his name was Sully. I then turned around and walked over to a table at a restaurant on the mezzanine level and had breakfast with David Anderson and one other.

Soon after this dream, I received an e-mail from David indicating that he would be coming to New York soon and would like to have a face-to-face meeting with me. Asking how I would like to arrange this, I told him that I would be occupied at Montauk but that he was more than welcome to come.

David warmed to this idea but had a question. He wanted to know if it was suitable for him to make a presentation to the group. Everyone, including myself, was amenable to this development. It was a complete surprise, and no one knew what to expect. I decided, however, to keep his appearance at the event a secret. Although it would boost attendance considerably, I knew that it could attract and bring out some of the lower characteristics of humanity. Besides those who had already signed up for the event, only close friends were invited but most of them could not make it.

In some strange way, or perhaps it was not so strange, the Medicine Man's presence was synchronously tied to David Anderson giving his first public viewing of the time reactor. The whole weekend event was rather enigmatic with elemental overtones. Although some people had flown in, the weather was absolutely foul on Friday evening. The wind and sea were blowing harshly. There were only about six or seven people, and I was the only presenter there. All I could do was give them a summary of how we had all gotten here by reason of my various investigations along with a promise to deliver a surprise the very next evening. At the end of the evening, I revealed that the surprise was to be a presentation from David. It was very exciting.

The next day, April 10th, was filled with energy, events and all sorts of different people arriving from different places, two of which were David Anderson and the Medicine Man. Synchronicity had smiled upon our gathering. The evening event, which featured David, turned out to be the climax of the entire weekend. He showed us a video of an early version of the time reactor. Inside the time-warp field of the time reactor was a tightly-closed bud of an amaryllis plant. Horticulturists ordinarily project a four-day window for such a plant to bloom fully. During this video presentation, it bloomed in under 3 minutes. David also mentioned that they were able to "reverse" its stage of blooming — to regress it back almost into a bud again — however, the field became unstable at one late point in the regression, and it was exposed to high-level gamma rays which destroyed the plant life. Although we did not see the regression, David said they had remedied the unstable boundary field. It should also be mentioned that there was a professional photographer in attendance whom I know, and he commented that what we saw could not possibly have been "time-lapse" photography due to the saturation of colors that was displayed in the video. Keep in mind that this particular video is several generations behind the more advanced work that has been going on in recent years. As David has said many times, the Government is always ten to fifteen years ahead of what it informs the public about.

It was a breathtaking event. David also indulged the audience by taking all of their questions afterwards. This was a very rare opportunity for people to Q&A with David, and it all came courtesy of the Medicine Man's return to Montauk. This last point should not be underestimated. The chances of the Medicine Man and David Anderson coming to Montauk by themselves were not good at all. That they should show up at the same time during a presentation of time control technology is all the more significant.

At some point during the evening, I had asked David what it was he had originally wanted to talk to me about. He said that he would like to do that the following morning, after which he would return to Rochester. So, I took him to breakfast the next morning at the health food store in Montauk. When he told me why he had wanted a face-to-face meeting, I was kind of taken aback. All he wanted to know about was what I would like to present at Atlantykron that summer. I say I was taken aback because it was not at all necessary to have a face-to-face meeting over this subject. Although I had no idea that it was happening at the time, our conversation was taking a very magical turn which would unfold in its own time over the next several years.

Responding to David, I told him that I was rather tired of hearing myself talk about the same old subjects. This not only includes the Montauk Project but the events in *Transylvania Sunrise* as well. While I do find the subjects of great interest, there is a certain saturation point when you keep talking about them to different audiences who do not have the same familiarity. I then told David about an event that had occurred at Atlantykron the previous summer. I had woken up from a nap in the middle of the afternoon. As I emerged from my cabin door, I saw two students sitting at a table and writing. When I asked what they were doing, they told me they were writing a movie script but were having some difficulties. I sat down and helped them resolve their difficulties. Later in the day, I saw them again and they asked me to be in their movie. Personally, this was the last thing in the world I wanted to do. As they were students, however, and I was there to help them, I agreed.

The cinematographer was Roberto Quaglia, a native Italian who attends Atlantykron every year. Roberto is also a writer and bills himself as the "Dean of Science Fiction in Italy." Roberto is a very special person, and I knew him from the previous year. As we proceeded to make this short movie, there were a lot of obstacles, the most challenging of which was no script. The students had an idea but there was no easy means of writing a script and getting it copied. Even though I was only an actor in this movie, I ended giving directions so as to resolve issues and move things along. Roberto and I found that we worked very well together. The movie, however, could not be finished due to a rather petty conflict. It had to do with a cape I had been wearing for the movie, and it had been lent to the crew by a third party who is still unknown to me to this day. After the first day of shooting, this third party decided that he no longer wanted us to use the cape, claiming he was upset at Roberto from the previous year. I was rather disappointed that someone would take out their upset at Roberto in such a way as to cut across what the students were doing.

Sharing the story about Roberto and the cape with David, I suggested that we form the Atlantykron Film Company which was really only a title to facilitate the making of a short movie that the students would shoot, produce and edit. This time, however, I suggested that we eliminate the factors which had hindered us the previous year. I would provide a script and bring enough copies so that everyone knew what they were doing. The only thing I requested from David, however, was that he would ensure that Roberto would partici-pate. We would be co-instructors, but I knew that I could not accomplish this without Roberto. David was very enthusiastic about the idea and the dream was born. He also said that he would get us some editing software.

I did not think about it at the time, but as soon as I arrived home, I was under the influence of a magical current that dovetailed precisely with the recent events at Montauk. This had to do with my friend, Tantra Bensko, who had accompanied me on my first trip to Romania. Tantra, who had also visited Montauk with me prior to our trip to Romania, was sending me carbon copies of an e-mail correspondence she was having with Eve Lorgen, the author of *Love Bites* and *The Dark Side of Cupid*. This correspondence concerned Transylvania Colony, an area designated by many of the Founding Fathers of the United States which was proposed to be the fourteenth colony of the United States. Although I probably learned about this in school, I had no recollection of Transylvania Colony and was very intrigued by how that name had been acquired. The history of Transylvania Colony is as follows.

In 1775, a judge of dubious reputation by the name of Richard Hen-derson formed the Transylvania Company with the intention of making the Transylvania Purchase, a huge tract of land that made up most of what is today the state of Kentucky. American frontiersman, Daniel Boone, was hired to trailblaze the Cumberland Gap so as to make the land accessible. Boone was also involved in the final negotiations to purchase this land from the Cherokees. The purchase was problematic because there were other Indians who claimed the land and Boone lost some family members over this. The purchase was eventually voided because the legislatures of both Virginia and North Carolina claimed parts of the land, citing an edict by King George III which stated that colonists could not purchase land from Indians.

After reading these curious facts about the Transylvania Purchase, a couple of thoughts occurred to me. First, King George III is well known for his documented insanity (see the book *The Madness of King George III* by Alan Bennett) that revolved around his struggle with porphyria, a disease that is also known as "blue-blood's disease," one of the symptoms of which is purple urine which is sometimes referred to as "purple rain." It is well known that the first recorded historical case of this disease concerned his ancestor, Mary Queen of Scots, whose lineage traces back to Transylvania. The second thing that occurred to me is that one of the most documented cases of "blue people" who possess Rh-negative blood is in Kentucky. If you wish, you can read about the Blue Fugates of Kentucky (on the internet) for further information.

I wondered if the area where these Blue Fugates were from was the same part of Kentucky that was part of the Transylvania Purchase. Sure enough, I found that the Blue People of Kentucky were located right in the heart of what was once referred to as the Transylvania Purchase. I also learned on the internet that a native by the name of Blue Otter stated that, according to his people, there was once an ancient race of Blue People who lived underground. It should be noted that Kentucky is studded with some of the most extensive and beautiful caves in the world. They were so special that Aleister Crowley himself made mention of these caves in his autobiography and went out of his way to visit them.

Contemplating these facts, I learned that there was another extreme element of synchronicity at play. The woman who was the event coordinator for our recent event at Montauk just happened to be from Kentucky. When I called her to tell her about the Blue people of Kentucky being connected to the Fourteenth Colony, she informed me that she was moving back to Kentucky that very week. Ironically, her father's land was right in the middle of this "Blue Blood Country" although she knew nothing about this until I informed her of it. She soon found that there were artifacts on the property of an ancient civilization and that some rogue archeologists had been removing them. I also contacted my friend Mary Sutherland who told me an earful.

Mary has a whole thread on the Blue People of Kentucky on her website and she has also visited the area. There is even a picture of her with a very large pre-Columbian statue of a Caucasian head who is referred to as the "Serpent Prince" and is recognized as either Sumerian or pre-Sumerian. She has said that there are a multitude of artifacts in plain sight but that only the locals know where they are and they are not that friendly with outsiders. She subsequently introduced me to Rick Osman by teleconference who is preparing an extensive video documentary on the pre-Columbian settlements of Prince Madoc. He has witnessed all of the old fortifications which are plainly in sight and were erected on previous fortifications from even more ancient times.

All of this is fascinating in and of itself, but it still does not explain how the name Transylvania came into play. Despite extensive searches, I have found no logical etymology and only a few admitted speculations. *Transylvania* is most often said to mean "across the woods" or "beyond the woods." The Hungarians, who once occupied Transylvania, called it Erdély which was derived from Erdő-elve, meaning "beyond the forest"). *Erdő* means "mountain deep forest" with the *elve* suffix being a derivative of the older form *elü* (meaning beyond). What I would point out in all of this is how it might have transmogrified into the English word *elf*.

110

Following this thread further, I looked to see if there was any common denominator between the Transylvania Colony in Kentucky and the region in Europe that we know as Transylvania. This led to a rather astonishing discovery about St. Germain (Rákóczi is his real family name), the famous Prince of Transylvania. According to Manly P. Hall's *Secret Destiny of America*, St. Germain was present in America during that time period and instigated the *Declaration of Independence* as well as the American Revolutionary War itself. Hall also asserts that St. Germain was a reincarnation of Francis Bacon, the author of *The New Atlantis* (as well as Shakespeare's plays) which positions America as the new Atlantis. Bacon and St. Germain were both Rosicrucians.

As Benjamin Franklin is also deeply tied to the Rosicrucians, I looked for a connection there and found out that he was a major investor in the Transylvania Company as were many politically influential colonists such as George Washington, Alexander Hamilton, and Thomas Jefferson. Franklin and Jefferson both travelled to Paris where St. Germain is also recorded to have resided during this general time period. St. Germain's presence in France is tied to the French Revolution. The common denominator in all of this is Rosicrucianism, a powerful secret society. Freemasonry and the Illuminati lurk in the background as well, and it is a well known fact that Jefferson commented on and corresponded with Adam Weishaupt, the founder of the Bavarian Illuminati. In such a scenario, it is anyone's guess what "illuminated" agendas were at work.

What you have just read is what I was able to find out about the namesake of the Transylvania Colony. Besides the converging tangents just mentioned, it is also important to note that I have written rather extensively, albeit on a separate research line than mentioned here, on the Blue Race. This information is mentioned in *The Black Sun: Montauk's Nazi-Tibetan Connection* which focuses on the blue-skinned gods of the Egyptians and Tibetans; and *The Montauk Book of the Living* which focuses on the Amazigh Berbers and Taureg of North Africa and their ties to Queen Antinea, an Rh-negative blue queen of the Amazons whose ancestry has been historically traced to islands in the Atlantic identified with Atlantis. *The Montauk Book of the Living* also features the first plausible scientific theory of parthenogenesis, meaning a virgin birth, in humans. The name *Antinea* was transmogrified by the Greeks into *Athena*, and she was recognized as a virgin goddess with the Parthenon, a word which symbolizes parthenogenesis, being erected in her honor.

After my conversation with David Anderson, I had agreed to write some sort of script so that the students could make a movie. There was no agenda on my part nor even any clear idea of what we should do. The research thread you have just read, however, made it a no-brainer. My muse was telling me to integrate the theme of the Blue People of Transylvania Colony in Kentucky with those of Transylvania in modern day Romania. As David Anderson had

111

helped precipitate all of this, I decided to throw his time travel technology into the mix as well. Besides that, I would draw upon the local geography as there was no budget for much else.

There was one other aspect which inspired the story you are about to read (which was to be put into a film). It has to do with two of my dear Romanian friends that both made very distinct impressions upon me. One was Stefan, a man from Brasov who lives in Rome, Italy. When I first met him, Stefan had very long hair and a substantial beard that I thought made him look like the Russian mystic Rasputin. I voiced this when I first met him, and it generated a lot of laughter. When I video-taped him, Stefan would even act like Rasputin for me in certain respects, happily expressing certain aspects of the lower chakras. Others and myself found it quite amusing, and although he was clearly clowning for us, it fit with his personality. The other Romanian friend that inspired me had an opposite character. Her name is Cristina Jalba, and she approached me after hearing a lecture that I had done with David Anderson. She had read *The Montauk Project* in the Romanian language and was also interested in Chi Gong. We became friends, but I was very struck by the fact that she looked like an elf. To me, she looked so much like an elf that I even video-taped her pretending to be an elf. She enjoyed the idea; and because there are so many Cristinas on the island, I started referring to her as Cristina the Elf so as to distinguish her from the other Cristinas. As I found Cristina and Stefan to be rather opposite in nature, I wanted to write the movie treatment around both of them. Accordingly, my muse told me to write this story about a magical island where vampires and elves, both of whom had evolved from the ancient Blue Race, would find themselves in a dramatic conflict. The conflict would come into view by a descendant of Rasputin whose ancestors had migrated to Kentucky but would find his way back to his Romanian homeland.

What you are about to read, *My Kentucky Cousin*, is the script that I put together to do the promised movie. Shooting the movie was quite an experience on the mundane level, but nothing about the experience was ultimately very mundane. Most importantly, my entire education and experiences with regard to seemingly diverse threads were synthesizing through the creative process. David Anderson, in some mysterious way, was serving as the catalyst for this synthesis to take place. What is even more significant is that this catalyzing process was serving a more exalted agenda that was being fostered by characters, embedded into the mythos of Transylvania itself, that I had not even encountered yet. You might say that the white bat itself was flying over me and steering me in a specific direction.

CHAPTER TWELVE

MY KENTUCKY COUSIN

PREAMBLE

In 1775, a group of highly influential American colonists invested in The Transylvania Company, an enterprise which hired frontiersman Daniel Boone to negotiate and secure the "Transylvania Purchase," a large tract of land which includes most of modern day Kentucky. The advertised purpose of the Transylvania Company was to create "Transylvania Colony," the fourteenth colony of America. It is known that powerful secret societies wielded a considerable amount of influence in the Transylvania Company through distinguished American investors such as George Washington, Benjamin Franklin and Alexander Hamilton. Despite the powerful people behind the Transylvania Company, the purchase was ruled null and void by the legislatures of North Carolina and Virginia because they each claimed a right to part of the purchased land. There was, however, an even more powerful authority behind this refusal and this was the Crown of England, ruled by King George III, who suffered from a disease that links him inextricably to the lore and actual history of the land known as Transylvania.

Scene #1 - A road, preferably a dirt road, somewhere in Romania. A provocative girl wearing a cape named Xina is looking around, appearing as if she is looking for something but also as if she is hiding and not wanting to be seen. She darts from behind a tree or a rock (utilizing whatever obtrusions are available in the chosen location) exaggerating her motions by utilizing the cape. She is waiting for something. As Xina waits, an archeology student from Kentucky appears walking down the road with his backpack. Xina watches him approach. When he reaches her, she makes a dramatic motion with her cape and appears to the student named Gregori. He is startled by her sudden appearance.

XINA
(she smiles at him seductively.)
Hello.

GREGORI
(reciprocating her greeting)
"Hello......Who are you?..... Do you speak English?"

XINA
Yes...and my name is Xina. Welcome to Romania.

113

GREGORI
Thank you. Maybe you can help me. I am a student of archeology
and have come all the way from America, from Kentucky."

XINA
You look Romanian.

GREGORI
Yes, that is why I am here. I come from Transylvania
University in Kentucky where I study archeology. My family
has ancient roots in this country.

XINA
(smiling)
I can see that in your eyes.

GREGORI
(looking very serious)
I come from a large but poor family. We suffer from rare
blood diseases, all of them related to an inability to properly
process copper. My family has saved their money to put me
through school and to come here and find some answers.

XINA
My uncle can help you. He is a professor and
he knows about these things. Come with me.

Xina makes a dramatic motion with her cape and they walk off together.

Scene #2 - Office with Xina's uncle, who is a professor named Flavio.

XINA
Uncle, this is Gregori. He is visiting Romania
and I think you could help him.

FLAVIO
(Speaking inappropriately, not the way you would speak to a guest)
You look like Rasputin!

GREGORI
My family tells me I am related to him.

FLAVIO
How so?

GREGORI
My great grandfather was a bastard son of Rasputin.
His mother knew him in Russia and she escaped
during the Russian Revolution and she eventually came to
America and married into the Blue People of Kentucky.

FLAVIO
Ah.....(he says showing recognition)....
the Blue People of Kentucky. Rh negative.

GREGORI
You have heard of us?

FLAVIO
Yes, I have studied about strange biology.

GREGORI
What do you know?

FLAVIO
They suffer from different diseases such as methemoglobinemia,
porphyria and Wilson's Disease, all having to do
with the biochemistry of copper in the blood.

Vampires are shown outside who begin to get curious and eavesdrop on
the conversation between Flavio and Gregori. They are trying to listen in
by whichever way they can.

GREGORI
Yes! This is what I want to discover.
Why do we suffer from such diseases. Is there a cure?

FLAVIO
Yes, these are very curious questions.

GREGORI
Yes, and there is also a strange history.
What else can you tell me about the history of my people?

FLAVIO

It will help if you first tell me what you know already. And why
do you come to Romania to get these questions answered?

GREGORI

Because there is a high incidence of these blue-blood or copper-
related diseases in Kentucky, I studied the history of the area and
I found out that most of Kentucky was part of what was called the
Transylvania Purchase of 1775. American frontiersman, Daniel
Boone, was hired to help negotiate this purchase from the Cherokee
Indians and he also helped settle the territory. It was supposed to be
turned into the 14th Colony in America and was to be called Transyl-
vania Colony, but it was overruled. But this is why I come to Romania.
The history books do not give me an adequate reason as to why this colony
was called Transylvania. There must be a connection to your country.

FLAVIO

Yes, it would seem so.

GREGORI

There is also a peculiar coincidence at work in this equation.

FLAVIO

What is that?

GREGORI

The Transylvania Purchase was revoked by North Carolina and Virginia
because they claimed the territory for themselves, but they were only able
to overrule it because King George III had a rule against purchasing lands
from Indians. This is ironic because King George III suffered from porphyria, a blue-bloods' disease. This is a common disease in blue-blood royalty and there is a huge case study on King George who was a descendant
of Mary Queen of Scots whose ancestry was traced back to Transylvania.
This is why I am here....to find some answers to this mysterious
legacy and to get help for my family.

FLAVIO

Yes, I agree that this is very curious.

GREGORI

In America, those to whom I have spoken to always suggest that these diseases might have something to do with shape-shifting, particularly when I

mention the connection to Transylvania, such as in the story of Dracula.
(Show vampires eaves-dropping again.)

FLAVIO
(becoming angry)
Stop! Do not talk of Dracula!
He was the prince of Wallachia, not Transylvania.

GREGORI
Yes, but he was born in Transylvania.

FLAVIO
But that is only because his father was under house arrest.
He spoke a different language and that was Romanian. There is too much
nonsense from Hollywood movies. He was not a shape-shifter nor a vampire. He was a stern ruler who used cruelty to enforce his rules.

GREGORI
OK, but I still want to know why our land in Kentucky
was called Transylvania. Do you know?

FLAVIO
The connection is through St. Germain. He was a prince of
Transylvania who was present in your country in 1775 and he instigated the
American Revolution. He presided over the Declaration of Independence.

GREGORI
How do you know this?

FLAVIO
I read it in a book.

GREGORI
What else do you know? Can you help me?

FLAVIO
He was a Rosicrucian as was Benjamin Franklin. They would
have known about the Blue Bloods of Kentucky because King Arthur
visited there also. The Blue People lived underground in caves. They fit it
into the mystery of the Holy Grail. That is why King Arthur went there. I
am talking about the real King Arthur and his brother, Prince Madoc.

GREGORI
Yes, there are many deep caves in Kentucky. But what is
this about the Holy Grail? I have not heard this before?

FLAVIO
I cannot tell you any further because this is a bigger
secret than I am able to share or even fully know.
(Show vampires eaves-dropping again.)

GREGORI
But what I can do? Where can I go to understand this?

FLAVIO
Although I cannot help you any further, I can send
you to a secret society who meets once a year.

GREGORI
A secret society? The Rosicrucians?

FLAVIO
No....more secret than that. My niece Xina can give you directions and take
you part of the way, but first you will need a secret code to gain entrance.

FLAVIO
It is a secret, but I will place the code on your palm. It is just
a number, but is also the secret number of the Illuminati.
(Flavio then writes the number "23" on the palm of Gregori)

FLAVIO:
Now go. See Xina and she will take you to a secret island
where this secret society will meet and teach you about
rare blood and other questions you might have.

When Gregori leaves the room with Flavio, Xina sticks her head in the door,
revealing vampire fangs. Camera shows Flavio then revealing his own vampire fangs as they both laugh in a mad/frenetic sort of way. Xina then (without fangs) takes Gregori outside. She then runs ahead of him, moving ahead
on the path and gesticulating in a provocative and seductive manner so as
to encourage him to follow. It is mostly inappropriate because Gregori is on
a mission and has a firm purpose. He moves ahead stoically as if not to pay
her too much attention.

Scene #3: On a road or path within a short distance or possible view of the island. As they approach the island, they confront a man who looks at them strangely.

MAN
(looking very concerned and bewildered)
Where are you going?

GREGORI
To that island (He points to it).

MAN
(looking more concerned)
That is known as Vampire Island. You should not go there.
God has put me in your path to warn you.

The man makes the sign of the cross and runs away, clearly frightened. Vampires who were eavesdropping now leave, run away or disappear.

XINA
(smiling)
Do not worry about him. He is full of superstition.
Just show them the secret code on your hand and
you will not be harmed. I will see you on the island.

Xina throws off her cape and jumps into the water and disappears. Scene fades out.

Scene #4: The island. Gregori comes to the island (either by boat or by foot...whatever is logistically easier to accomplish). He is greeted by someone who looks imperious. Gregori stops before him and the man raises his hand, exposing his palm. Gregori does the same, revealing the 23 on his palm. Camera focuses on the palm. The man looks at the palm and nods in recognition.

MAN
(looking solemn and professional)
You are welcome on the island. Come with
me and we will prepare for your safety.

This man leads Gregori to the nurses tent where he meets the nurse.

119

Scene #5: The Nurse's tent. The nurse looks at him seriously and professionally as he reveals his palm with the number "23" on it. She inspects it carefully.

NURSE
Welcome to the island. You have a rare blood type. For your own protection and for study, we will need a sample of your blood. The nurse begins to bring or prepare apparatus to take Gregori's blood. As she does this, camera shows Gregori who is looking bewildered and somewhat upset.

GREGORI
My blood! Why do you need my blood?

NURSE
(trying to sound comforting but not too convincing)
Don't worry. You were given this sign, the number 23, to tell us to protect your blood. We cannot only study it to answer your questions, but it is a rare type of Rh negative blood that you have and we need a sample in case of emergencies on the island.

The nurse then jerks her hand as if making a hypnotic gesture and Gregori falls limp as if hypnotized. She then takes a pint of blood or enough to fill a glass. The prop can be Kool-Aid or whatever is available from the snack bar that is red. Scene does not require actual needle poking, but a needle can be shown and then the nurse holding the blood and putting his name on it before placing it with other blood samples. Glasses can be used. Gregori is then shown sleeping.

The nurse then goes outside of the tent where there are vampires (ideally clothed in cloaks and with fangs) sitting at a table. There are already glasses of blood there, like cocktails. Again, Kool-Aid or red juice can be used. (If the right drink is available, we can even make Gregori's blood blue in color but this is not too important). The nurse then brings what is Gregori's blood to the table. She speaks.

NURSE
I have a new sample for you to try. It is Rh-negative, type B.

The vampires get a little frenetic and are eager to try the blood. Each one sips a bit and nods in approval. Camera now switches back to Gregori who is awaking from his stupor. He looks around and gets up, walking out of his tent and is surprised when he sees the vampires. A close-up of his name on the glass is seen by the camera and then he sees it. There is a look of shock on his face and the camera captures that.

GREGORI
(pointing)
That is my blood! What are you doing? You are drinking my blood! Camera now focuses on the vampires, who are smiling. One of them speaks up.

VAMPIRE
You are becoming one of us!

The vampires descend upon Gregori as he falls to the ground and the nurse goes to his neck and begins to bite it as the scene fades out.

Scene #6: It is day time and Gregori is sleeping. He wakes up and looks around, looking disoriented. "Where am I?" he asks to himself. He sees a path on the island and begins to follow it. Before long, he sees an elf who is moving rocks around in a circular pattern.

GREGORI
What are you? You are not a vampire!

CRISTINA
(looking irritated)
What do you think?! (she asks adamantly) That there are only vampires in Romania! There are many strange things in this country and especially on this island, and they are not all vampires. I am an elf!

GREGORI:
I came to this island and it was full of vampires. I was bitten by one last night or had a dream that I was.

CRISTINA
(almost scolding him)
So you think vampires are the only strange things on this island?

GREGORI
I don't know what to think. I was told there was a secret society on this island but when I came here yesterday, my blood was taken,

and I was bit by a vampire. I just woke up and don't know
what to think. Now, I meet you. What is happening?

CRISTINA
You are at Atlantykron.

GREGORI
I was told I would find a secret society here,
but someone said yesterday this was Vampire Island,
and I certainly did run into many vampires.

CRISTINA
You have entered an overlap between two realities.

GREGORI
You mean Atlantykron by day and Vampire Island by night?

CRISTINA
Something like that.

GREGORI
Tell me, what is Atlantykron? Is it a secret society?

CRISTINA
It is a place where science fiction becomes reality....
where scientists meet with writers, artists, and students.....
and also strange creatures like myself!

There is a rush of sound (depending on what is available in terms of sound
effects) and a vampire appears from nearby the stone circle that the elf had
laid out before. The vampire speaks to Gregori.

VAMPIRE
You are one of us now! Come!

Cristina the elf then motions her hands so as to stop the vampire dead in
his tracks. He freezes in response to her magic and then falls down.

GREGORI
What did you do?

CRISTINA
I can handle vampires.

GREGORI
Where did he come from? I thought they only came out at night.

CRISTINA
The circle I was making is not finished because you interrupted me. This is a medicine wheel of stones. I have placed it in an area where there is a great surge of energy entering the Earth from outside. These occur all over the Earth. The stones ground the energy and distribute it in an even manner. I need to place a stone in the center. The vampire came in because I had not finished. (She puts a stone in the middle and finishes).

CRISTINA
There. That is done now.

Suddenly, two elves come running up to them with a device that is a Temporal Tremor Detector (prop can be a cell phone or ideally something better).

ELF #1
Cristina, the TTD is giving a signal.

GREGORI
What is a TTD?

CRISTINA
It is a Temporal Tremor Detector, a device developed by the Anderson Institute who has a presence here on the island.

ELF #2
Yes, they have developed time control technologies and are experimenting in time.

CRISTINA
Where does the TTD indicate that something is taking place?

ELF#1
It is coming from across the river, from the ruins at Capidava.

CRISTINA
We must go.

Scene #7: The ruins at Capidava. Get a long distance shot of the elves and Gregori making their way to the ruins. Have the elf with the TTD (Temporal Tremor Detector) pointing the correct direction to go in. As the elves approach, a single vampire comes from behind a rock and begins to attack Cristina.

ELF #2
Look, a vampire!

CRISTINA
Do not worry. I will take care of him. Cristina makes magic motions with her hands. Her energy is enough to stop the vampire who falls down inert.

ELF #2
Maybe the TTD was signifying that a vampire had penetrated this dimension.

ELF #1
No, the TTD is still going off. Something is over there.

ELF #1 points in the direction of some rocks. As they approach, they see a runestone. A close-up of the runestone is focused upon. The runestone is a prop which will have runic type writing on it. The group gathers around the stone as Cristina picks it up. She speaks.

CRISTINA
This is a runestone. It is an artifact from ancient Atlantis and ties to a network of other stones placed along ley-lines that tie across Romania and the entire world. They are like memory chips in a computer becoming activated, but they are telluric forces of the earth that are activating consciousness. These include the Sphinx in the Bucegi Mountains and Sarmizegatusa in Transylvania.

ELF #2
But why does it appear now, just as we have discovered a displacement of time?

CRISTINA
Energy comes out of the earth here and this stone holds many keys. It is like a keystone in a building as it will explain many things.

GREGORI
Maybe it will explain the rare blood disease in my family
who are from Transylvania, Kentucky - and why I
ended up on an island of vampires in Romania.

CRISTINA
It is not an island of vampires. Only by night and then only
sometimes. During the day, there is a secret society called Atlantykron
and you now have the key to admission by finding this runestone with us.
Atlantykron means "Time of Atlantis". We are activating the consciousness
of ancient Atlantis and fitting it into modern reality. Our theme is where
Science Fiction Becomes Reality. We are also studying time and how
to shift from one dimension or reality to another. We study something
called the space-time interval which teaches us that all factors of
time can be converted to distance. We have a time travel research
group here who have studied how to manipulate time. They are
still learning but they can do amazing things and can
move forwards and backwards in time.

As this explanation comes to a close, Elf #1's Time Tremor Detector goes off
indicating another alert. Scene then fades away.

ELF #1
The TTD is giving us a signal again. There's a big disturbance
back on the island. We've got to get back there.

CRISTINA
Fine. We will go.

Scene #8: Elf #1 and Elf #2 run over to the Tesla Coil where a deluge of
vampires are flooding in. The vampires come out of or nearby the Tesla Coil
in quantity. As the elves neutralize them with their "magic hands" by shooting energy at them, there soon become too many. Then Count Dracula himself comes out.

ELF #2
Cristina, there are more vampires than we can handle.
I am afraid there are too many.

CRISTINA
You might be right. I can only do so many at once.

Cristina is captured by the vampires who take her to where she is tied up. The vampires then began to goad her as they ignore the other two elves.

VAMPIRE #1
You are helpless, there is nothing you can do.

VAMPIRE#2
Yes elf, you are quite helpless and now we can feed off of your blood.

CRISTINA
(speaking to the elves)
Go to the Time Travel Research Group on the island and
see if there is anything they can do to change this outcome.
It might be our only hope! Hurry!

The elves run off while the vampires continue to goad Cristina. There are several vampires around her.

VAMPIRE #1
You think the time travel group can save you?
No, you are now in our clutches.

VAMPIRE #2
Where are your scientist friends now?

VAMPIRE #3
We are going to bite your neck, drink your
blood and take all of your energy!

All the vampires begin to goad and mock in unison as Cristina struggles to get away but she cannot.

VAMPIRES
(collectively and in a mocking tone)
Time Travel Group!?.....Ha ha ha ha ha ha
Camera then shifts to Count Dracula who
is searching around looking for the blood.

COUNT DRACULA
Where is the blood? I understand there is new blood already waiting.

Scene fades out.

Scene #9: The remaining elves run to an office that says "Atlantykron Time Travel Research Group". There will be a sign outside of a tent. ELF #1 speaks to a representative at a technical setting. Perhaps the music tent would be serviceable for this.

ELF #1

Cristina has been caught by vampires and they are taking over the island. She wants to know if you can use time reactor technology to change the outcome by controlling a field generator of closed time-like curves.

TIME TRAVEL RESEARCH GROUP PERSON
(who just smiles as they speak)
Our staff already alerted me to the potential problem. I have already seen the outcome and there is no need for intervention. Don't worry. Just make sure that Cristina reads the rest of the runestone.

Scene #10: Nurse's tent as before. Count Dracula is there to sample the blood. The blood he samples has Gregori's name on it. When he drinks Gregori's blood, he begins to react differently and starts to lose his power. This can be dramatized as suitable.

DRACULA
What is this blood? Something is wrong with this blood.
Where did it come from?

GREGORI (who is nearby)
It is my blood. I hope you can tell me what is wrong with it because this is why I came to this island.....to find out.

DRACULA
Rasputin! You are Rasputin! This is bad blood! It is from the genetics of Rasputin. I cannot take it. It has magic in it and I am losing my power!

By this time, all the other vampires are circling him and wondering what to do. Some of them are losing their power. ELF #1 AND ELF #2 come and free Cristina and they all come and subdue the vampires with their magic hands until all the vampires are still.

GREGORI
Are they dead?

CRISTINA
No. They will remain dormant for a good while.

GREGORI
But what do we do with them?

ELF #1
We were told to make sure you continue reading the runestone, Cristina.

CRISTINA
Do not worry for now. We will read the runestone.
(ELF #2 comes forth with the runestone. Do close-up of runestone.)

ELF #2
Here it is. You can read it now, Cristina.

CRISTINA
(reading the runestone)
It says that we must study the past to see the future;
then it says we must study the future to see the past.

GREGORI
What does that mean? It sounds circular.

CRISTINA
It is, but it means that the answers to the future lie in the past and
vice versa. I should also tell you here this is also the real secret of Atlantykron. The ancient stones point to a time in the future when Atlantis would
reawaken and with that, all of its ancient knowledge. But also, as we look
into the future and begin to understand the technology of time control, we
discover that these things were also known in our ancient past.

ELF #2
It is a balancing act between the past and the future.

CRISTINA
Exactly, and when you can balance the past and the future you
are mastering the present and that is your every day life.

GREGORI
But what about those vampires? Are they dead? And what of
my questions about my own family?

CRISTINA
These are very delicate questions. Once again, balance is
very important. Let me see your palm.
(Gregori shows his palm which displays the number 23 on it.)

CRISTINA
This number, number 23, is also displayed on the runestone and
we can now call it the biological secret of Atlantykron.

ELF #2
What does it say?

CRISTINA
It says there are 23 gene-pairs in ordinary
human beings but there used to be 24.

GREGORI
I have studied biology. It means 23 pairs of chromosomes.

CRISTINA
Yes, and this 23rd gene-pair is sometimes errantly but colloquially
referred to as the 23rd chromosome. It is the sex chromosome which
makes human beings. The runestone calls it the magic chromosome or
gene pair because it was fused together long ago in the history of man.
Originally, men were more like elves. They had 24 gene pairs instead of 23.

ELF #2
What else does the runestone say?

CRISTINA
It says that to look into the human body is to look into a time
machine. It also says that there are time chromosomes.

GREGORI
What does that mean?

CRISTINA
Look at it this way. The two chromosomes of the 23rd gene pair
are like guardians. When they separate and create a new gene pair, which is
really representative of an the original template of the human body,
the 24th gene pair, it gives rise to multiple realities and different
permutations than ordinary humans of today would be used to.

ELF #1
You mean like shape-shifting and other paranormal phenomena.

CRISTINA
Yes, there are infinite possibilities.

GREGORI
But what about my family and their diseases?

CRISTINA
When chromosomes combine with each other in ordinary biological
functions, it results in disease. I am referring to the chromosomes of
one gene combining with that of another. Diseases, including
hereditary disease, are the result of an admixture of chromosomes.
It therefore becomes apparent that if the magical 23rd sex "chromosome"
is really the result of two collapsed or fused gene-pairs, then this
affliction is representative of a master disease in the human body that is
shared by virtually all of humanity. This is what the runestone says.

GREGORI
So my family has this disease?

CRISTINA
Your relatives have an over-active pair of chromosomes as do the
vampires; but they both express themselves in different ways. As I
already said, there are many other potentialities from this as well.

GREGORI
What do I do for my family, and what do we do about the vampires?

CRISTINA
The runestone gives us a solution. It refers to something called Mania
or sometimes Manna, and this represents a way to access our ancestors
through our DNA. It is monatomic white gold, sometimes called Manna
from heaven, but in ancient days, it was known as Mania
and was the active spirits of our ancestors. It is part of the name
of Romania. It also has to be mixed with other sacred substances and
is an alchemical formula we can give the vampires, one by one, to heal
their DNA, and teach them to find balance within themselves so they do
not have to suck energy or seek it from others outside of themselves.

Scene #10: Cristina is preparing a formula which she gives to the elves who start feeding it to the vampires who begin to recover and lose their fangs.

CRISTINA

The exact formula can be a bit different for each one as everyone is an individual with different needs. (She then makes a healing motion over one of the vampires before speaking.) He will be healed in three days.

ELF #2 enters the scene in an interrupting fashion.

ELF #2

We just got a message saying that Atlantykron Time Travel Research Group has located artifacts from the past which require a DNA sequence.... called a method sequence....which is a key to protecting the planet.

GREGORI

What does this mean?

CRISTINA

It is something we are going to have to study. (She turns towards the camera and speaks to the viewing audience). We do not know everything here but we have a good head start. Remember, at Atlantykron we study the future to understand the past and we study the past to understand the future. And if you can balance the past and the future, you will be in the eternal present of NOW. We hope that you can come to Atlantykron and learn this for yourself. And if you are lucky, maybe we can bring Atlantykron to your country.

CHAPTER THIRTEEN

MOVIE MAGIC

Before you read *My Kentucky Cousin*, I mentioned that my entire education and experiences with regard to seemingly diverse threads were synthesizing through the creative process. I did not intend it that way. Atlantykron has its own magic, and many of the people who attend the camp, particularly those who attend year after year, often comment upon it. They do not necessarily, however, write about it; and if they did, it would not be in English.

My Kentucky Cousin was written to facilitate a learning experience for the students at Atlantykron and, at the same time, promote the spirit of Atlantykron. It was literally inspired by my own amplified lens or *mis en abyme* of two of my favorite but rather opposite people who attend Atlantykron: Cristina (as the elf) and Stefan (as Rasputin's great grandson). The timing of my 2010 meeting with David Anderson had also mysteriously synchronized with the dialogue of Tantra Bensko and Eve Logren, to which I was made a party, all of which concerned the history of the Transylvania Colony in America. It was a natural no-brainer for me to try and connect this to Transylvania in Romania. The prospect of Rh-negative blue-bloods was staring me straight in the face, and the timing was rather propitious. A year earlier, I had just published *The Montauk Book of the Living* which discusses this subject in great detail. As this book also featured my introduction to the Montauk Medicine Man, Artie Crippen, it was clear that the carrier wave generated by this book was making its presence felt in my subsequent adventures and also doing it in a rather dramatic and intriguing way. Before I touch on these aspects, I will briefly discuss what transpired during the actual shooting of the movie.

In what would prove to be the first of a string of disappointments, Cristina Jalba wrote to me before my departure from New York and said that she would not be able to be in the movie due to other pressing responsibilities. She was disappointed as well. So, I would have to find another elf, and it would be challenging to find someone who looked the part to the extent that Cristina did.

As soon as I arrived, the script for *My Kentucky Cousin* spread fast throughout the island and was read by many. There was a huge turnout on the first day of those who had signed up for the film workshop. I found out later that many people did not attend because they figured all the parts would soon be taken. The first person cast actually did not attend the initial workshop. She had read the script though, and we thought she would be perfect for the part of Xina, the temptress. Her name is Veronica, and she was already a trained actress and performer. Without worrying too much about who would play who, we began shooting immediately with Veronica. We only had a few days to shoot if we were going to finish in time to show it on the last night of Altantykron. After shooting the film, finishing it would require a lot of post production work as well.

Although Veronica's portrayal of Xina was plagued by mosquitoes, it otherwise went smoothly. Unfortunately, Stefan could not remember his lines in English. Although he speaks serviceable English, memorizing lines was too difficult. I then recruited my assistant to play the part. He had no acting ability whatsoever, but after a day, he caught on and was doing a good job. Unfortunately, the script had been found its way into the hands of his parents in a nearby town, and they hit the roof over his son being in a bloody movie. This was an extremely odd if not ridiculous reaction as the movie is not really bloody, but we had to eliminate him for public relations reasons. This required finding a new star and reshooting all of those scenes.

Originally, we had a producer and a director. It was my intention to have the students literally do everything. The major problem I had was that all of the participants would disperse to go to other seminars. This made things extremely difficult as those who were responsible for scheduling the shooting were not even available to do that. In the midst of this, I recruited my brand new assistant, Cristian. He had better editing software than David had provided, and he would take care of that in addition to helping me supervise the entire movie. I ended up having to cast him as Gregori as he did not desire to attend too many other workshops or seminars. Cristian dedicated most of his time to working on the project, even when we were not together.

After a few days, one of the elves I had recruited — and it took a lot of flattery and convincing to get this shy girl to play Elf #2 — stepped on a thorn during filming. The thorn drew blood, and I could not help but consider the symbolism. In all of my time at Atlantykron, I have never seen someone step on a thorn to this extent. I bodily carried her to the medical tent. Although she would be fine, she no longer wanted to be in the movie.

When I spoke of the troubles and resistance we were having in shooting this film, one of my esoteric friends on the island said that if two people go down during the shooting of the film, it is not a coincidence. There were plenty of other challenges I will not relay for brevity's sake, but losing these two people was representative of a culmination of other frustrating incidents.

In the meantime, we had decided that Veronica would not only play Xina but Cristina as well. As there was really no one else, I changed the script a little to merge the two characters into one character with a good and evil side. It turned out to be a serviceable if not a very good idea. If it were not for Cristian and Veronica, this movie would have died right there.

I made nightly reports to David who was not at the camp that year. In addition to David, I wrote to a friend who works in the theater in New York. She advised me that anytime there is a production of either *Dracula* or *Macbeth*, there are similar problems. Cast members fall ill or become injured. Well, I wish I would have known. I only had a cameo appearance of Dracula, and this was only done to tie in as many threads as possible with regard to

Romanian history. Even though this Dracula was based upon the Hollywood representation, it was intended to be a fictional synthesis of various themes concerning Romanian history. I even asked for permission to include this representation of Dracula as it can be a touchy subject with certain Romanians. Vlad Tepes is, after all, considered a national hero for protecting his people from the slavery of the Turks.

The morning after we had lost Elf #2, Veronica came to me and was very upset. Her face had swollen up as an allergic reaction to the makeup. This was extremely odd as the makeup was hypoallergenic. She said that this had occasionally happened to her before, even with hypoallergenic makeup. It looked as if this would be the final frustration that would shut things down for good. As we were finally ready to call it quits, Veronica came to me and said she had put so much effort into this film that she wanted to finish it. This was great news, and we went across the river to the ruins of Capidava. It turned out to be a completely extroverting experience for everyone. I think it was the best day of Atlantykron for those of use who participated on this adventure. I know it was for me. Everything came together on that day. There were only a few more scenes to do, and some of these we were able to do at night. A lot of it required chopping up the script, rewriting at the last minute, and especially consolidating some of the long-winded passages.

Despite a Herculean effort by Cristian, he could not finish the editing. Although he was able to show a preview, the final film was not finished and never shown. As I write these words now, it is almost five years since the filming of *My Kentucky Cousin*. Although it was meant to be campy and fun, it was disappointing that we did not get a finished product. Although Cristian took the footage with him and vowed to complete it, he never did nor has he returned to Atlantykron since. Roberto Quaglia, my co-instructor who also did the cinematography, has the footage as well but has not done the editing. He did not do anything the first year as he expected it to be done by Cristian. The next year, he said he did not have the script. By the following year, in 2012, I had sent him the script but it still was not done. By 2013, he had lost interest. Veronica has tried to persuade him as well. For all of her hard work and professionalism, Roberto and I gave her the equivalent of Atlantykron's first Academy Award.

While I some day hope there will be a finished product, I have let it go. What is more interesting to me, however, is that the themes in the movie have carried on in my own adventures. This includes the appearance of a "real elf" as well as a member of the blue race. Both of these creatures are inextricably connected as you will learn later on in the book. Before I discuss the more esoteric aspects of what transpired after I wrote *My Kentucky Cousin*, I will first give a few basics with regard to screen writing. I am not at all a seasoned screenwriter, but I will share what I do know.

As an author and publisher, I have had several run-ins with Hollywood, but I will concern myself here only with the alchemy of the writing process. If you have any aspirations of becoming a screenwriter yourself, I suggest you read a book on that specific topic. There are several on the topic and they will assist you in the protocol that is required by the industry.

Those who are already familiar with screen writing will notice that *My Kentucky Cousin* does not conform to the current bureaucratic protocol of script writing. Personally, I just did not have the time. In actuality, the script was also serving as a treatment. For those of you who are unfamiliar, a treatment is basically a short story style description of what is to be filmed. It contains directional details. It is the first draft of what will be eventually be a movie or taped show. There are also adaptations of the original treatment called a presentation treatment for purposes of selling a story to the industry. A real film would require outlines and story boards, all of which is an extensive and time consuming process.

Hollywood has been around for about a hundred years and has developed into a very bureaucratic industry, and this includes all the various aspects of what is required to make a film. It means employing and paying all the various casts of characters and guilds who have their hand out. While one can debate the pros and cons of guilds and unions, there is a key challenge to anyone who works in Hollywood and that is creativity. There is so much money at stake that the process has become cumbersome and has turned the average director into a traffic cop rather than a creative player. Changing a script is not just something one can do before moving on to the next scene. The easiest way to get around this is to be the writer and the director yourself. If you can finance the picture, all the better. For all of its remarkable ability to make magic, Hollywood suffers from a tremendous lack of artistic creativity. This is to be expected in any industry. It has very specific standards, and while this is understandable, it incurs tremendous liability with regard to creativity. With this in mind, look at the definition of creativity below.

> **creativity (n.)**
> the ability to transcend traditional ideas, rules, patterns, re-lationships, or the like, and to create meaningful new ideas, forms, methods, interpretations, etc.; originality, progres-siveness, or imagination: the need for creativity in modern industry; creativity in the performing arts.

This definition says a tremendous amount in a few short lines. It is important to remember that, archetypally speaking, movies and/or Hollywood are ruled by Neptune which is all about deception and illusion. Actors are paid and encouraged to be people they are not. Film makers are creating history that is designed to create a dramatic impact upon the audience. Accuracy, even when it is sincerely pursued, is a ludicrous proposition by the very nature of what one is doing. At its worst or best, Hollywood is creative drama. It is never history. When agendas and control issues are at hand, it only exacerbates the situation. So-called creativity is often used to reinforce traditional patterns and ideas rather than to transcend them.

What is important with regard to *My Kentucky Cousin* is that the creative process had an agenda all of its own that was living up to the definition of creativity you have just read. While I was fully allowing the creative process to take place, I was only trying to write a finite script for Atlantykron. This is why I have encouraged you to write down your thoughts, impressions and ideas while you read this book. The creative process is far greater than your own controlling and logical intellect. Writing it down allows it to take place.

My own creative experiences as a writer began as a result of my interest in the time phenomena surrounding the Montauk Project. All of this concerned the prospect of manipulating time. This manipulation was coincident with the desecration of the indigenous people of Montauk, known as Pharoahs, whose traditions indicated they had descended from the Egyptians. The Egyptian pharaohs themselves, particularly the ancient ones, identified with an even older race of blue people who had Rh-negative blood. All of this coincided with Dr. David Anderson, a rather remarkable time scientist who said he was woken up spiritually when he read *The Montauk Project*. His interest in my own work led him to invite me to Romania. Likewise, the interest of Radu Cinamar in *The Montauk Project* led to my collaboration with him. This, in turn, led me to the realization that the antecedent civilization to Egypt was in Romania. Besides Zalmoxis, there was a sphinx and a hall of records.

Whether you think these statements are correct or incorrect, they have been my experience. The same could be said about any author. Life is a series of experiences, all of which revolve around a certain pattern of different archetypes. The fact that we have these archetypes at all is a testament to their recognized existence. The elements I have encountered happen to be particularly rich archetypes. None of these experiences, however, would have ever happened if I did put my experiences into writing.

When I studied the Blue Race during my research for *The Montauk Book of the Living*, I was immersed in the realm of occult biology. There is a certain point where regular science just cuts off. From all of the data I had researched, however, there was a very obvious conclusion to make. As disease is caused by an irregular combinations of different chromosomes, it was logical to intuit that the devolution of Mankind from a Blue Race was the result of a master disease. All of this dovetails with the very sound theory of Mankind once having twenty-four gene pairs with two of these gene pairs eventually collapsing or fusing into one gene pair. While my basic statement remains a hypothesis to the conventional world of science, there are pockets of information indicating it is far more than a hypothesis.

A further point here is that Mankind is generally in a state of denial with regard to its very existence. So many, if not all, of the world's problems can be reduced to the world of politics which is replete with denial. It is not much different than a family having to deal with an alcoholic father. In the United States, we recently had a president who was an alcoholic. While everyone in the media knew this — it was a matter of public record — they never emphasized that many of his responses to political situations were symptomatic of an alcoholic. We have a society of enablers, and it applies to so much in our day-to-day world. The case of the twenty-fourth gene pairs, however, is a far deeper issue of denial than a mere alcoholic. One is faced with the prospect of awakening from a long sleep of deprived mental faculties. The path of denial is often considered more comfortable. In the long run, it is not.

As I have already alluded to, *My Kentucky Cousin* was a synthesis of various threads instigated by the writing process. It was also a lot of fun and was an adventure within the bigger adventure of my Romanian experiences. When we finished the shooting of *My Kentucky Cousin,* I took a plane from Bucharest to Sofia, the capital city of Bulgaria. I was to meet with my Bulgarian publisher for a ten-day tour of sacred sites in Bulgaria.

CHAPTER FOURTEEN

THRACIA

My trip to Bulgaria was the result of my collaboration with my publisher in that country. In 2008, prior to my first trip to Atlantykron, I had received a request to publish *The Montauk Project* in the Bulgarian language. As was the case in Romania, *The Montauk Project* would be their first book and would launch the publishing company. At that time, there were two individuals involved. After I was invited to Atlantykron by David Anderson, I asked if they could come to Romania and meet me there. David and the people at Atlantykron were accommodating to them, and they spent a few nights with me on the island. After Atlantykron, David travelled to Bulgaria to visit them.

It was now two years later (2010), and I was going to spend ten days in Bulgaria. After being picked up at the airport in Sofia, we drove about two hours to Plovdiv, a large city that is known as the intellectual capital of Bulgaria. It is modern but also quaint and beautiful. If you turn the page and look at the map, you will see that Plovdiv is more or less in the southern central part of Bulgaria. Like the city of Rome, Plovdiv is built upon seven hills. The Roman style ruins are still there amongst the hills. Plovdiv is also known as the city of cats, and you will find cats most everywhere. For the most part, they seem to be honored and respected.

Travelling back and forth from the mountains to the Black Sea, we visited many ancient sites, and there are many stories and legends to tell. In this book, I will give only a very short synopsis of ancient Bulgarian culture before focusing on what I consider to be the most exciting part of the trip: a visit to the Tomb of Bastet, broadly recognized as the cat goddess of Egypt.

Bulgaria is due south of Romania, the two countries being divided by the Danube River. The Black Sea is to the east and Turkey to the southeast. Greece is due south with Macedonia to the southwest and Serbia to the west. Bulgaria is the home of many mysteries, all of which have been kept secret for political reasons. The Bulgarian language has been improperly categorized and undervalued by academics, mostly because they do not understand the language. It is a root Indo-European language. By this, I mean that it is so fundamental to so many languages that it is sometimes construed to be either synonymous to the original Indo-European language or at least very close to it. For those who think the Romanian language is difficult to understand, Bulgarian is much more challenging. Much of this has to do with the fact that they use the Cyrillic alphabet. Although many academics might have a fit over this statement, it is not a stretch to state that Bulgarian is the original language upon which the other Cyrillic languages are based. It is far older, and this has to do with the mostly unrecognized fact that Bulgaria was situated at the crossroads of the ancient world and served as its capital, once ruled by a priest-king named Sham. It is from Sham that the word *shaman* was derived.

This alone should give you some idea of the impact the ancient "Bulgarians" had upon cultures as geographically and culturally diverse as the Mongols and the Native Americans, both of whom used the word *shaman*.

Many of the intriguing cultural ties to ancient Bulgaria are tied to the proto-Thracians, the prehistoric people who preceded the Thracians. The term Thracians refers to the people from Thrace, an ancient territory with vague and varying borders that occupied most of today's Bulgaria as well as some of Turkey. Historians consider the Trojans to be the first Thracians recorded in history. The words *Thrace* and *Troy* are both related to the word *three*, the most obvious explanation for this being the concept of the triple goddess (crone, mother and virgin) that was recognized by the ancients.*

While the Thracians are an interesting people, we are concerned here with the proto-Thracians who were a very advanced forerunner civilization that occupied extensive caves throughout Bulgaria. It should be pointed out that these caves extend right up through Romania with Transylvania being the ancient root source of such a civilization. It is from the proto-Thracians that many of the great traditions of Mankind emerged. These include the Vedic civilization of India, Zoroastrianism of Persia, Lao Tse of Ordos (a northern province of China), and also various pyramid-building civilizations that extended across the globe.

I realize that what I have just written might shock the sensibilities of many, but it is true and can be verified historically. The man who is often identified as Lao Tse (which means long-living wise man in Mandarin) was of Bulgarian extraction. The province where he was an administrator, which was known for its orderliness, was Ordos, and this is where we get the English word *order*. Bulgarians have been known to visit this region of China; and when they mention that they are Bulgarian, they are accordingly dealt with a great deal of respect. The third letter of the Bulgarian alphabet is pronounced *vede* and is meant to signify "knowledge." It was adapted by those who migrated to India and wrote the Vedas. Ayurvedic medicine, as practiced in India, is based upon Bulgarian folk medicine.

Although what has been said here is virtually unknown to the general public, it has never been so to those who control the world stage. Like Romania,

---

* Another explanation for the etymology of *Thracian* is in the book *The Thracian Script Decoded I* by Dr. Stephen Guide. Most of this book is in Bulgarian but there is also a summary in English. Dr. Guide sites hieroglyphics to demonstrate that the First Dynastic king of Old Egypt was named Tzer (later anglicized to Djer). Tzer came to and set up Buto, the first city of the Egyptian Civilization (lower Egypt). King Tzer is also the same as Tiras from the *Bible* (son of Japhet, the son of Noah) and Tiras's tribe are the Tirasians (same as the Thracians).

The most common derivation of *Thracian* is from the god *Thrax*, the son of Ares or Mars. Thrax is commonly identified as Tiras from the *Bible* and also as the father of the Getae, Trojans, Etruscans and Germanic people.

Based upon the above scholarship, it is logical conclude that there is a relationship to the titles Czar, Caesar, and Tzer.

BULGARIA

A small country geographically, Bulgaria is sandwiched between Romania
on the northern border and Greece and Turkey to the south. Macedonia
and Serbia are on the western border while the Black Sea is to the east.

Bulgaria has huge gold deposits. As soon as the Iron Curtain of communism
fell, the United States began establishing military bases around these deposits,
all of which have hidden esoteric significance as well. None of this should be
too surprising if you take stock of the fact or remind yourself that Bulgaria or
Thracia was situated at the straits of the Bosphorus and Dardanelles and ruled
the ancient trade routes. The obfuscation of Bulgaria's extremely rich history
is a deliberate effort to reduce its political significance and cultural influence.

As I already alluded to, there is also an argument to be made for the
Bulgarian language being the original Indo-Aryan or Indo-European language
or at least very close to it. Convincing scholarship has also indicated that
Romanian is closer to the original Indo-European language than others. It is
challenging for me to reconcile the differences and similarities between the
two languages because I am not fluent in either. Although I know different
Bulgarians and Romanians, I have yet to find someone who has such a com-

141

mand of both languages that they can give me a better understanding of these matters. The two countries have remained rather friendly with each other for years and English serves as an easy bridge language between the two peoples. Although the Romanian language uses the Latin alphabet, it originally used the Cyrillic alphabet until the Crimean War changed that. Instigated by the British and French over a dispute about a chapel on the Mount of Olives in Jerusalem, the Crimean War set the boundaries of Romania and made it a nation. Changing the alphabet to Latin helped perpetrate a fiction that Romanian was not an original language but was instead derived from Latin.

In more recent times, the land we know as Bulgaria was known as the origin point for the people we know as Cathars or Bogomils. Although they clearly originated in Bulgaria as a form of alternative Christianity to the Church, the Cathars are more known for their history in France. In the name *Cathars*, you have a direct reference to the phoneme *cat*, and it is not an accident. As I have elsewhere covered the ubiquitous reference and adulation to the cat throughout history, I will keep it simplified in this particular work.

Let us first consider the word *Thracian* or *Thrasian* which can easily be construed and converted into *Tirasians*, a phonetic combination of TAO + IR + ASIANS. When we consider the actual history of this land, this phonetic iteration is not a coincidence. *Asia* is from an old Akkadian word *asu* meaning "to go out, to rise" and refers to the land of the sunrise. The iteration *su* refers to "source" and that is why it has been adopted as an expression for the sun. *Ir* is an expression for the word *cat*, and the Erie (*IR + EE*) Mound Builders or "cat people" are just one example. The continent of Asia or where it borders Europe, the Caucasus area, is where historians have always considered that the human race as we know it arose from. As Leo is both the astrological symbol for the cat and the sun, the word *Thracians*, when we interpret it as TAO + IR + ASIANS, can be construed as either "the Rising of the Cat"; "the Way of the Rising Cat"; or the "Way/ Source of the Cat." Those of us in the West commonly associate Asia as the land of the rising sun. When we also consider that the Akkadian word *asu* means "to go out," the word *Asians* can also be construed as those who emerged from the underground.

When we consider the ancient Thracians, it is also important that we grasp how the aforesaid phonetic etymology relates to the Precessions of the Equinoxes; and in particular, the Age of Taurus. The phonetic break down of *Thracian* into TAO + IR + ASIA also ties into TAU+RUS or *Taurus*. Although the words *Tau* and *Tao* are homonyms and their relationship cannot be overlooked, *Tau* is tied to the constellation Tau Ceti. *Ceti* is the same as *siddhi* or *sidhe* which means "cat." In Ireland, a *sidhe* was a fairy mound which cities were eventually built around and even named after (*sidhe = city*). We all know that Taurus also signifies the bull, but there is more to this meaning than might readily be expected. Etymologically, the old word *bull* comes from *tora*. This is the same as the Torah or the Hebrew holy scroll. An edict from the Pope was known as a bull or Papal Bull, meant to signify a holy writing, just as the Torah was considered to be holy.

The word *Taurus* consists of *tau* and *rus* where *tau* represents the ankh or tau cross, the symbol for everlasting life, and *rus* signifies "red" or "blood." Besides this being considered the red cross or blood cross, it could also be considered the Rosy Cross. The tau cross or ankh also represents the cross of space-time turning into a curved space-time or vice versa. In addition to all of this, the ankh also represents the yoke placed around the neck of an ox or bovine creature. This is the harnessing of the bestial energy. Mundane etymologies suggest that the word *yoga* derived from *yoke*. Yoga is also known to mean "union," but we cannot dismiss the concept of a yoke for the very reason that the practice of yoga is designed to harness or control the bestial energy of a human. Yoga fosters and cultivates the Tao.

The Thracians have an intriguing but mostly lost history that is equal to the various etymologies presented above. When we consider the Precession of the Equinoxes, the seeds of this legacy took place during the Age of Taurus. So that you have a clearer perspective of ancient history and what the Age of Taurus represents, I will now delineate how certain astrological signs played out in the drama of human civilization. Each age represents approximately 2,000 years or a little more.

> **The Age of Pisces** signifies the dying god, most often identified with Christ but also Osiris. The Age of Pisces is symbolized by the Vesica Pisces which represents two interlocking spheres or realms.

> **The Age of Aries** is ruled by the planet Mars and represents war in the name of monotheism and is represented by the ram. This age is strongly identified with the Hebrew religion and Rama in India.

> **The Age of Taurus** represents Mithras or Marduk with the ankh of everlasting life being identified with the thoracic vertebrae of the bull. Featuring the sacrifice of a bull, this age culminated in Moses metaphorically killing the Golden Calf.

> **The Age of Gemini** is identified with the god Mercury or Hermes including communication and trade. We also know to identify it with Zalmoxis, the swastika, and the Hyperboreans, those beings that the Greeks referred to as gods.

The Age of Cancer represents the great flood of antiquity. Water represents the emotions and the matriarchal nature of this time period.

It was a time of sea-faring but also settling into homes or that which represents the hearth. This included the domestication of animals.

When we consider the great flood and the legend of Noah, we can consider that Sham, the ancient priest-king of Bulgaria, is identifiable with Shem, the son of Noah in the *Bible* and also the father of Melchizedek.

The Age of Leo represents the cat but also great heat, something the Egyptians identified with Sirius. This time represents global warming and the melting of the ice prevalent during the preceding Age of Virgo (a cold sign which can be identified with the Ice Age).

I have now given you a summarized precursor to an incredible tale whose seeds would most definitely trace back to the Age of Leo. This tale concerns one of the most enigmatic and revered goddesses in ancient history. In fact, you could make an argument that she is the Mother of All. I am referring to the cat-headed goddess known as either Bastet, Bubastis or Bast. Most of her notoriety is centered around Egypt, but the ancients knew a different story. I will now share the story of one of the greatest mysteries of both modern Bulgaria and ancient Thracia.

CHAPTER FIFTEEN

THE TOMB OF BASTET

This tale involves two exotic Bulgarian women and one of the most enig-matic areas in Bulgaria, a country that is laden with mystery that has been complicated for millennia by various political agendas. While this story is still news to most of the world, it has been familiar to Bulgarians for many years. For whatever reason, this great mystery has also found a way to weave its threads into my own work.

The enigmatic area referred to above is known as the Strandzha Moun-tains, a rather extensive massif of approximately 3,681 square miles which straddles the border of Southeastern Bulgaria and reaches into the European region of Turkey. A Thracian stronghold throughout antiquity, there are abundant ruins with columns, sanctuaries, dolmens and countless archeologi-cal artifacts. The name *Strandzha* is a transliteration derived from *Istranca*, the former name of the Municipality of Binkılıç in Çatalca district, Istanbul province. As we are dealing with the cat goddess Bastet, take due notice of the name Çatalca. There is, however, a much deeper legend behind the name Istranca or Strandzha.

According to legend, Strandzha was a woman of nobility who never mar-ried. Leaving her family and settling far from home with her closest allies, she found that throngs of people followed her, seeking protection. Living in the tradition of an Amazon woman, she obliged them. She refused all of the many suitors until many black men, including their king, came and refused to leave until she yielded to having a mate. Strandzha was at an impasse as she could neither refuse the proposal nor use force against them. What hap-pened at that very moment of impasse was a substantial earthquake with the rivers and seas in upheaval. Chaos ensued until finally there was calmness. When everyone looked out, there were brand new mountains and the sea had turned from crystal white to dark or black. Both Strandzha herself and the black men were consumed by the new mountains. It is from this tale that we have a metaphor for how the names of the Strandzha Mountains and the Black Sea were derived. It is important to comment here that black heads are often found on Romanian heraldic shields. The largest town close to Atlantykron is Cernavodă, a name which can be construed to mean "black king." Whatever the actual truth of these legends might be, there is no question that this area was once the home of a substantial civilization. It is no wonder by reason of the fact that it is adjacent to one of the major trade routes of the ancient world, the Bosphorus Strait. Despite its very rich cultural history and strate-gic location, Strandzha has been very quiet, the last political volatility being the Balkan Wars of 1912-13, the result of which was the western Strandzha Mountains being awarded to Bulgaria. Much of this had to do with the Brit-ish wanting to neutralize the strength of the Ottoman Empire.

The largest peak in the Strandzha Mountains is Golyamo Gradishte. Many people consider it to be a pyramid, but others like to insist it is not. This is similar to the pyramid frenzy in Bosnia. Both areas are the center of ancient cultures, possibly from the Age of Taurus. It is the pyramid in Strandzha, however, which concerns the tale at hand. In the 1970's, a huge chamber in the shape of a perfect cube was discovered in this mountain through use of Ultra Long Frequency wave scans which can penetrate the earth's crust.

I will now share how this information came into the hands of our first "exotic woman" that I mentioned at the beginning of this chapter. Her name was Lyudmilla Zhivkova, and she probably enjoyed more freedom than any other women on earth at that particular time. Lyudmilla was the daughter of the Bulgarian communist dictator, Todor Zhivkova. Treated like a virtual princess by her father, she not only had money to spend, she could travel throughout the entire world. In the 1960's and 1970's, it was not possible for people in the free world, particularly women, to travel to and from the Communist Bloc countries. As a dignitary, she would not only have been able to travel throughout the capitalist world but also amidst the communist countries as well. In any event, she graduated with a degree in history from Sofia University, studied History of the Arts in Moscow and finished her studies at Oxford. It was at Oxford that Lyudmilla met a man from MI6 who told her about the Ultra Long Frequency wave scans indicating there was a hollow cube beneath the Strandzha Mountains of her home country. It was a curiosity but nothing more at that point. For the most part, the information was forgotten until further developments took place.

It is obvious that Lyudmilla was not only a culturally diverse woman but also a powerful one. Her father appointed her as Minister of Culture, and she created a powerful Committee of Culture. She then opened up Bulgaria cultur- ally with an array of international exhibitions and events. High profile artists, musicians and writers from all over the world visited Bulgaria as a result.

After Lyudmilla suffered a very serious car accident, she developed a very strong interest in occult matters and physics. She even refused modern medicine in favor of Eastern medicine with good results. This resulted in frequent trips to Tibet and India where she became very close friends with Indira Gandhi. Her strong interest in these Eastern cultures led to her being initiated into several different disciplines.

Lyudmilla was not only an exciting, intriguing and highly intelligent character, she was extremely popular with the people. One of her most famous initiatives was the Flag of Peace. Many times, she would have large contingents of children from across the world come to Sofia and gather around a specially constructed children's train, each placing and tolling a small bell that represented their respective country. This and all of her other remarkable characteristics and activities stuck in the craw of the

GOLYAMO GRADISHTE

Above is Golyamo Gradishte, the pyramid mountain and highest point in the Strandzha Mountains in southeastern Bulgaria, only a short distance from the border with Turkey. The site of ancient Thracian ruins, this is the area where the ancients are said to have buried Bastet, the famous "cat goddess" who is more commonly thought to be of Egyptian roots.

ultra-restrictive politics of the Soviet Union, and they marked her as a dangerous enemy. Here was a woman in the Communist Bloc exhibiting more freedom and progressive activity than might be imagined. It was certainly not something any "good communist man" was going to do. She further aggravated the Russians by associating herself very closely with the Ryorih family. The Ryorih's were a Russian family that developed a philosophical-social system called Agni Yoga. It was heavily persecuted through at least 1987.

How the discovery of the tomb of Bastet fits in concerns a series of somewhat complex events which will be tightly summarized. For Lyudmilla, it began with a man who had come across a strange and rather unintelligible schematic of geometric figures and hieroglyphics which he thought was a treasure map of the ancients. Pursuing this mystery, he arrived one day at the doors of the Bulgarian Academy of Sciences, and this is how this "map" came into the hands of Lyudmilla Zhivkova. As the Minister of Culture and the exalted daughter of the dictator, this was only natural. With regard to the "map", there was another reason it came into her hands. Lyudmilla maintained steady relationships with many diverse spiritual leaders from across the world. If Lyudmilla and her contacts could not figure out the puzzle of this "map," perhaps nobody could. Lyudmilla, however, did not have to go far. The person who would help her in this matter was the other exotic Bulgarian woman I mentioned earlier. Extremely well known in Bulgaria, Romania, and Russia, her name is Vanga.

Vanga lost her sight when she was struck by lightning at a very young age whereupon she acquired strong prophetic abilities whose accuracy still makes people marvel to this very day. Probably the most famous Bulgarian of all times, throngs of people would gather outside her door to receive readings from her. There has always been much hyperbole and either inaccurate or false writings surrounding Vanga, and even though she has long since passed, many books are still written about her. One aspect of her life that might tend to be overlooked is that she was regularly visited by various heads of states and important political figures. In this respect, she was something akin to the Bulgarian version of Father Arsenie Boca, the Romanian priest who was often consulted for his ability to see into people's future lives.

Completely independent of Lyudmilla, Vanga had come across this mysterious "map" herself. It occurred when the same man (who had come to Lyudmilla) arrived at the home of Vanga's sister in hope of getting a reading on the map. As Vanga has a reputation for neither encouraging nor helping treasure hunters of any kind, the man made a special appeal to Vanga's sister, thinking he might be able to persuade her to convince Vanga of his merits. Complaining that professors were dismissive of these geometric shapes and hieroglyphics, he showed her a crumpled piece of paper upon which they had been copied. Being as pleasant as possible, Vanga's sister suggested that her daughter, Vanga's niece, who had studied Egyptology, have a look at these ten lines of characters as she might be able to read them.

Overhearing their conversation in the next room, Vanga's niece was not happy to hear any of this. Feeling under-qualified to interpret these figures, her observation of the paper soon confirmed what she had thought. Patiently listening to the man, she suggested that they copy the writing so that she could show it to various professors that she knew. He agreed and soon left.

The niece's name is Krasimira. When she next saw Vanga, they enjoyed small talk whereupon the subject of the "map" came up. When it did, Vanga took an unexpected and very keen interest in the text, saying it had been copied many times for many years. This had gone on for generations, but no one was able to decipher it. According to Vanga, this was not about a treasure but was rather a written language unknown to this world. It is, she said, a script from the inner walls of a stone sarcophagus that was buried deep into the Earth thousands of years ago. Even if they found this sarcophagus, she said, they would not be able to read the script which includes the history of the world, two thousand years into the past and two thousand years into the future. The sarcophagus, she said, was buried and hidden in these lands by men who came from Egypt. There were slaves, warriors and high priests and they walked with camels. One night, under full darkness and silence, the sarcophagus was buried with large quantities of earth, and the people who took part in this work were all killed on that same spot. In this way, the secret was cemented with streams of innocent blood in order to wait for the time when it will be found and exposed to the world and deciphered by the people. This was thought to be a one thousand year old message with immeasurable value.

Despite Vanga's enthusiasm and Krasimira's own awe over Vanga's reading, Krasimira was skeptical. After showing it to some of her colleagues, they concluded it was a joke and Krasimira tore the paper and destroyed it. When she met with her aunt again, Vanga showed continued interest in this matter but said that no one would be able to read the map because the time had not come yet come. Then, after seeing some other people, Vanga was again alone with her niece and began to vividly describe an area in the mountains. She was going into detailed descriptions of the area before saying that they had to arrive there on May 5th.

When asked why, Vanga said, "Because of the celestial bodies. You have to look for the first rays of the Sun and Moon."

Vanda then said that she never wanted to speak of this again.

As a result, Krasimira and four colleagues made their way to the mountain by May 4th. Following Vanga's instructions, they noticed that her descriptions of the area were impeccable, and they knew they were not lost. Specifically, there was a rock on the northern side of the meadow that they had been guided to. After suffering two hours of heavy rain and getting wet, they decided to light a fire and spend the night. All of this, however, was against the better judgment of Krasimira. The next morning, as they gathered around the fire and chatted, the sky cleared itself of clouds as the sun began to make its presence felt. Without even realizing why, they ran across the meadow and stood at the foot of the rock. The previous day, however, one of her friends had noticed that the upper end of the rock had been carved with three "solar" circles. They were about the size of a small coffee plate; and together, they formed a triangle with a sharp peak pointed at the Earth.

After about a half hour, one solar ray played upon the rock and came down to the solar circles and began to move on them left to right, depicting a solar triangle. They witnessed this play of the light for about twenty minutes until most of the whole rock was in sunlight. The fact that Vanga had told them to observe the first rays of the Sun exactly on May 5th, that very same day, offered a strange proof that they were onto something.

They talked about what happened for the rest of the day, patiently waiting to see what the rays of the moon would reveal. In some respects, it was a repetition of the previous day. It rained heavily again but the skies cleared again at the last moment. Skeptical that they might see anything else, they soon saw the first star in the evening sky. At this moment, the lunar ray repeated the play of light of the solar one they had witnessed in the morning.

It was nine o'clock in the evening and it was dark everywhere. The lunar ray touched the tip of the rock and then again touched the solar circles from left to right for about fifteen minutes. Once again, it depicted a triangle with a sharp angle pointing downwards. The ray soon disappeared, and they all stood silent in the darkness, two or three meters away from the rock.

Soon after, the smooth southern side of the rock, in front of which they stood, began to glow from within, emitting a color of bright gray as though it were a television screen. Two huge figures then emerged on the screen, occupying at least fifteen square meters. The figures were so real that Krasimira felt they were actually going to disembed themselves from the rock and approach their party. They were all petrified with fear. In the foreground, there was an old man standing. He was in a robe that reached the ground and his hair was shoulder length. His left hand was resting along his body, but his right one was extended forward and hiding some object, an unknown device that was something round like a ball but was not a ball. In the background, elevated higher and a bit to the right, there was a second figure who was sitting. For some reason, it appeared to Krasimira as a pharaoh. This figure was a young man sitting in something like a coach with his hands and feet collected together and resting along his body. His hands were resting on the hands of the chair. He was also wearing a tall hat, but there things above his ears that were sticking out like antennae. The figures remained on the rock long enough to be studied and well remembered. After that, the rock "switched off" and everything became dark again. After they recovered, they reasoned that the whole event had taken place in twenty minutes. As if under some unspoken command, they packed up and headed back to the city using only flashlights. When they started talking again, they all agreed they had seen the same thing.

Krasimira went to Vanga the next day and told her what had happened in detail. Vanga, however, did not make any further comment. Krasimira wondered if this spot was the place where the sarcophagus was buried. She remembered well that Vanga had said, "The time of the 'miracles' will come and science will make great discoveries in the field of the immaterial. All the hidden gold will come on the surface of the Earth, but all the water will hide. This is pre-determined!"

When Lyudmilla eventually saw the map and connected it to Vanga's information, she suddenly recalled what the British man from MI6 had told her about a hollow cube being found beneath the mountain. As the chair woman of the Committee of Culture, Lyudmilla gathered her closest entourage, under a full cloak of secrecy, in order to conduct an expedition to the "hollowness in Strandzha." From one of her many trips to India, lamas had already told her that the sarcophagus of the goddess Bastet was in Bulgaria. The lamas also said that this information would have a very positive effect on Bulgaria in the future. As you will soon learn, the Tibetans were not the only ones aware of this ancient and mysterious repository of archeological artifacts.

For various reasons, little has actually been revealed about Lyudmilla's expedition up this point. We do know that the expedition included the following personnel:

Krastyo Mutafchiev — Chief of the "Cultural Heritage Service" at the Committee of Culture

Krasimira Stoyanova — Administrator in the Committee of Culture and niece of Vanga; graduated in Egyptology from the New Bulgarian University.

Ilya Prokopov — Senior Scientific Cooperative, Second Degree; historian; and specialist in numismatics. He became the curator of the museum in Kyustendil and later of the National History Museum.

Tseko Etropolski — A journalist from Sofia.

Georgi Pantov — Chief Mechanic in the local Strandzha coal mining complex.

A local man, Iliya Petkov, who was a participant in the events of the time period — he was the party secretary and also known as a local "collector of stories" — has provided further information on the expedition. Saying that the mining began slowly, the expedition first discovered a wooden winch and also a copy of an old Russian *Pravda* newspaper. It turned out the Russians had excavated this area in 1940-1950 as the result of old documents from a hermitage in St. Petersburg. At the very least, they found torsoes of statues and also stone inscriptions, all of which were transported back to Russia.

Sometime around the 1800's, when the Ottoman Empire ruled over Bulgaria, two high-ranking and very knowledgeable priests were sent from Istanbul to the same spot. They arrived with a group of workers who worked both at the Tomb of Bastet and a nearby area for six months. What they found was believed to have been taken back to Istanbul as well as Greece.

There were also two groups of Nazis stationed in the area during World War II. The activities of one of the groups included the installation of an antenna on Golyamoa Gradishte. Their ostensible reason for being there was that they were monitoring the telephone lines, but with the Nazi's predilection for ancient artifacts and their cozy relationships with the Tibetans and the prior German collaboration with the Ottoman Empire, it is probable that the Third Reich was knowledgeable about the Tomb of Bastet and desirous of any artifacts or information regarding it. Verbal reports indicated that all of the excavations done by the Nazis in Strandzha were transported to Germany where they remained, even after the war ended.

Lyudmilla's team then came to an entrance that looked like a mining gallery which led to a deep tunnel that had been sealed with a constructed rectangular stone. Inside the tunnel, they found a pulley and the decomposed wooden handles of cutting tools. There were also two stones of black garnet. One was flat with the profile of a male engraved upon it. The other was spherical with twelve sides. Garnets are known to serve the same function as microchips as they can store information. The expedition's findings were sent to Germany with specific instructions from Lyudmilla, but there is no further information.

The expedition team also made other unusual discoveries. Two meters beyond the entrance, there was a circular well on the floor that was filled with stone pieces. In the meantime, on the peak of Gradishte, they found signage on the rocks which was actually ancient script just like that found on the map that had been presented to Lyudmilla and Krasimira. These enabled the team to find another entrance to the underground complex from the southern side. On the eastern side, they found a huge cave with amazing acoustics.

During the excavations, some border officers were employed to help with the digging, but they experienced severe physical reactions which included the whites of their eyes turning blue and paresis of the limbs. Rumors indicated that some of them went crazy and died. After this, no more outsiders were used. It was later determined that there was a very high level of radiation at the site. It was speculated that this could either be from alien technology or perhaps a defense shield set up by the ancients who constructed the complex. One of the more interesting reports concerned the finding of a scepter made of "alien matter" which depicted different holographic images based upon where one would hold it. This was allegedly illegally exported as an artifact and ended up in Vienna where it was sold to a Western space agency, presumably NASA. Whether this is true or not, we do know that America has assumed a dominating military presence in Bulgaria. Part of these finds in the Strandzha Mountains also included bones that belonged to a giant.

Not too much more is known about the expedition, and most of this is due to the untimely death that Lyudmilla suffered just a few days before her fortieth birthday. Due to her "obstructive" presence in the Communist Bloc, it gave rise to speculation of her death being a political assassination by the KGB or others. It is known that, just four days before Lyudmilla died, a Russian academic by the name of Stanislav Shtalin — a man who was soon to become Michael Gorbachev's right-hand-man — arrived in Malko Tarnovo with an entire party of subordinates. Malko Tarnovo is a small village of only a few thousand people that is a reasonably short drive from the archeological site. For these people to go to Malko Tarnovo is something akin to the Queen of England sending a contingent of MI6 Oxford academics to a small village on Prince Edward Island in Canada. One is forced to ask, "Why?"

When Lyudmilla died, her excavation team was just about to return to Sofia in order to analyze what they had found. As they now had no patron, Krasimira turned to the Minister of Mineral Resources, an engineer by the name of Stamen Stamenov, who promised to provide them with men and equipment so that they could get to the bottom of this ancient site. As soon as the team returned from Sofia to Malko Tarnovo and emerged from their vehicle, they were approached by the mayor.

"Engineer Stamenov has died!" he said excitedly.

Krastyo Mutafchiev, who was a part of the excavation team, then had a nightmare where steam emitted from his body as an eagle flew above him in the sky. Based upon similar dreams experienced by those who had dug up King Tut's tomb, he took this as a warning to stop the digging. During that same year, the architect who studied and laid out the terrain for the excavations suffered a near fatal car crash.

The official version of Lyudmilla's death is that it was an accident in the bathroom. Later on, it was added that she might have suffered a brain hemorrhage. In her last months, Lyudmilla had suffered serious weight-loss associated with a long-term illness. While a clever assassination of Lyudmilla cannot be ruled out, it seems that a very strange energy surrounded these events, and we have to consider that the deaths of Lyudmilla and Stamen might be attributable to a protective occult factor.

Despite the security surrounding the expedition, rumors and reports had circulated and caught the attention of the Bulgarian State Security Agency. The expedition was suddenly terminated, and the site was placed under the guard of the Bulgarian Army's border patrol and members of the special forces. The area was soon surrounded by a "live fence" with poisonous snakes.

After the deaths of Lyudmilla and Stamenov, her policy line was not inherited by anyone and most of her initiatives were discontinued. All of the materials from the expedition were locked in the safe of Leonid Katsamunski, a cousin of one of Lyudmilla's staff. He is the former chief of police whose title translates as "Main Police Inspectorate Directorate General."

In March of the following year, a court case was lodged against Krastyo Mutafchiev of the expedition and others for illegally confiscating and embezzling state properties. Others named in the suit included the former Vice Minister of Foreign Affairs, Zhivko Popov, who also was a general from the First Main Directorate of State Security. Mutafchiev was sentenced to fifteen years in prison. The entire matter was sealed and the file was stamped: "Strictly

Confidential! State security!" Those members of the excavation party who were not imprisoned have remained silent for a very long time.

Mutafchiev served over eleven years before being released upon the fall of communism in Bulgaria. Before he died from cancer, Mutafchiev regretfully admitted that he felt that he had unwittingly killed his close friend, Stefan Haritanov, a film director he had invited to shoot footage of the mysterious tomb complex. Mutafchiev attributed Haritanov's death to a "pharaonic curse" as the director later caught a fever of 106º Fahrenheit, suffered hallucinations and became unconscious. Haritanov's film and all material evidence revealing the existence of the Tomb of Bastet were hidden away in a safe as per above, save for one exception. It is a triangular pediment featuring a relief of two outspread hands. It decorated the portico of the corridor leading to the tomb, and is now a major exhibit in the Malko Tarnovo History Museum.

Five years after the trial, it came to light that the Cultural Heritage Department was being used as a cover for a large-scale misappropriation of funds under the direction of General Mircho Spasov, the director of the Staff Unit of the Central Committee of the Bulgarian Communist Party. These funds were being spent on improper or illegal activities, all of which benefited certain intellectuals. Besides Mutafchiev, none of the other above-mentioned members of the expedition were charged.

There are many conflicting theories. What we do know is that the area has long been recognized as the Tomb of Bastet, a cat-headed goddess who was returned by the Egyptians to her homeland in the Strandzha Mountains. There was also an expedition which uncovered material and/or phenomena that was so highly sensitive, it created one of the most intriguing stories in Eastern Europe if not the entire world. Most Westerners and Europeans, however, have never heard about this story nor the persistent but obscure legacy behind it.

Besides the above, there is also the story of Krasimira, Vanga's niece. With regard to the revelations concerning this incredible find, Krasimira said that it will be revealed in the future, but it is not yet time. Vanga has long since passed away, but as each second ticks on the clock, the time is coming closer.

I will now share the story of my own visit to the Tomb of Bastet which, much to my surprise, plays into the future revelation of this great mystery.

CHAPTER SIXTEEN

BULGARIA

I am the first to admit that the legends and stories of Bastet's Bulgarian roots appear to be obscure and enigmatic. If they were not, there would be no need for me to even write about them. Plenty has been written about Bastet from an Egyptian reference point. My travels into Eastern Europe, however, have taught me that Mankind's understanding is significantly lacking when it comes to the influence upon Egypt from northern cultures. Although I was armed with the data you have just read, supplied to me by my Bulgarian publisher, I had neither great hopes nor aspirations of unraveling this mystery any further. Visiting the site of the tomb, even though it had been blown up so as not to leave a trace, was of great interest to me.

I flew from Bucharest to Sofia on a propeller plane and it took about an hour. Upon my arrival in Sofia, I was picked up by my publisher and driven for two hours to his home in Plovdiv. His friend, Michael, who would serve as our driver, met with us there and the three of us would spend all of the next week together. Michael, who was a student in Scotland at the time, had the use of his father's Mercedes and this was to afford us optimum transportation as we crisscrossed the country.

Our first night was in a mountain chalet which was breathtakingly scenic, very comfortable, and cost about $30.00 a night. The economic disparity between America was astonishing. I was told that one could buy a decent house there at that time for just over $10,000. Many Brits choose to retire or to have a second home in Bulgaria. I found Bulgaria to be an extremely beautiful country that features fertile plains and many mountainous regions. There is also a coastal area on the Black Sea.

An esoteric historian named Constantin accompanied us to the chalet, and he shared all sorts of information with me about the proto-Thracians, some of which is included in Chapter Fourteen. The next morning, we hiked to Belintash, an old Thracian sacred spot which features a stone shaped like a man's face. There is also a nearby stone with countless niches and holes that are supposed to represent the stars in the sky. Scientists cannot figure out how the holes were cut. The entire country is saturated with such holes and the nearby ring on a cliff suggests to some that it was an old Atlantean wharf. Alexander the Great visited Belintash in order to learn his future from the Thracian elders. There is also a vast underground cave system that is tied to the many caves beneath Romania. These underground tunnels were the realm of the proto-Thracians. It is definitely an energy spot and attracts people for that reason alone. There are also stories of UFOs and orbs emitting from the site. I invite you to do an internet search on Belintash when you get a chance so that you will be able to truly appreciate this rich Thracian sanctuary. As with the rest of sacred Bulgaria, it remains virtually unknown to scholars.

Guardian of Belintash

Above is the figure of a man's profile carved in stone at Belintash, an ancient sanctuary of the Thracians. There are many ritual sites and stone memories of the ancient Thracian culture. The face is often referred to as a "guardian" of the sanctuary.

Our next destination was the Strandzha Mountains and the little town of Malko Tarnovo. This was an arduous all day drive. The countryside of Bulgaria was absolutely breathtaking. Personally, I find the terrain of Bulgaria to be less intense than Romania. Both are beautiful but Bulgaria has a more gentle beauty. I also observed that the personalities of Bulgarians tend to be less intense than that of Romanians. During our trip to and through the Strandzha Mountains, we did not encounter any of the strange phenomena that is attributed to it and arrived at our hotel at Malko Tarnovo without any fanfare or disturbances. Having not eaten much all day, we went to a sidewalk cafe where they offered us a large menu with all sorts of different pizzas on it. When I chose one and my request was translated to the waitress in Bulgarian, I was informed that they had only one of the pizzas so I simply ordered that.

When I asked why they had so many pizzas on the menu but could only sell me one, my publisher said, "This is Bulgaria."

What you take for granted in America or Europe cannot be taken for granted in Bulgaria. They do not accept credit cards, at least at the time when I was there. When I later wanted to cash a traveller's check from American Express, my publisher said to forget it and that I would not be able to. On the internet, I did find four banks in the large city of Plovdiv that would accommodate me, but it is not like Paris, Munich or even Bucharest. Bulgaria is a cash economy, and I share this with you in case you decide to travel there. Do your research and do not assume anything.

Another point about visiting Bulgaria is safety. David Anderson, who had travelled alone to Bulgaria in 2008, was very concerned about my safety and monitored my activities throughout the entire journey. I wrote to him via email every chance I got and told him about our activities. There was not one incident of any concern, and I attribute this to the fact that I had excellent hosts. I think when you to do not speak the language in any country and are not familiar with the customs, you are vulnerable. If you are travelling to Bulgaria, I would highly recommend that you travel in the company of Bulgarians that you are familiar with and can trust. You should also purchase travel insurance in case of any unfortunate incidents.

After sleeping in Malko Tarnovo, we awoke early in the morning and had breakfast with Stefan and his lady. Stefan is a Bulgarian who lives in London. He was kind enough to make arrangements with the historical museum where the five of us joined regular tourists who were also making the journey to visit the Tomb of Bastet. If you want to go to this area, you contact the historical museum at Malko Tarnovo and tell them you want to see the Tomb of Bastet. I think we paid something just under $20 per person for the guided tour.

We all got in an old but very functional jeep that was originally intended as a personnel carrier. It was a carry-over from the communist days and was built in the Soviet Union. The roof had a huge propeller with vents to counter-act the supreme heat of this area in the summer. While the fan makes it comfortably cool, it was also extremely loud. It took about 45 minutes to get to the border area. The tour guide, who was female, was accompanied by a male border guard the entire time. He wore military pants and a T-shirt and was extremely friendly, even taking us on a short excursion for a quick snack where we picked ripe plums off of a tree.

The area where the tomb itself had been excavated had a very special energy. There were concave repositories that were black but not quite caves as one could not descend into them. Existing cracks that would enable a lizard or snake to enter the underground were too small for humans. The only evidence of the expedition or mining operations that I saw were remnants of stanchions that had been used in conjunction with pulleys.

We spent a lot of time in the area and walked around the entire area as well. It was definitely a special place, but it is hard to say anything concrete or to relay any proof of the remarkable accounts you have read. The area itself is in "no-man's land" and is between the fenced borders of both Turkey and Bulgaria. After all of the scandals settled and the communist era was over, the controls on the area were loosened, and it is now a limited tourist attraction. Turkey was geographically so close that if I had a baseball and bat, I could have hit the ball over the fenced border. There is a long-standing prediction that Turkey will someday retake this land and assume ownership of the ancient Tomb of Bastet. It is assumed that such a development would prohibit any further investigations.

Not far from the Tomb of Bastet is a Thracian complex that was much more interesting in terms of finding tangible ruins. It included a cupola-like tomb surrounded by low circular walls and sacrificial basins. It has been dated, correctly or otherwise, to about 40 BC, and it seems to have been honored by the Romans as well as by occupiers in later times. It is possible that there was something in common between the Thracians and Romans here. According to legend, Aeneas founded the Roman Empire by escaping the siege of Troy with the Trojan women and bringing the flame of Electra to what became the sanctuary of the Vestal Virgins. This signified the eternal flame of the Eternal City. I would also like to note that the very spot in Rome where Julius Caesar was stabbed is now overridden with cats to this very day. Perhaps the last laugh belongs to Bastet.

It is apparent that the area in and around the Tomb of Bastet is psycho-active and that the technology within is similarly aligned with if not from the same source that created the technology in the Bucegi Mountains of Romania. While it is impossible to make a final conclusion, the Tomb of Bastet appears to be a huge multi-level complex that once served as the repository of a very ancient civilization with remarkable technology. Such repositories are often the result of one civilization being erected upon another. They usually feature a necropolis because the wisdom it represents is from the ancients.

My publisher and I contemplated the above and hypothesized that there might be a Bulgarian Radu Cinamar in the mix who was destined to come forward. After all, Bulgaria is loaded with underground sacred complexes. The Tomb of Bastet was only the second of many other astonishing sacred sites I would visit in Bulgaria. Asking my publisher if there was anything we should do at any of these sites, he said we should just visit them to perceive the energy. His non-assertive wisdom on this point was very profound, but I did not realize how profound at the time. We just went about our business and visited the Black Sea and a nearby sanctuary and eventually made it up to the Madara Horseman in the north and later to the very impressive Temple of Orpheus in the south, only a short distance from Greece. There were many other sites and adventures, but they are not so important to tell right now.

What is important is that my trip to the Tomb of Bastet was to play a very strange dividend many years later. I had written about Bastet in the past, and travelling to her tomb was the most efficient way I could honor her within the context that I have to work with. It was also hard for me to believe that such a story did not somehow play into the drama described by Radu Cinamar in his books.

Little did I know, the White Bat was flying over me and keeping out a watchful eye. I was in for a big surprise, but it would not surface for another four years. In the meantime, I was left with many pleasant memories of Bulgaria and the land that was once known as Thracia. I still long to return.

CHAPTER SEVENTEEN

ART

As this book is designed to be creative and interactive, I feel it significant to relay a dream I had as I finished the chapters on Bulgaria. In the dream state, I found myself amidst ruins that were reminiscent of the Tomb of Bastet. I saw Dracula, and he was the same Hollywood version I had dreamt about years earlier in my dream about the white bat. This time, however, he was strictly evil and sinister looking. He was accompanied by an assistant of some sort who I will refer to as Renfield. The assistant did not look like Renfield from any of the movies. Before I could contemplate any horror, Dracula had suddenly and unexpectedly acquired a Siamese twin version of himself. They were joined together at the side. Surprisingly acting like a vampire himself, Renfield then bit the neck of the Siamese twin version of Dracula which began to shrivel up like an old corpse. Dracula was so horrified and confused by what had happened that he did not know what to do. There was so much confusion going on between the three entities that it was like an explosive pinball game. I was able to exit without being noticed.

I then found myself on an athletic field with a friend. I could not recognize his face nor identify him in anyway. I only knew that he was a friend. It was nighttime, and I am not sure whether we were in Romania or America. It could have been a combination of the two. We then saw two phosphorescent green streaks in the sky which we recognized as UFOs that were probes sent to look for us. Telling my friend that we should move so that they could not find us, he said they would find us anywhere we would go. The green streaks then became recognizable as skyrockets, and one crashed and exploded into flames about twenty yards in front of us. Despite the flames, nothing caught fire and the apparent probe had utterly failed. The other sky rocket fell far away and was even more harmless. We were free and unencumbered.

After sharing with you what I already have about the Tomb of Bastet, I feel the dream signifies an exorcism surrounding certain events that took place during the excavations and aftermath of the Strandzha expedition. This suggests, along with other experiences I have had, that we might indeed receive some revelations and further information about the expedition.

With regard to what the Bastet expedition suggests, the only pragmatic explanation I can give is to evaluate it against all of my previous work. In the past, I have written considerable information (thanks to the scholarship of Sid Catlett) about the importance of the cat and how the name *Moor* derived from the Old Greek *Mauresh*, a hybridization of *mau*, the Egyptian word for "cat" and *resh*, the Hebrew word for "king" or "head." The implication of the expedition combined with the legends of Bastet herself suggest that this highly revered goddess either had the head of a cat or a cat-like head. Further, her own genetic configuration is suggestive of being a by-product of the DNA bank beneath the Romanian Sphinx in the Bucegi Mountains. It is important to remind you that Bastest was considered to be the Mother of All. She smiled upon all forms of creation and DNA experiments. This is the essence of who Bastet was as an archetype. In this respect, she would be a prime suspect for being a progenitor, rather than a by-product, of a complex like the one beneath the Romanian Sphinx which is, after all, part griffin or lion (if viewed from the right or eastern profile). As you will learn, I do not think it was an accident of fate that circumstances were such that I would be afforded an opportunity to visit her tomb. I will say, however, that this experience was so intense that it has taken me four years to utter a word about it publicly save for a scant mention in the *Montauk Pulse* newsletter and perhaps on a radio show or two. The significance of my actual experience took years to sink in.

Upon my return to America, I had two priorities. First was to catch up on my routine business responsibilities for Sky Books. Second to that was to secure a translation of Radu Cinamar's second book, the American title for which is *Transylvania Moonrise: Twelve Days in the Mysterious Land of the Gods*. It was challenging to find a translator, and I am very grateful that Radu himself intervened and finally found one for me. It was a personal friend of his who had emigrated to another country. Although the translation was adequate, I found it very challenging to edit. Another Romanian translator once explained to me why. She said that Radu sometimes writes in a style that features rather complex sentence structures that gives way to run-on sentences. Perhaps the most challenging aspect was that these passages dealt with equally complex esoteric information. In the end, Radu wrote to me that he was very happy with the English translation. Other Romanians told me that it was clearer and easier to understand in English than in the original Romanian version. If this is true, I can only attribute such clarity to myself applying what I wrote earlier in this book about words and concepts.

What I found most interesting about this book was the data presented, particularly in the first chapter. Prior to that, however, *Transylvanian Moonrise* actually begins with an Editor's Note from Sorin Hurmuz which includes all sorts of excerpts from the Romanian news media that corroborated aspects of *Transylvanian Sunrise*. The Romanian people, particularly those who had retired from the intelligence community, were telling the editor that the story in the book was true.

With regard to the first chapter of the book itself, it left me rather awe-struck, and I should be quick to point out that I am not easily awestruck. Being in the profession I am in, people frequently send me all sorts of strange or far-out data. Most of it is rather "more of the same" and while it might or might not be true, it does not garnish much serious interest on my behalf. This first chapter of *Transylvanian Moonrise*, however, really made me stand up and take notice. It was about a subject that has been much written about but never well understood: alchemy. While I had written cutting-edge revelations, at least in terms of popular thinking, about alchemy in books such as *The Black Sun* and *The Montauk Book of the Living*, this work was on a different track than any others I had seen before.

The first chapter starts out with Radu's editor, Sorin Hurmuz, receiving persistent phone calls from a man named Elinor, which is a pseudonym, who wants to talk to Radu. As Radu has given Sorin specific instructions to deflect all such communications, Elinor is turned down. His persistence, however, finally encourages Sorin to ask why it is so important for him to talk to Radu. Elinor then tells him that he is speaking on behalf of a Tibetan lama who would like to meet him. Sorin feels obligated to communicate this to Radu who is surprised that a lama would like to meet him. An arrangement is soon made for Radu to meet with the lama at Elinor's house in an exclusive area of Bucharest. I should add in here that I have come to know Sorin well over the years. As we have spent significant time together and done various favors for each other, we have become good friends. Sorin has verified for me that Elinor is indeed a real character who called him on the phone to make the aforesaid arrangement. He told me that Elinor had a regular voice but that he has not had any further communication with him since.

When Radu arrives at Elinor's home and meets him, he is informed that the lama will be late. This affords the two to have a conversation which I found to be the most remarkable aspect of the book. I am referring to their discussion about alchemy. Although Elinor is over sixty-years-old, he has a youthful appearance and looks like he is twenty-seven. His driver's license indicates he is over sixty. Elinor explains that he has been initiated into a rarefied alchemical tradition facilitated by an ancient ancestor. It is a fantastic and intriguing story.

This ancestor of Elinor's was born hundreds of years previously and was initiated into this tradition himself after a series of misadventures that began when his father, a trader of renown on the Asian trading routes, and mother were killed when their caravan was attacked. Travelling with the caravan and still a young boy of fourteen, the ancestor was subsequently awarded to a small time Persian king. When the king was visited by a travelling maharaja from India, the latter took the boy back to India where he met a magician friendly to the maharaja. With the maharaja's blessing, the magician became the ward of the boy, Elinor's ancestor. After twenty-three years of preparation, the magician apprenticed him into a very secret science whose profound mysteries were known only to the truly wise. It was an alchemical tradition which would prolong his life for hundreds of years. Before he parted with him forever, the magician gave Elinor's ancestor a very strange object made out of a special metal alloy. He had been told that as long as he remained around that object, he would never grow old and live for thousands of years. Not only did he not grow old, he became younger than when he received the mysterious alloyed object. During the four centuries that passed, he experienced a profound change in his perspective and way of perceiving the world. His consciousness was greatly elevated and his priorities totally changed. Part of his initiation included learning how he could obtain the special alloy for such a longevity device as well as precise directions on how to construct one. Eventually, he was contacted though occult channels by representatives of a superior civilization. At the same time that this occurred, he achieved the ultimate desire of any genuine alchemist: the Philosopher's Stone. It would not have been possible, he said, had he not first been able to grasp a profound understanding of the essence of life and the universe as well as other mysteries of knowledge that had been revealed to him during his existence.

What I have said here is only a tight summary of what is involved in the first chapter of *Transylvanian Moonrise*, but the content and the way it was written peaked my interest in a way that no other book ever has. While there are plenty of details omitted, it was apparent that they were discussing an actual alchemical tradition and not simply spouting off at the mouth about it as is the case with most pontificators on this subject. There was also an aura of maturity in the approach to the subject that was accompanied by a genuine knowledge that would preclude accomplishing such a feat.

As I said, I am not easily impressed, even when I receive a lot of so-called leads and information that is perceived as cutting-edge. Most of it is rejected for one of two reasons. Either it is worthless in its own right or it is not specifically applicable to what I am working on, even if it has merit. Whether the information from Elinor was true or not, I experienced an uncanny intuition that I was receiving a personal initiation into his alchemical tradition just by reason of reading the original translation of the first chapter. As a matter of fact, I had paid a significant sum for the translation of the book, but I felt that paying the sum would have been worth it just to read that chapter alone, let alone my responsibilities for publishing the entire book. Even though I knew the book had already been published in the Romanian language and I would be circulating it in the English language, I still contemplated the peculiar notion that this was a personal initiation for me and perhaps just me. It is now over four years since I first read that chapter, and experience since then has suggested to me that I was probably either right about that assumption or at least close to it. People in our civilization are not only dismissive of such an idea, they are neither physically, mentally or spiritually prepared to take such longevity seriously. By reason of my own life path and specialized Chi Gong practice, which I take very seriously, I am already being prepared to live a long life that is far beyond routine expectations. Such longevity, however, is projected to be somewhere in the range of 120-200 years. Elinor's words were stretching my mind to view beyond my already stretched horizons.

In order to make you better appreciate what I am saying about people not being ready, I will give you an example. On those rare occasions when I give a lecture for forty-five minutes about Chi Gong, people typically learn more pragmatic information than they have ever heard before about Chi Gong and the healing applications of the martial arts. This sounds good except for the fact that everyone is more inclined to walk away like Humpty-Dumpty bloated with information. It does them no good if they do not apply it and do the routines on a daily basis. It is better to talk for five minutes and have them work for forty minutes. People, however, are generally predisposed to their own pre-conceived ideas and might prefer a power-point presentation, particularly if they do not have to do any real physical work. The natural tendency in popular workshops and seminars is to make snazzy presentations. These are appealing to the visual centers of the brain, and while you can certainly learn data, there is something wrong with this equation when it comes to Chi Gong. It takes work, and it has to be done every day and for a considerable amount of time. Ten minutes of exercise, however, can do a great deal of good, too, but it will not get you to the higher levels. Even so, it is an acceptable starting phase.

There is nothing wrong with going to seminars that teach you how to organize, how to do public relations or any manner of other subjects. That, however, is not the type of learning I am talking about. Serious longevity is a subject that has never really been taught to any significant extent. It requires that you drastically change your viewpoint of how you approach life. People will usually tell you they do not have time. While this is readily understandable from a normal human perspective, there is one gaping hole in this mind-set. If you learn and practice a genuine tradition of longevity, you will have a lot more time in which to live your life. In other words, you are buying time by taking time. When faced with such logic, one is prone to visualize their personal foibles and what they would have to sacrifice or do in order to engage in such training. This will cause both a mental and emotional reaction inside of you which will be accompanied by resistance. This resistance has force behind it. You can either yield to the force and ignore the call or you can martial your energies and overcome the force. This, in essence, is your first lesson in martial arts. You are overcoming an internal force that is working against you. The next step is getting such force to work for you, and this begins by engaging in an actual breathing posture and/or routine that will circulate energy throughout your entire system. I could go on, but I am just trying to give you an example of what serious training entails.

Most important to my diatribe is that longevity training requires a drastic change in attitude. With regard to Elinor's tradition, I was already in the throes of a dedicated discipline that is drastically different from what ordinary human beings, highly-educated or otherwise, usually cannot take too seriously due to their own dubious creature habits. After over three years of very serious Chi Gong training, my own personal discipline was being rewarded by the mere suggestion that I could elongate my life considerably longer. Since learning about Elinor's tradition, I have now been studying Chi Gong for seven years. Rather than slowing down or backing off, I have lengthened my workout and take Chi Gong even more seriously than I did when I first learned of Elinor's tradition. All of this is preparation for radically changing my orientation to life yet further.

As interesting or daunting as all of this might sound, Elinor's discussion of alchemy and longevity was only the first chapter of the book. The influence was profound. The momentous meeting Radu had with Elinor, however, had an equally interesting ending. Very late in the evening, the mysterious lama showed up at Elinor's door, but he had a very strange creature with him. Standing about seven-feet high, the lama's companion looked like something out of the *Arabian Nights*. By comparison, the lama was small. According to the Tibetan tradition practiced by the lama, this creature is referred to as a yidam, an independent "extension" of a lama's mind that is the successful manifestation of an involved sand mandala ritual. It is a high level operation performed by only the most exalted lamas. The purpose of creating a yidam is to enable a lama to negotiate realms of existence, which might or might not include the regular physical universe, that would destroy an ordinary human body. You might say that it is somewhat akin to creating Superman to protect you rather than becoming Superman yourself. What a yidam looks like is completely dependent upon the individual lama who chose to create it. It could manifest as a hulking giant, a fairy, a fire-breathing dragon or anything else you might imagine. It could even be a sasquatch, an abominable snowman or a talking parrot. Possessing telepathic abilities, yidams can talk but only if they are specially trained to do so. The only reason this particular yidam accompanied the lama was so that Radu could become familiar with him and avoid any possible shock or psychological reaction that might ensue during an upcoming trip that the lama had prepared for Radu, himself and the yidam. The lama was there to encourage Radu to take the trip.

After a lengthy discussion about the yidam, the lama finally apologizes and introduces himself as Repa Sundhi, an official lama who had once served in the palace at Lhasa but escaped prior to the Chinese invasion in the late Fifties. After further discussion, the lama reveals that he is also known as Dr. Xien, the same man who had created Department Zero and was the mentor of Cezar Brad. Having important political connections throughout the entire world, the lama had somehow reinvented himself as a doctor in Communist China who was recognized to have extensive experience in the paranormal. Unbeknownst to Radu, the lama had prepared to take him on an exotic journey to a very remote and rarefied area of Tibet.

CHAPTER EIGHTEEN

THE HIGH PRIESTESS

When we contemplate either the pathways or archetypes of the Tree of Life, there is a rather remarkable correspondence with regard to the previous chapter and what was to ensue in regards to Radu's experiences. I referred to the last chapter as "Art" as this is the name used in the *Thoth Tarot* for the card that is called "Alchemy" in the *Rider-Waite Tarot*. Earlier in this book, it was said that The Lovers (also symbolizing Gemini or Zalmoxis) is considered to be the precursor to Alchemy, but it should also be pointed out that the latter is, in turn, the precursor to the High Priestess.

To be a little more specific with regard to the Tree of Life, Alchemy is the path that leads from Yesod (symbolic of the moon or astral realm) to Tipareth (symbolic of the sun as either Mithras, Apollo or Christ and also represents the harmonious beauty of nature). It is from Tipareth to Kether that we have the card or pathway known as the High Priestess. After Radu is introduced to Elinor's alchemical tradition, he is led on a path that takes him directly to the High Priestess. Art imitates life and vice versa. This principle alone should encourage one to face the prospect of taking alchemy seriously as well as all the others aspects of the Tree.

As Radu's conversation with the lama continues, he is convinced that he should take a trip to the Apuseni Mountains in southwestern Transylvania. In a few days, they take the trip in an SUV that is driven by Elinor. In the Apuseni Mountains, they meet up again with the yidam who materializes in front of them. A very well described space-translation takes place which propels all of them to a rarified region of Tibet. It is unclear whether or not the space-translation is specifically engineered by the yidam, the lama or both of them. As the yidam controls the forbidding temperature, they reach a cave after a reasonably short walk. Radu is not allowed to enter until after Repa Sundhi and the yidam first enter by themselves. When they emerge, Radu is invited in along with Elinor.

Inside the cave, Radu is in awe as he sees a beautiful blue-skinned goddess whose name is Machandi. She is presented as a very evolved soul who also lived as a close ally of Rama and Sita, two exalted characters featured in the *Ramayana*, one of the two epic tomes of the Hindu religion, the other being the *Mahabharata*. We eventually learn that the *Ramayana* is based upon actual events that took place in Transylvania rather than India. This is backed up by the statement that the flora and fauna mentioned in the *Ramayana* were present in Transylvania and were not known to exist in India. Most beautiful to the eyes, Machandi is an exotic creature who, according to the text, accumulated immense experience in manifestation, always evolved, and at present, governs a big part of our galaxy and has a superior place in the hierarchy of celestial beings. After giving Radu a brief esoteric initiation, she leads him to an ancient manuscript many hundreds of years old that had been deposited in Tibet for safekeeping so that it could be released at an appropriate time in the future.

The parchment was written by one of Guru Rinpoche's closest disciples and at his direction. More commonly known as Padmasambhava, Guru Rinpoche is one of the most exalted personas in the history of Tibetan Buddhism and is known as the Divine Sovereign Sage of the Three Worlds. Guru Rinpoche, sometimes spelled Rimpoche, is considered to be an emanation of the Buddha and is regarded by the Nyingma school to be the Second Buddha. The Nyingma are also known as the Red Hats and were centered in the area of Tibet known as Kham. (Note the phonetic similarity to *Khem*, the ancient name for Egypt).

The parchment given to Radu by Machandi is one of many parchments that were hidden all around Tibet over a thousand years ago. Each one has its own importance and destiny. The one given to Radu is significant because its discovery and translation would not only lead to initiation but also a series of actions and events which will have a very profound impact upon humanity. The translation of the manuscript and the aforementioned actions and events are the subject of *The Secret Parchment — Five Tibetan Initiation Techniques*, the fourth book in *The Transylvania Series*, all written by Radu Cinamar with Peter Moon. A synopsis of important points and how they relate to my own adventures will be given later on.

As Radu finishes with Machandi, she tells him that he will meet her again in several days time for a very special initiation but this time in his country. With the manuscript in hand, Radu then returns to Transylvania via another space-translation and then back to Bucharest, accompanied by Elinor and the lama. The yidam has other business to attend to and departs by means of dematerialization before their eyes.

After their return to Bucharest and the manuscript has been determined by Repa Sundhi to be written in an ancient Tibetan script, the three soon return to Transylvania in Elinor's SUV. Their destination is Gugu Peak, a holy site to Romanians that is a very important energetic center of the country. As they arrive in Transylvania and set out on their long hike to Gugu, they encounter a group of young Romanians, mostly in their early twenties. All of them are there because of a series of initiatory dreams they have had with the goddess Machandi. She is the one who told them when and where to go. Repa Sundhi had already advised Radu that they would meet these people and further stated that they would all play an important role in the amazing transformations of the nation of Romania. Each one of these young people experienced their dreams with Machandi independent of each other.

On their way to Gugu Peak, they have been joined by the yidam who materialized. He is there to protect them from the rather severe and negative forces which soon besiege them. Part of these negative forces include thunder and lightning. When they finally get to Gugu, a spectacular event occurs when the entire group becomes draped in a sort of light that covers and completely isolates them from the terrible atmospheric phenomena. Not even the pouring rain penetrates this bubble of light. Thundering "apocalyptic" lightning and flying shrubbery is seen, but they remain unperturbed in a safe bottle of protection. The stone of the mountain then becomes transparent and reveals a great cave inside the peak. Machandi then appears from inside of the cave and comes outward. Her presence subdues the storm, and Radu refers to this as a "wonderful apparition of the goddess." The experience then becomes rather subjective as Radu then receives a transmission from Machandi offering them all precious teachings about humanity and the way they have to act in order to be completely successful in their missions. Machandi then comes forward and places her hand on Radu's head and he goes into a profound state of consciousness that I can only compare to something called the Great Stillness in Taoist Chi Gong. He feels that he becomes one with everything and has touched eternity. When he finally opens his eyes, Machandi and the young people are long gone, and he finds out that he was absorbed for more than seven hours. His friends, Repa Sundhi and Elinor, are waiting for him, and he is told that the very special experience he has just gone through will have great importance in his spiritual evolution.

Radu's narrative ends here. I asked him to write an epilogue for the American edition, and he did so. He reiterates that the experiences were indeed real and mentions what a profound experience it all was. After a good period of time, he mentions a meeting with Repa Sundhi who is accompanied by his assistant, Shin Li. We learn in *The Secret Parchment* that Shin Li will help him understand the subtle aspects of the parchment itself so that he can write a book to explain it.

What you have just read is a summarized version of a much more in-volved and very fantastic tale by Radu Cinamar from the book *Transylvanian Moonrise*. While I enjoyed the narrative about Machandi very much, it did not move me in quite the same way that the meeting with Elinor did. Perhaps this is due to the fact that his journeys to see Machandi required me to stretch my mind even further in order to accept the proposition that what Radu said did indeed happen.

Although Radu's experiences have to be considered highly subjective experiences to an outsider, there are aspects that connect them to the everyday reality of the earth. The concept of Machandi, let alone the reality, has to be put into context, and this requires integration. The word *integrate* means to bring all the parts together or to make whole. It is easy to be dismissive of intangential or irreconcilable experiences and far more challenging to inte-grate them into a cohesive stream of consciousness. Once again, we will find the Tree of Life a useful metaphor for actual states of conscious existence. As

Machandi precisely fits into the category of High Priestess, it is prudent to explain some characteristics of this card, particularly as it is depicted in the *Rider-Waite Tarot*. On either side of the High Priestess are two pillars, a black one on her right designated with the letter *B*, and a white or gray one on her left that is designated with the letter *J*. These pillars are representative of the pillars that once stood before Solomon's Temple, and they are meant to signify Boaz and Jachin respectively. Scholars are candid about the fact that they do not really understand the etymology of these two words, but they do try.

Boaz is traditionally defined as strength but strength based upon faith. It is the struggle of the spirit and is related to the word *Tibet* which really refers to a prayer bead or a means of prayer. The pillar of Boaz represents people praying by whatever means. It is a request to or consultation with the Creator. In reality, this is really a request to the primordial energies of the Creator. This prayer invokes duality, sometimes represented by black and white.

The word *Jachin* yields to understanding if we consider that *Jachin* = *Ja* or *Ya* as in *Yahwah* (Jehovah or tetragrammaton and/or the four elements of fire, water, air, and earth) + *chin* = *shin* (referring to the "son" or missing piece of tetragrammaton by giving us *yod-he-shin-vau-he* or pentagrammaton where *shin* represents the ability of spirit to act upon and change the four elements).

These phonetic etymologies tell us that the two pillars before the Temple of Solomon represent two core aspects of existence. Boaz is faith, the faith we experience every day when we wake up, walk out into the world and trust it will be pretty much the same as yesterday. This sort of faith is more fundamental than the ordinary concept of religious faith which has to do with belief. Every creature who has awoken to find himself juxtaposed in space-time is faced with the conundrum of existence. He or she not only has faith that he or she is in this self-propagating continuous paradigm but that there is perhaps a method to create a better circumstance. This gives rise to prayer and a conversation with the a priori Creative Principle. This interaction between man and the Creator, through prayer or intent, gives rise to the theater of life and is symbolized by the two pillars of Joachin and Boaz.

This interaction of Joachin and Boaz manifests on the path of the High Priestess, and it is actually representative of all the myriad crisscrossing of opposites that the mind can imagine, all flowing down the Tree of Life to Tipareth. This realm, assigned to Christ by cabalists because it is meant to signify ultimate harmony, includes the reconciliation of opposites, whether they be black or white. I choose to emphasize black and white in Tipareth, not only because it is mentioned in classical interpretations but as it is also a central theme of this book. This embracing of one's opposite nature is the key to transcendence and is represented well in the archetype of Zalmoxis where we have transcendence from a man to a god. As I would eventually learn, this is also the message of the flapping wings of the white bat.

CHAPTER NINETEEN

INTEGRATION AND EDITING

I am choosing to write this chapter at this juncture for a few reasons. First, prior to the last several chapters, every other chapter was about the mechanics of writing as opposed to the content itself. This was an arbitrary structure that I created which flowed with the points of view I was trying to get across. As I got more into the narrative aspect of this book, the story took off and I felt like it was best to follow it and abandoned the arbitrary structure that I had become comfortable with. Whatever one is writing has to have a structure. If not, it just chaotic information. Whether or not one wants to conform to the generally accepted formats of either fiction or non-fiction, one has to choose how they are going to present their information. One has to become circumspect about what one is writing as well as who one is writing for. Many books can easily conform to a standard format. Others can be tricky, particularly when you are writing about the topics that I typically write about.

Many books about the paranormal are expository, seeking to demonstrate a remarkable story and very often trying to convince you of either the plausibly or objectivity of what has been presented. It has gotten to the point in today's world that there are many such books. The shock and awe of what has been presented is neutralized by the sheer quantity of people that are pretty much in sympathy with the idea that paranormal factors are real. Even so, there are still countless people who think their story is special and want to tell it. Do we need any more? That is a question that one has to ask if they choose to write and tell their own story. My advice to anyone who wants to write and publish a story is to offer something that is unique and also of value to the reader. With regard to it being valuable, I have encountered very many people in recent times who are impelled to tell their story in order to help others learn something about a specific area of life. What I have noticed about such people is that they are actually working out some issue they need to process and their passion to teach others is really more about themselves and their own process of self-discovery. There is nothing wrong with that, but it is not always necessary and sometimes inadvisable to teach others your own life lessons. It is important to identify the precise reason why you are writing a book. When I have pointed out to people that they are actually just working out their own issues in their manuscript, they are usually in agreement with my observation and quite content to simply work out their own process. Most things in life are really about yourself. This is the *mis en abyme* mirror at work.

I have designed this particular book to have a certain 360º aspect. By that, I mean that I am very circumspect about what I am writing, why I am writing it, and who I am writing it to. This includes the *mis en abyme* principle. There are mirrors or virtual mirrors placed all around the consciousness involved.

If you have not already noticed, there are five major threads in this book: 1) the original dream that inspired this book as well as the other dreams and stream of consciousness that flows with all of this; 2) my personal narrative and experiences; 3) Radu's stories; 4) the theme of writing and how to do it; and 5) the Tree of Life as a working model or mirror of life. While there are other sub-threads, all of these major threads are interactive and crisscross with each other.

Whatever you are writing, unless it is just simple and straight forward, delineate your various threads. This is a matter of identifying what it is you are actually writing about. It has to be clear in your mind, particularly if you are writing about a complex subject. Any good attorney has to be very astute at this as legal cases can be more complex than nuclear physics.

Outside of obvious or boorish mistakes, integrating or organizing your various threads is one of the first impressions that you will make upon a reader. If the threads are clear, the fact will often go unnoticed because there is no confusion induced in the reader. When you do not integrate the various threads, you are going to either confuse, irritate or raise questions to anyone who attempts to read or edit your writing.

If at all possible, it is advisable that you become proficient at editing, particularly if you want to be either a professional or serious writer. Most editors will say more or less the same thing about a given manuscript, provided they are not psychologically disqualified by reason of prejudice. I am assuming that such editors are not emotionally triggered by the material. In the spirit of understanding the editing process, let's look at the etymologies of the following words.

editor (n.)
1640s, "publisher," from Latin *editor* "one who puts forth," agent noun from *editus*, past participle of *edere* (see *edition*). By 1712 in sense of "person who prepares written matter for publication;" specific sense in newspapers is from 1803.

edit(v.)
1791, perhaps a back-formation from *editor*, or from French *éditer*, or from Latin *editus*, past participle of *edere* (see *edition*). Related: *Edited*; *editing*. As a noun, by 1960.

edict (n.)
late 15c., *edycte*; earlier *edit*, late 13c., "proclamation having the force of law," from Old French *edit*, from Latin *edictum* "proclamation, ordinance, edict," neuter past participle of *edicere* "publish, proclaim," from e- "out" (see *ex-*) + *dicere* "to say."

Other than to clarify the meaning of what an editor actually is, I have included these words because they show the relationship of *edit* and *editor* with the word *edict*. An edict is a very forceful word which is quite literally a law. While the word *law* conveys a rather somber and heavy tone, it basically means to lay down something. What these words show, however, is that when you write you are essentially making a proclamation. While you might or might not think of it as law, it is your own truth, at least for the moment you are writing it. The editing process is different than the writing process. In the writing process, you have unlimited capacity to experiment and play. You can test ideas all you want. When you edit, you are writing it down in a much more permanent and serious fashion. It extends a mirror out into the world. If you do it lamely, with hesitation, or hoping an editor or someone else can improve the content, you are fluttering in the wind. Do not expect others to pick up or correct your mistakes. Even so, it is advisable to have others read your manuscript and help out and make comments. This is always very helpful. One of the worst disservices I have ever seen, however, is when people read another's work and tell them how good it is when it really is not an appropriate comment. Although the manuscript might be "good" or even interesting to the person who made the comment, I have too often seen instances that while the writing in question might have some excellent qualities, it has no potential whatsoever for being sold. This is perfectly fine if you do not want to sell what you are writing, but such comments by people who are not in the publishing world can give false hope or encouragement to someone. Therefore, if people like your work, that is fine. In most instances, do not count on them for professional advice with regard to the marketability of what you have written. They might, however, have some good points or astute comments about the marketing of your manuscript, so while you should not discount them utterly, be careful about becoming overly enthusiastic about such endorsements.

There are plenty of good writers in the world. Many, if not most, college graduates are fully capable of writing clear and concise literature of almost any type. Those who will get their material sold is an entirely different prospect. We currently live in an age where the technology of print-on-demand has created more published authors than there has ever been in the history of the world. Anyone can publish these days, but marketing and selling is an entirely different matter. Counting on others to do this is also quite risky. Writing and the marketing of what you write are two separate art forms.

None of what I said should discourage you from writing. Ideally, your writing should be chronicling the adventure of your soul. If you are writing a resume, you are writing down the aspects of your soul that you want others to recognize so that you can integrate your talents with the world. A teacher or instructor can write to share his knowledge and make learning fun for his students. If you are a CEO, you can totally change the mood of your organization in an upbeat way by firing out carefully thought out memos and edicts through your secretary. If done callously or stupidly, it can ruin morale, create confusion, and lessen the productivity of everyone.

Those of you who do not have any particular professional aspirations for your writing might be the luckiest of all. First, you will not have to deal with the prospect of failure. More importantly, as said before, you can begin to chronicle the adventure of your soul. Why? Well, if you do, you will be transferring information from one side of the brain to the other, and you will also have a record that you can refer back to. This also stimulates your creative thinking, and creativity applies not just to writing but to all aspects of life. We all need to be more creative in the kitchen, with our families, and with our various life projects. Just as a sports coach or an engineer does better when he puts things down on paper, so will you.

According to conventional history, the first writing was done on papyrus. The Egyptians were big on writing, and their mystery schools included the Right Eye of Horus and the Left Eye of Horus. These were two separate paths, but one needed to learn both in order to fully integrate both sides of the brain. According to their religion, a fusion of the two hemispheres of the brain would demonstrate itself by an isotope of white gold emitting out of the forehead. This was a testament to the Third Eye having been activated, but this exceptional ability was only achieved after a full integration of both sides of the brain. This means the intuitive aspect of consciousness was synchronized with the linear aspect. Do not forget that the Hebrew letter *shin* is also symbolic of the unification of both hemispheres of the brain. It is the key secret of the universe, bridging the higher and lower aspects.

Editing is all about integrating. Do not, however, expect a professional editor to integrate your work. Whether or not you use an editor, you still have to do a considerable amount of editing yourself. After all, it is your work and you are the author and therefore integrator of a vast body of data.

With regard to editing, I will give you an anecdotal story from my own life about the most important technique I ever learned and how I learned it. This concerns a colleague I had acquired during my days in the computer and advertising businesses. Her name was Odette, and she was a native Parisian who became a medical doctor in France. A very versatile woman, she was an artist who emigrated to America where she hosted a French radio show in New York. I believe it was called the Voice of France. Odette had also worked as an editor for a major publisher of science fiction. I think it was Bantam Books. An interesting side note about Odette is that her radio show was piggybacked with a show of Ayn Rand, the famous author of *Fountainhead* and *Atlas Shrugged*. Ayn Rand, according to Odette, was a strong believer in UFO's emanating from the inside of the earth. Rand talked about this subject adamantly. I do not recall, however, if it was just in private conversations or on the radio. If I recall correctly, it was broadcast on the radio. UFOs are what Odette remembered the most about Ayn Rand.

Odette also told me about working with most of the prominent science fiction authors of the day. She said that most of them were either in tears or close to tears as they would complain that their publisher would not put any marketing efforts behind their books. This is a pitfall to any author. Publicity and marketing budgets are seldom viable unless it is a big named author with a built-in audience, such as a president writing his memoirs. Marketing is even more difficult in today's publishing world save for the internet which is everyone's easiest route to success.

When I was working on the original draft for *The Montauk Project*, I remember speaking to Odette one day about what I was working on. In her French accent and in an adamant voice, she told me to bring her the book. To my surprise, she was in a hurry, and I was not even done with the book. I thought her eagerness was odd, and it had nothing to do with her being interested in the subject. It was like the jinn were propelling me to get the help of a professional editor. She gave me very good advice over the phone and said not to change anything. Everything I had written up to that point were simply transcriptions of taped interviews with Preston Nichols. It included none of my own reconstruction of Preston's very complicated and sometimes challenging explanations of space-time phenomena. She was insistent that I not change anything because this would make me psychologically immune to any criticism she might offer. Odette said she would introduce me to the technique of line editing. When I finished transcribing all of Preston's data, I took a two hour drive to her new home in New Jersey.

Line editing consists of one person, her in this case, reading out loud to another person (myself). She would read out a sentence, and more often than not, she would have a problem with it. As we were dealing with Preston's spoken English, the existing format was not even how he would express himself in written form. One just listens to what is being said and evaluates whether it makes any sense or could be said better. Almost all of what we accomplished was her talking out loud and making corrections. It was my job to write them down and make the actual written corrections later. As she spoke out loud, only occasionally would I pitch in and deal with specific issues that required further scrutiny and explanation. After an entire afternoon, we were only half way done. It was a grueling and laborious process, but it was edifying. I returned in a couple weeks after making the necessary corrections. We then went over the second half of the book. After a little more of this, I realized I had long since grasped the actual process and the nuances of it. It then turned into a grind, and I no longer needed her help. I was done. What I learned during this process, however, was invaluable.

I already had a good sense of how to write and edit before I learned about line editing, but I cannot over emphasize how enlightening and helpful this process was. When one writes, one has to be very conscious of everyone who might pick up your book. You have to assume the viewpoint of how they would or might receive the information as you are presenting it. A good way to deal with this aspect is to turn on the television and channel flip for a long time. As you do, write down all the different characters you see on different shows. This might include a mother, a soldier, a banker, an actor, a truck driver, a foreign national, and anything else under the sun. As you write and/or edit, keep such people in mind. Think if they could understand what you are saying and how they might relate to it. When you read out loud, even if only to yourself, it will objectify your writing and enable you to perceive it from a different perspective. It is ideal to have someone to read it to, and particularly someone who knows language and grammar. If you are beginning this process, it might also help to have them read to you and listen to their input.

Unless you have a really exceptional story or ground-breaking data, I do not suggest you hire a professional editor. They are expensive. Most college graduates or literate people are fully capable of editing if they bone up on the subject. If you need an editor to correct your mistakes, you probably should not be writing professionally or formally. Proofreading is an entirely different matter, and one should utilize a proofreader, even if it is in software format. A friend with a good understanding of English can proofread for you.

Looking back, it appears to be in the hands fate that put me together with Odette, a woman who had hobnobbed with so many of the great science fiction authors. When I was young, these people were my friends, at least in my own mind, even though I did not know them. They were frequenting the same noosphere that I was interested in. It seems that the creative process put me together with Odette. She was very helpful and also very creative herself.

One of the most beautiful aspects of the creative process is that it can be used to integrate disparate factors of existence. It can take desolation or failure and turn it into something better. This is alchemy. Remember, *The White Bat* was originally a failure as a story, at least in commercial terms. It has taken over two decades for it to bear fruit.

Integrating disparities is one of the biggest challenges I have faced as a writer. Much of what I have sought to explain exists on the far horizons of ordinary consciousness, including my own. Radu's stories are no exception. They have, however, shown themselves to have traction as far as being able to connect them to real events. Radu's third book, however, required me to stretch my horizons even further. Even so, the contents of the book were more than a little interesting. If they are not exactly true, and I am not saying they are not, they were highly entertaining and well worth reading.

CHAPTER TWENTY

MYSTERY OF EGYPT

At this point in the narrative, it was 2011 and I had been to Romania three times. *Transylvanian Moonrise* had been published, and I received a Skype message from Nicole. She wanted to know if I was going to Atlantykron in the summer, and I told her, unfortunately, no. I had raised money for my previous trips by arranging special sales packages through Sky Books. While this definitely got the job done, these sales had run their course. There was not much more that I could do. While I could easily have purchased a ticket, I did not feel it was financially prudent to make any expenditures in this direction. When Nicole received my response, she answered back with a big sad face. I then told her that maybe she could make one of her Christian prayers and maybe we could have a miracle. Nicole said she would do just that. I did not find out until later, but she actually fasted for a certain period before the prayer.

The next morning, I received a phone call from Marta Thomas, a tour operator whose business is known as *Body Mind Spirt Journeys*, and she wanted to know if I would be her guide in Romania. Marta had read *Transylvanian Sunrise* and understood the importance of the area and what I was doing. There was, however, too little time left for her to gather a group who might want to go with us. She offered to pay for my flight and transport as well as Nicole's transportation throughout Romania. I told her Nicole was vital as we needed someone to negotiate the language. The prayer worked! If it was not the prayer, one could not deny the synchronicity.

Nicole greeted both myself and Marta at the airport. We stayed at a nearby hotel. The next day, we took a bus to Bușteni and checked into a hotel where four of my Bulgarian friends had checked in. Bușteni is a mountain village where one can take a cable car to the Romanian Sphinx. Another man from America and a couple of other Romanian ladies joined us, and we had a team of people for the adventure. It was a lot of fun for all of us.

The most notable part of the adventure was when we went to the Sphinx the first morning. As is typical, we were prepared to wait for two hours to get on the cable car that would take us there. One of our Romanian friends instead secured the driver of a van who took us up there for about thirty dollars each. It was well worth it. I did not know previously that one could make their way up the mountain via a road, the last part of which is extremely bumpy and best suited for an SUV.

When we arrived at the Sphinx, we were greeted by my friend Lenutz, the woman I had met at Sarmizegetusa in 2009. She was accompanied by her husband and an assortment of Romanian dowsers and people of an intuitive persuasion. As everyone took in the Sphinx, people began to drift in different directions. I remained with Lenutz and her friends as she would only be able to visit for a short time. Nicole soon drifted off, and I had no translator.

As Lenutz and her friends did not know English, one of them had a ten-year-old daughter who did. She was an excellent translator and even did a good job with the metaphysical terms and concepts being shared with me. It was explained to me that there were two sets of rocks to the west of the Sphinx that are considered doors or gateways. If one were to follow them and walk, one would eventually reach the Iaolomita Valley. One can either walk to the valley, which is a very long hike down the mountain, or one can take a cable car. It is smaller than the one to Bușteni, and there is no waiting line.

When Lenutz said good-bye, two of my Bulgarian friends were sitting on one of the "gateway" rocks. In their own way, they were dowsing and feeling the energy. They said we must go to the valley below. We had hoped to hike northward to Mount Omu, the mountain of humanity, but we learned it would take at least three hours to arrive there. There was no way we could get back in time to take the cable car. Instead, we decided to take the cable car to Iaolomita Valley where there was also a cave. This cave turned out to be the highlight of the entire trip.

When we emerged from the cable car, we had to walk for maybe three quarters of a mile to get to the cave. The first thing I noticed, however, was a nice hotel, the Pestera Hotel (pestera means cave in Romanian). It is a spa, and I was happy to learn of this. If one has a car, van or SUV, one can travel to the Pestera Hotel and take the nearby cable car to the sphinx. It is so much easier than going via Bușteni, mostly because there is no or very little human tourist traffic. It is also very beautiful. On this trip, we only had time to visit Iaolomita Cave.

In front of the cave is a huge wall that was built by a monastery. They regulate traffic in and out of the cave, and you are expected to make a small donation. One can also stay overnight in the modest rooms at the monastery. The cave itself is absolutely magnificent. You could drive about three tanks into the beginning of the cave. It then becomes smaller, and one follows a lighted path that leads about a half mile into the earth. Some of the passage ways become rather small, and you have to crouch low to get through. Passages that are very awkward have been facilitated with wooden steps and planks that make the cave navigable. As you travel, there are at least two huge spaces that are picturesque and unlike anything I have ever experienced.

The cave is also supplied with a continuous water source. The path diverges at one point. After a short walk, you find an underwater river or brook with a flowing pool of water. When you get to the very end of the cave, it does not really end. The man-made boarded pathway ends, and there is a very slim opening. You can feel the energy but that is about it. A few days later, I would arrive at Atlantykron where I met a man who had gone beyond the so-called end to the cave. Using boards and lighting, he made it about eighty yards beyond the point where tourists are wise to stop. He said there is water, and one has to account for that. After eighty yards, he said the cave opens up and one would need spelunking equipment to go any further. This, quite literally, is supposed to be a path to the Inner Earth. There are many such caves in Romania.

Although I did not realize it at the time, the exposure or "communication" with the Inner Earth is very important in Romanian lore. This cave is sometimes held to be the locale where Zalmoxis remained for four years and came out transformed into a god. There is another cave in Transylvania, however, that leads to Sarmizegetusa and that might have a more authentic claim to this legend. What is important is that such exposure to the inner part of the earth can have a profound effect upon your consciousness. One option is communicating with the resident spirits.

After examining and experiencing this cave, it is very easy to imagine or feel the reality of what Radu Cinamar writes about in *Transylvanian Sunrise*. This spectacular cave is just a short distance from the Sphinx itself which is on top of a mountain. The entire area itself is studded with underground pockets of natural phenomena.

The following day, we had hoped to return to the mountain and climb to Mountain Omu, but it rained and was not to be. I went with the Bulgarians to the Julia Hasdeu Castle. This castle is the result of a true story about actual spiritual phenomena. Julia was a remarkably talented progeny of Bogdan Petriceicu Hasdeu, an extremely brilliant and internationally recognized writer of Romanian nationality who was originally born in the Ukraine. B.P. Hasdeu was a philologist who knew 26 languages. Philology is the study of language in written historical sources and is a combination of linguistics, history, and literary criticism. Hasdeu's daughter, Julia, was reading and writing at age four and graduated the conservatory at age eleven, majoring in piano. She was slated to complete her doctorate at Sorbonne in France but died of tuberculosis at age eighteen. To say that he was tragically affected by his daughter's death is a severe understatement.

Hasdeu turned to the spirit world and received a commensurate answer to his grief. Julia appeared to him and conversed frequently. She dictated the plans for Hasdeu Castle, a unique structure which is said to be a combination temple-castle, and the only one of its kind. Visiting the castle is not a light experience, and while it is said to be the only one of its kind in Romania, it somehow seems typical of Romania. It is hard to explain.

Neither Marta nor Nicole went with us. Despite my strong admonitions not to do so, they visited Bran Castle, more popularly known to tourists as Castle Dracula. I do not recommend this to anyone, and I have never gone myself. It is not Dracula's Castle, but it is a tourist attraction that is designed to imprint one with a very negative vibration. There are lurid stories about what goes on there as well. These also have nothing to do with Dracula and are not shared with the general public. Romania is a land that is full of primeval spirits. If you go on a journey, you are going to be tested. It is not wise to start off by putting yourself in a suggestible or vulnerable position. There are far more positive angles to purse. Nicole, who has a very pure natural energy, was energetically discombobulated when she got home, and I spent some time doing a Chi Gong technique on her. She definitely felt the difference. Marta was in even worse straits. She came to the realization that her expensive video camera had been stolen in Bosnia, and there were other elements connected to her recent trip to that country that were now coming to a negative culmination. While Bran Castle did not cause those factors, everything came to a head after her visit there. She was up late into the night. Go at your own risk.

Despite my adamance about Bran Castle, I am not at all down on anyone visiting the Poenari Citadel, a fortress on the border between Wallachia and Transylvania. Although it was not built by Vlad the Impaler, he repaired it and used it. The area and structure is of significant historical importance, and it is also the inspiration for my story *The White Bat*. I would also not be surprised if there was something significant underneath the mountains there.

The next morning, the Bulgarians drove back to Bulgaria while Nicole, Marta, and I took the train to Bucharest and then to Cernavodă where we got a ride to Capidava and attended Atlantykron. There were only a few days left at Atlantykron, but this was a new experience for me. I soon found myself communicating and networking nonstop. Over the last three years, I had made so many friends and contacts that I felt like a major transformation had taken place. The landscape was becoming more and more familiar; nevertheless it was a short trip, and I would soon be back in America.

My top priority upon returning home was to get a translation of Radu Cinamar's third book, *Mystery of Egypt – The First Tunnel*. Very fortunately, I was able to do this through Monica Grigorescu. She had written to me a year earlier encouraging me to put Radu's books up in ebook format (which I have since done). I thought this was odd as her native language is Romanian, but she said that there were many Romanians who liked to read the books in English as well as read about my adventures. When I asked her what she did, she mentioned that she was a translator. I hired her. She did a very good job, and I am very grateful for her help and friendship.

Like all of Radu's books, *Mystery of Egypt* is different than the others although the background story and context remain consistent. The book begins with Elinor, the alchemist, having to leave the country for security reasons. Repa Sundhi suggests to him that Radu might stay in his house as a custodian where he will have access to Elinor's extensive occult library. Elinor accepts the suggestion but does not give Radu access to his rather extensive, exotic and classical alchemical laboratory in the basement. Before he leaves the country, however, Elinor facilitates a transformative experience for Radu by giving him two drops of a "yellowish copper-colored" elixir. This substance creates a profound reaction in Radu which resulted in him feeling "reborn" with his soul flooded with joy.

Soon thereafter, as he read from Elinor's library, Radu found himself longing for Cezar, his old mentor, in order that he could answer his questions. It had been a long time since he had last seen Cezar. Much to his surprise, and by pure synchronicity, Cezar called him and said he wanted to meet with him that very night. Overjoyed, they soon meet and Radu is recruited to join Department Zero on a journey with Cezar into the mysterious "first tunnel" in the Projection Hall of the Bucegi complex. This tunnel leads to a hidden chamber beneath the Giza Plateau in Egypt.

The journey requires a certain amount of physical training on Radu's behalf. As he prepares, he meets Cezar's superior, General Obadea, who tells Radu why he has been chosen to participate in this highly secure operation. The Romanian government, who has lost touch with Repa Sundhi, is very desirous of speaking with him again due to political developments that have taken place. As Cezar's efforts to contact Repa Sundhi were not successful, they are hoping that Radu, who was recently with the lama, might be able to facilitate a connection. While they fully understand that it is not a matter of Radu calling the lama on the phone, they recognize the aspects of quantum affinity and are hoping Radu's involvement might precipitate a reconnecting.

While Radu's entire adventure is high sci-fi, the story is both entertaining and plausible. To me, the most exciting aspects were Radu's descriptions of the advanced American technology required for the journey through the tunnel to Egypt. This included rubberized suits with biosensors and high tech vehicles, but the most interesting technology was in the hands of a gawky American savant named Aidan who has a laptop computer that projects holographic readouts. It was a super-genius device that tied into an even bigger holographic computer at the Pentagon. Aidan explained that he felt emphatically "wired" into the circuitry of the computer itself.

Radu and Cezar are accompanied on their mission to Giza by Aidan, another American and another Romanian. This was a follow-up mission to a previous one two years earlier. A a result of intense feedback submitted from the original expedition to research and design labs working for the Pentagon, a remarkable high-tech vehicle was designed. With an optimum cruising speed of 125 km per hour and a capability of reaching up to 200 km per hour, the vehicle was designed so that the cruising speed could remain constant, even if ascending or descending slopes in the tunnel. The design included an aerodynamic flow of air on the body, redundant laser guidance systems, control systems for the outer atmospheric parameters, cabin pressurization with oxygen reserves, and even a sophisticated system that could artificially support life for a certain period of time in case of serious accidents.

The target of the expedition was to recover neatly organized slate-like tablets that are in fact a type of ancient "DVD" that project holographic "memories" of the history of the world. The tablets do not require a projector and are so numerous that they could only hope to return a portion of them to their home base, after which they would be sent to America for detailed study. Even though they could not recover everything in one mission, what they did retrieve would take a team of viewers a considerable amount of time to view.

There is also an occult chamber containing a device consisting primarily of huge crystals that facilitates the projection of one's consciousness back into time. It is not a physical time travel device and requires a certain amount of psychic and esoteric development to be able to withstand the rigors of projecting oneself into time, even if the physical body is not being utilized. We also learn that this device is bioresonant in that it is tuned to the physiological, mental and emotional conditions of the subject as well as their own past experiences. In other words, you would have different experiences than would I and so on.

Another intriguing aspect of the time device is that there is a certain amount of censorship present. When Cezar attempts to project his consciousness into time in order to see who created the device, he encounters blockages. While it is informative and useful in certain respects, it contains mysteries which it does not want penetrated, at least at this particular time.

These circumstances encourage interesting speculation such as the nature of those in the Pentagon who might be given access to these holographic recordings. It is likely that the recovered disks were somehow downloaded into the master holographic computer in the Pentagon, as alluded to by Aidan, and/or the NSA's mega-warehouse for data at the Utah Data Center. While all of this is an attempt to emulate the ancient data base for purposes of political control, I suspect that the Americans overlooked the prospect that the builders of the Bucegi Complex and its satellite chambers were installing a Trojan Horse in the Pentagon and/or NSA that is designed to overcome any negativity which these organization might be prone to precipitate.

At the same time as I was finishing the editing of *Mystery of Egypt*, rioting began to break out in Cairo. I could not help but think that what was going on was due to political infighting behind the scenes and that it might have to do with the intrigue Radu writes about beneath Giza. After all, the Egyptians were realizing that Romanians and Americans had access to an area on their territory that they did not. Radu confirmed my suspicions in a letter; but he also told me something else that was of far more interest. He said I could expect a short meeting with Elinor in the next ten months. This was exciting. Perhaps my feelings about receiving a personal initiation into this ancient tradition were going to come to pass. Never in my wildest dreams had I ever contemplated an actual meeting with Elinor.

CHAPTER TWENTY-ONE

THE SECRET PARCHMENT

Quite specifically, I was told to expect to meet this remarkable man within a ten month time frame. In other words, it would take place by the end of October 2012. It was to be only a ten minute meeting or so, but I would have the opportunity to extend it to thirty minutes if I wished. Not much more was said other than the location of the meeting place. I viewed such a meeting as a window of opportunity to find out more about as well as possibly participate in the esoteric tradition of alchemy that Elinor was a part of. If we can judge by the data as has been presented, this was not an opportunity of a lifetime but rather an opportunity of many lifetimes.

In the meantime, I was contacted by a woman named Jonette Crowley (no known relation to Aleister Crowley) who is an extremely popular channel who came upon this ability by happenstance. Although she is an American, most of her clientele are internationally based. Jonette wanted me to accompany her on her upcoming trip to Romania in 2012 which was entitled *The Transylvania Tour*. Visiting sacred spots all across the globe, Jonette's messengers directed her to go to Romania. On a previous visit to Romania, she was in the Bucegi Mountains and her intuition told her there was something underneath, like tunnels and more. One of the women in the group was from Denmark, and she knew about Radu's books as well as my involvement with them. The long and short of it was that Jonette's channeled source told her that it was very important that I accompany her on her next trip to Romania.

While I have certainly witnessed a certain amount of channeling, I have never been affiliated or a big fan of this sort of thing. For me, however, it was a great gift to accompany her. It would be the second year in a row that spirit was literally pulling me back to Romania. In both of these years, I would otherwise have probably decided to forego the expense and simply stay home and work on my next project.

Jonette was an executive in the business world before she started channeling. I found her not only to be a big sweetheart but that she was also extremely practical and functional when it came to planning what we would do. Asking for my input, I was insistent that we avoid Bran Castle and that we go to Sarmizegetusa for three days. When I told her the story about the so-called Dracula's castle, she definitely got the message, but she was not able to accommodate my request for three days in Sarmizegetusa. While there were valid logistical reasons for this, I was a bit disappointed; but only because it had been ground into my head from my Romanian friends that you must spend three days to get the full experience. Most special of all, however, was that Jonette and her husband, Ed Oakley, generously accepted my invitation to attend Atlantykron before we departed on the spiritual journey itself. I therefore got plenty of time to get to know both of them better.

Before we left, however, I had been soliciting my translator, Monica Grigorescu, to supply me with the translation of Radu's fourth book, *The Secret Parchment — Five Tibetan Initiation Techniques.* Monica was extremely helpful in this regard, and I read it as each chapter was translated. She completed the job about a month before our departure. I was then able to supply Jonette with a fully translated but unedited manuscript before we left. This was very important to me because I wanted Jonette to know as much as possible about where we were going. I will now give you a quick summary of what *The Secret Parchment* is about.

The Secret Parchment begins with a power struggle over Department Zero. For some time, certain members of the Romanian parliament have been attempting a coup to take over control of Department Zero in order to get their hands on the accompanying technology that it was created to protect. Cezar's boss, General Obadea, avoids this crisis by utilizing a loophole based upon their working agreement with the Americans. By sending Radu to America for a very special training program in remote viewing, diplomatic stipulations mandate that Department Zero must stay intact as it is. Radu not only gets to visit America, but he excels in the remote viewing program and is one of only five people who are allowed to remain in the program. As soon as he achieves this status, he is interrupted by a phone call from Romania. It is Cezar telling him he must return immediately on the next plane out.

When Radu returns to Alpha Base in Romania, he is both startled and pleasantly surprised to see Repa Sundhi there. The lama is accompanied by a female assistant named Shin Li. Repa Sundhi informs Radu that it is time for him to actually complete the translation of the manuscript. Shin Li is there to help him understand the meaning so that he can properly communicate it in his own native language.

It is important to point out at this juncture that the uncovering of such a manuscript is a monumental event in Buddhism. Such a document is referred to as a terma in the Tibetan tradition. It is recognized by both the Buddhist and Bön religions. A terma means "hidden treasure" and refers to key teachings that were written down and esoterically hidden by various adepts such as Padmasambhava (aka Rinpoche or Rimpoche) and his consorts in the 8th century. It was intended for them to be discovered in the future at auspicious times by other adepts, known as tertöns. As such, they represent a tradition of continuing revelation in Buddhism.

The secret parchment itself is rather short and sweet, but it required much study and dialogue between Radu and Shin Li before he was ready to present the translation and commentary. The commentary is very important and should be read for a full understanding. In the epilogue of *The Secret Parchment*, I took the liberty of summating the parchment in the format of crib notes for fast ready reference. At the same time, I commented that one should also read the full text as written by Radu. My personal and individualized summary of what the parchment contains is as follows.

1) Compassion — There is a divine source of compassion in this universe, and we need to recognize it and link to it.

2) All we are is a result of what we have thought — what you think is what you get. This is also representative of the principle of quantum affinity or the Law of Affinity.

3) Synchronicity — There are no coincidences. When events or experiences coincide outside the ordinary bounds of probability, this is a meaningful coincidence and there is an intention behind it.

4) Vibration — Everything is connected by vibration.

5) Will — Align yourself with your own Higher Will and the Divine Source of Creation.

These are simple but potent precepts which can create tremendous harmony in your personal life, particularly if they are reviewed on a daily basis as you continually cultivate and refine the finer aspects.

While *The Secret Parchment* is focused upon the actual translation of Machandi's manuscript, the release of the manuscript into the world is accompanied by an assortment of impactful global events. The first hint of this occurs as Radu begins his work with Shin Li on the translation. Department Zero is under siege again; but this time it is from the Americans. Cezar and General Obadea are surprised and disarmed when they learn that their strategic partners in the Bucegi operation, the Americans, have become inexplicably indignant and suspicious towards Department Zero. The entire issue is over a secret operation that took place in the Orăştie Mountains near Sarmizegetusa. Cezar and General Obadea have only a very thin file on this specific issue, and they are more in the dark themselves rather than hiding something. It develops such a wedge that General Obadea is forced to resign his commission. The future of Department Zero remains uncertain and blowing in the wind.

Just after Radu completes his translation, and it is being prepared for release to the world in the Romanian language, a stunning development takes place that reunites the Romanians and Americans as it begins to explain the mystery that the Americans were so upset and distrusting about. The Americans report that not far from their Macor Base in Antarctica, a huge antenna-like structure began to reveal itself through an internally driven process which facilitated the melting of the snow and ice it had been wrapped up in for millennia. Nobody was quite sure what it was, but it appeared to be a device that was placed there in ancient history for a specific purpose. What the Americans did notice, however, was that it was facilitating signals that revealed a triangulation between three areas: Jupiter's moon Europa, Sarmizegetusa in Transylvania, and an area near Mount McKinley in Alaska. As the Americans are seeking help, Radu joins a remote viewing team and travels to Antarctica. General Obadea comes out of retirement and also joins the team, eventually becoming a liaison to the Joint Chiefs of Staff with an office at the Pentagon.

We finally learn what is behind all the drama when Cezar reveals to Radu the contents of the thin file previously referred to. Up to that time, it had been the top state secret of the Romanian government, a topic that was even more sensitive than the holographic technology chamber beneath the Sphinx. Cezar showed Radu the file and also explained it to him.

After the fall of communism in Romania, archeological professors began to do various digs, looking for clues to the past. One was Professor Constantin, and he was working in the area of the Orăştie Mountains. One day, at the end of digging, the son of the contractor who was helping him accidentally discovered a chamber while putting tools away. As everyone else had left for the day, the two investigated the small chamber and soon discovered that it led to an even bigger underground space. Soon, they found a very gradually sloping surface that was descending deeper and deeper into the earth. Eventually, they discovered tunnels containing substantial veins of gold. As they continue, they eventually find tunnels of pure gold. Cezar explains that this is an extraordinary find because gold is seldom found in its pure state. When it is, it is seldom bigger than a foot or two and usually much smaller, often in the form of small nuggets. The fact that these veins of pure gold go on for miles is enough in itself to make this a top state secret. Had this information been revealed at the time it was discovered, Romania would have been a target of invasion from many different sources. It was accordingly kept quiet. There were, however, other factors which made it an even more potent secret.

The golden tunnels they pursued eventually led to a bed-like edifice made of pure gold. Accompanying it was a slab with hieroglyphics that was eventually studied by three major universities and reduced to the lowest common denominator and interpreted as follows:

KR–IO; SAL-MOŞ, HERE IS FOREVER, THE WORLDS UNITE

Based upon what was offered at the universities, Cezar explained to Radu that KR signified Cronos, the god of time and that this mysterious locale signified the holy place of Cronos. It is where the god Cronos is alive and present and unites the worlds. As such, this site represents the origin of time. A pointed and rather impeccable scholarly discussion ensues to demonstrate that this area of the Carpathians, modern day Transylvania, was the cradle of all civilizations and nations now existing and that the language they spoke was the source of the primordial language, the Romanian language. Cezar sites one of the greatest contemporary linguists as saying that it is the only natural language in Europe; and further, that it is exactly what scientists look for and do not find: the Indo-European language which is common to all nations which make up our modern civilization.

What was just stated above is not only considered controversial in academic circles, it is downright rejected by virtually all academics outside of Romania. The Romanians know better for they, as a people, have been witness to the politics that has surrounded the attempt to dominate their resources as well as their very ancient culture. They possess an unbroken memory, at least in some quarters. Cezar tells us about the political motivations for undermining the true history of the Romanian language. There is also an interesting history that should shed any doubt for those without prejudice.

In the 18th Century, certain academics went to the bizarre lengths of creating their own word, *protochronism,* in order to explain away and undermine the incredibly spectacular legacy of Romanian history. Quite ingeniously, however, typical academic scholarship blames the creation of this word on the Romanians themselves. Here is a definition from Wikipedia:

> **protochronism** (anglicized from the Romanian: *protochronism,* from the Ancient Greek term for first in time) is a Romanian term describing the tendency to ascribe an idealized past to the country as a whole. While particularly prevalent during the regime of Nicolae Ceaușescu, its origin in Romanian scholarship dates back more than a century.

Academics have explained that *protochronism* is part of an inferiority complex present in Romanian nationalism and one which also manifested itself in works not connected with protochronism, mainly as a rejection of the ideas that Romanian territories only served as a colony of Rome, void of initiative, and subject to an influx of Latins which would have completely wiped out a Dacian presence.

I cannot tell you how laughable and insulting this is to Romanians, especially when their nationals have contributed so much to science. Henry Coanda and Herman Oberth are just two examples. Romanians are not void of initiative at all. If the Dacian presence was wiped out, how come there is such a strong identification in the Romanian people that has persisted for centuries? Did they just look around one day, see how the modern world

185

surrounded them and say, "Gee, we have to make up a history about ourselves to explain why are not as good as the rest of the world?" In actual fact, Romanians are some of the most brilliant people you will ever meet. There is, however, considerably more behind this story.

The groundwork for modern Europe was laid, in many respects, with the Revolution of 1848 in Europe. In what has been called the most widespread revolutionary wave in European history, this was an uprising of the peasant and middle classes against the national governments and especially any remaining monarchies. It was basically set into motion by the Jesuits in conjunction with the Freemasons. Part of this was the Communist League who authorized the publication of the *Communist Manifesto* by Karl Marx. The entire communist ideal was based upon a Jesuit community in Paraguay.

Romania comes into the picture with the Crimean War in 1853. This was theoretically caused over a dispute about a chapel on the Mount of Olives in Jerusalem. Said to be the precise spot where Jesus ascended to heaven, the French and English wanted access, but it was in the custody of the Russians. There were, of course, other political issues at stake, and much of it had to do with reducing or removing the influence of the Ottoman Empire over the Holy Land. The Crimean War, however, literally gave birth to the nation of Romania as we know it. The boundaries of this new country were based upon the primary uniformity of language spoken by the people, i.e. Romanian.

The political machinations of the Crimean War resulted in the formation of the Junimea* Society in 1863, a secret society that was predominantly ruled by Masons who belonged to a lodge in the city of Iasi, Romania known as "The Star of Romania." It consisted of 150 members known as the Brotherhood of Junimea. The most influential intellectual and political association in Romania in the 19th century, the Junimea was the major impetus behind establishing the basis of the modern Romanian culture. At its peak, the Brotherhood of Junimea held the reins of power in the Romanian government, the parliament, journalism, and cultural affairs. They also had a magazine entitled *Literary Conversations*. The Junimea Society was actually a branch of the Masonic Lodge known as "The Great Orient Of France." The members of the French lodge were Masons from all countries in Europe, including some Romanians.

Up until the Revolution of 1848, the people of what we now know as modern Romania, save for a minority of Hungarians and a few others, identified themselves with the old Dacian empire and spoke what is referred to as archaic Romanian or archaic Dacian. After this, there was a major restructuring and alteration of the language, largely under the French Masonic influence. This included changing the Romanian alphabet from Cyrillic to Latin and eventually, after the Union of Transylvania with Romania on December 1st 1918, the final establishment of modern literary Romanian. Accompanying

---

* Junimea is derived from the Romanian word *juni* which refers to youth.

this was the deliberately created fiction that Romania and the other Romance Languages derived from Latin as opposed to archaic or classical Romanian.

All of these shenanigans amount to a rather obvious and successful effort by secret societies to steer the general culture, Romanians included, away from the esoteric power of their ancient past and to make them subordinate and willing puppets to the ruling elite. One of the more brilliant aspects of the coup was that it was fostered by Romanian nationals themselves. All of them were, however, educated in either France or Germany under the tutelage of Freemasonry.

While the language conspiracy is profound and its impact upon the culture of Mankind is too easily underestimated, it almost pales in comparison to the abundant and remarkable archeological finds in Romania. Archeologists have barely scratched the surface. The implications of these are enormous and are capable of completely turning the world's view of itself upside down. You will often see people getting excited over Egypt, Turkey, Bosnia as well as other sites of ancient culture. This is all well and fine, but it is sort of like getting excited about all the toys, diapers, bassinet, and other accoutrements of a new baby without examining the baby itself.

Let me now revisit what I said earlier about this magical location signifying the holy place where Cronos was alive, present and united the worlds. It should be noted here that long before the legends of St. Nicholas, the Romanians also recognized Cronos in his more cheery aspects as Santa Claus, the god of time, who appeared at the end of the calendar and ushered in the new year. This concept was later borrowed by the Greeks and transmogrified into Saturn by the Romans who celebrated their Saturnalia festivities. It is really important here to reiterate that this locale was quite literally considered to represent the origin of time. This, in turn, is indicative that this area, Transylvania, is the cradle of all civilizations and nations existing now and that this is the source of the primordial language. There is more to Cezar's story, but so that you better understand it, let me give you an analogy.

John von Neumann, the brilliant mathematician who is also recognized for his engineering of the Philadelphia Experiment and Montauk Project, is also the father of game theory. Studying the weather, stock market, as well as games in general, von Neumann stated that no matter what theory you devise with regard to games, it will always be subordinate to the eventuality that someone is going to cheat. Cheating is a way of life in this world and you see it all the time in the stock market, pro sports, politics, insurance fraud, and so on. In any endeavor that you undertake, you have to be aware of the potential of being cheated and take it into account in your planning. What I am going to suggest to you right now, however, is a concept you might not have thought about in the above context. I would also tell you that this concept of cheating applies to the field of physics and/or quantum physics. In other words, the perception of quantum phenomena and all the infinite potential that it represents, the Many Worlds Theory being just one prime example, has been manipulated to the point where people, and that includes scientists, cannot even think clearly on the subject. Physicists work mostly in a box; and when they do venture outside, they are continually frustrated by their failure to ascertain the ultimate resolution to the proposition of the physical universe. The reason for this is that either their perceptions and thinking capacity have been shut down in some regard or they are being denied information which would lead to a resolution.

I am suggesting here that the denial of information, coupled with censorship of its free flow between interested parties over an extremely long period of time, is directly responsible for the stuck paradigm that physics has been rolling around in. The corollary of this is that if there is unlimited access to information, it would have a quicksilver effect upon the mechanized apparatus of the physical universe as well its supporting structure; whether that supporting structure involves the spirit realm or otherwise. By quicksilver effect, I mean that the universe would be susceptible to "liquefying" and would exist in a more malleable state.

Whether you accept my hypothetical proposition or not, what I just said dovetails with the story that Cezar Brad reported with regard to Professor Constantin. The golden "bed" referred to earlier was called a bed because close examination in a photograph suggested that people had once used it to lay down in. I concluded that as it was made of gold, it was used for out-of-body travel. Cezar also states that because gold is the best superconductor, it literally facilitates super-consciousness in human beings.

As fascinating as the golden bed with the hieroglyphics was to them, Professor Constantin and the young man pursued this grand adventure into the golden tunnels even further. Following more golden tunnels, they eventually arrive at their most remarkable find of all. Following a blue light that gets stronger and stronger, they find themselves in a dome-shaped recess where they see six massive thrones made up pure gold that are imbedded into the ground and smoothly polished. Three of the thrones are facing the other three thrones, all of them surrounding a parallelepipedal (think of a rhomboid) table placed at the center. This configuration, which was artistically symmetrical and incredibly impressive, was completed at the end of the table by a seventh throne which appeared to be the throne of spiritual rulership.

In addition to the thrones, Professor Constantin was particularly astonished by an ensemble of huge plates that had been engraved into the corridor wall. These were actually huge panels, also parallelepipedons, that were symmetrically placed behind each throne with three on each side. On their perfectly finished surface, a text of thousands of unknown characters and signs was engraved. The signs were very clearly and orderly engraved and covered the plates almost entirely with the exception of a kind of curb on each side which was approximately ten centimeters large.

According to the prestigious international institutions that Department Zero had collaborated with, graphic analysis indicated that the writing on the huge panels was older than the unknown one previously found near the "bed" by Professor Constantin. The analysis also stated that the effort to engrave the plates was utterly remarkable and must have come from a very advanced level of civilization. It was concluded that the texts probably described a history of that place and its true meaning or that they referred to the occupants of each throne, offering elements of a certain nature about each person.

While we cannot precisely state at this juncture what those thrones represent, they are suggestive of the archetypal Throne energies. While these are most popularly depicted in Western culture as relating to the Abramic religions, most of what has been exposited by writers has been rendered in a Christian context. Even so, there is much diversion of opinion and commentary. Accordingly, my following description is an attempt to reduce this to the lowest common denominator based upon archetypal function.

Thrones are angels of the Third Order (first sphere).* Beings of tremendous power and movement, Thrones are keepers of the higher, more expanded energies. It is their job to ensure that these higher energies maintain connectivity and flow throughout the different realms of existence. Thrones create, channel and collect incoming and outgoing positive energies. It is also their job to pass messages to men and the subordinate angels.

Like the Cherubim, Thrones come the closest of all angels to spiritual perfection and emanate the light of God with mirror-like goodness. Due to the fact that these angels are living symbols of God's justice and authority, these angels are called Thrones. They send healing energies to victims while shining a light on injustice and bring it to our attention. Despite their greatness, they are intensely humble, an attribute that allows them to dispense justice with perfect objectivity and without fear of pride or ambition.

What is particularly interesting with regard to this narrative, as you will soon read, is that Thrones are assigned to planets. They are also direct conduits to the physical universe. Thrones are often depicted as eyes as is described in Ezekiel's vision of the chariots.

The experiences of Professor Constantin are certainly in accordance with the archetype of the Throne energies, and they become more so when we contemplate what happened next. Cezar explains to Radu that the throne area

---

* The first sphere of angles are the Seraphim, Cherubim, and Thrones. The Seraphim are the highest angelic class and serve as the caretakers of God's (think of God as the Prime Mover) throne and continuously exalt or recognize God. Cherubim are the next class of angels; and they are said to have four faces representing the fixed signs of the zodiac: one each of a man, an ox, a lion, and an eagle. Cherubim guard the way to the Tree of Life in the Garden of Eden and the Throne of God, actually sustaining the latter.

probably represents some kind of conversion of space and time, accomplished in a way which completely exceeds normal understanding. Saying that the Antarctic buoy connecting this area with Europa and Alaska is something like a cosmic knot that probably represents the end of a journey, he shows Radu the last photograph taken by Professor Constantin. Taken from an angle placed behind the right side of the main throne, it showed an empty space shaped like an ellipsis at the level of the ground. The ellipsis was about two meters long on its long axis and about one meter and a half on its short axis. It was marked by a small wall on the edges, like a curb.

Gazing into this ellipsis, Professor Constantin then began to lose his normal reference frame for consciousness. Looking into the empty space, he saw another universe. Looking at black cosmic space and the glitter of the stars, he said it was like looking through the porthole of a space ship at the surrounding cosmos. The difference was that the respective 'porthole' actually did not exist, but the access was free, as if through a fountain. Downwards and a bit to the side, Professor Constantin noticed a great planet with formations similar to the ones on Earth when seen from space. He compared the size of that planet with that of Earth as seen from the moon. The difference was that the color of that planet combined blue with different shades of yellow and orange.

In the process of witnessing all of this, Professor Constantin fainted, but he estimated that it was only for a couple of seconds. When he woke up, his companion was standing on the edge of that ellipsis and looked downward towards the planet as if hypnotized by it. The professor then saw a kind of shining funnel which was rising towards them from a point on the planet. The funnel emitted a light which became very intense until the surface of the ellipsis began to shine strongly. His companion then stepped over the edge and disappeared through it before the funnel withdrew back towards the beautiful planet. Frightened by what he had witnessed, Professor Constantin stepped backwards. He is uncertain of all that happened there or what happened next, but the professor did leave the scene and emerged from the underground whereupon he called the authorities. This resulted in an immediate response by the R.I.S. (Romanian Intelligence Service) in Bucharest.

A team was sent to investigate the tunnels once again as Professor Constantin showed the way. The R.I.S. people were in shock, and one of them died during the exploration. It was immediately decided that the entrance to this incredible find should be covered up. A cement mixer was hired to fill the area, but the man driving it became crazy and left. He was, however, always kept a safe distance from the site so he never knew exactly where it was. The R.I.S. people were able to cement up the opening themselves. They had taken four photographs and the professor had taken five. At least this is how many actually revealed anything, including the thrones and golden bed.

After leaving Professor Constantin under house arrest with the local police, the remaining three R.I.S. agents took a file with the photographs and headed back to Bucharest in a car. They did not make it, however, because they suffered a fatal car crash. All three died in the accident. In the meantime, General Obadea had ordered Cezar to go to the scene and investigate what had happened. Although all of these spectacular events were in the jurisdiction of Department Zero, they did not quite have the political clout that they would later develop, particularly after the Bucegi discovery. All Cezar was able to do was to recover the file from the crashed car. A thorough investigation indicated that the accident was not a human conspiracy. Fate had stepped in.

Cezar was also able to interview Professor Constantin and tape record their conversation. Although the professor was in shock, he gave Cezar what information he could. After being interviewed by Cezar for only a couple of hours, the R.I.S. took Professor Constantin away, and he has never been heard of again. Cezar gave the agents the tape recorded interview but made notes of everything that he heard, and these ended up in the file with the photograph. This file became Romania's top state secret. There is more about the file and its implications in *The Secret Parchment*.

This is pretty much where the story ends, at least in terms of Radu's published works. I have, however, received considerable correspondence from him since that time. While regretting and apologizing at the same time that he could not provide more substantial proof, he took considerable lengths to sincerely convey to me that these events in his book were indeed real and not merely fiction. Many people have been quick to question Radu's sincerity as well as to suggest that his work is the collaboration of a team. None of these people, however, have had the experience or circumstance to deal with Radu on any sort of personal level, nor to critically examine his writing style, particularly in his personal letters. There are also tangible and intangible factors concerning Radu, his existence, and what all of his writings might mean. Based upon my experiences with him, which cover a period of about six years now, I can tell you the following with confidence. Radu is a real person with his own personality who uses a pen name. His published works have always been subject to a filter of censorship. Whether this censorship is from a committee or Cezar Brad, I cannot say.

In all of these correspondences, the most noteworthy personal comment he made to me, if not the most interesting, was that Cezar had left his day-to-day activities at Department Zero in order to serve in the capacity of an ambassador to the beings in the Inner Earth. This puzzled me when he first said this as our cultural indoctrination inclines us to be dismissive of such a statement. The more I have become involved in this entire scenario, however, the more it makes sense to me. As all story writing is based upon the various permutations of core experiences, as are depicted in the Tree of

Life, I would say that Cezar himself is tied to the mythological archetypes of Hyperborea (Transylvania), and these include beings of the Inner Earth who have traditionally sought out various humans throughout history and tested them to see if they were worthy to receive initiation in order to transform to a higher level of existence, sometimes termed to be god-like. Born with an extraordinarily thick umbilical cord, Cezar was most definitely born with a different role than that of ordinary human beings. In Chi Gong, all chi or life force comes through the navel. This story indicates that Cezar enjoyed an extraordinary amount of chi.

While Radu's mention to me of Cezar in this regard might stretch his credibility, it is no less remarkable than any of his published writings. Anyway we look at it, Radu's stories are over-the-top when it comes to feeding that part of your mind which either enjoys or recognizes the incredible and fantastic elements of consciousness. What I have appreciated most in his writings is that there is a certain consistency and integration of different characters, global events, history, and esoteric lore. If it were merely creative writing, I would be very impressed and happy to read it as such. I have found out, however, that there is much more going on here than mere fiction. Much to my own surprise, I would find myself more involved in his characters and story elements than I had ever anticipated or even desired.

CHAPTER TWENTY-TWO

FINISHING

Whatever you write, always have a view on the finish line. The beginning of this book featured encouragement for you to write if only to integrate the two sides of your brain toward a more complete and functioning consciousness. As I got more into the book, however, the story took over. This is the way any story will develop. It will take over whatever confines or structure you have placed upon it. This is, in fact, how life works. At some point, however, you have to wrap things up, at least if you want to publish your work.

For those of you who wish to write with the purpose of publication, I want to relay an important story with regards to your potential audience. Keep in mind that any writing has an audience, even if it is only intended for yourself to read at a future date. Never disregard that fact and always think of your audience when you write.

Earlier in this book, I mentioned my friend, Roberto Quaglia, the man I worked with on the production of *My Kentucky Cousin*. When I first met him, I was very endeared to the fact that he had brought Robert Sheckley to Atlantykron in its early years. Most of you probably have never heard of Robert Sheckley, but I certainly had. He was a science-fiction writer who came to prominence in the Fifties. There is a considerable and distinguished write-up on Wikipedia about him, and while he did attain a certain amount of literary success, mention of his name results in a blank stare by most people; unless you are in Romania or Russia.

Although I had never heard of Sheckley's later successes in life, I had read some of his early science fiction in high school and found it very special. To this day, I remember reading a story of his about a character who was very thirsty for water on the parched desert of the planet Venus. Even though I knew there was no such desert on Venus, he told the story with such reality that I felt transported into the story itself. I thought he was a good writer, and I think that is what any reader wants: to be transported into another world that is not his own. Now it was about forty years later, and here I was meeting a man who actually knew Sheckley.

Roberto was impressed that I even knew who Sheckley was. As I said, his name earns you a blank stare from most people. Roberto explained to me that Sheckley had a huge fan base in Russia, and he would be driven around in a special limousine when he toured the country. Sheckley was also popular in Romania. I did not fully understand, however, the whole story between Roberto and Sheckley until a few years later.

In 2012, I was asked to take part in a seminar with Roberto and Sorin Repanovici, the director of the camp. Each of us were to give a ten to fifteen minute talk on dreams which would be followed by a question and answer discussion with the students. It was very interesting for me to hear their stories. Sorin talked about how his father took him fishing on this island when he was a young man. He had big dreams and as he got older, he and his friends would camp out on the island and have discussions about science fiction. It grew and grew to the point where Atlantykron is just about to have its 25th anniversary. It is now an international event.

Roberto told the entire story of his involvement with Sheckley and how he had once written him a letter. As Sheckley had moved, it was returned to Roberto about a year later after having found its way through both the U.S. and Italian postal systems. Although it is easy to get discouraged under such circumstances, Roberto was able to trace Sheckley's address to Oregon. It required both good luck and good fortune. The two took up a correspondence which resulted in Sheckley visiting and staying with Roberto for some time. They toured together through Europe and Russia. It also facilitated Sheckley's visit to Atlantykron. When Sheckley passed away, the latter's wife made a comment to Roberto that he was really his only friend. What is more important than the mechanics of all of this is the story Roberto eventually wrote and published. While it was not received particularly well in terms of sales or getting much attention of any kind, it did get the attention of one man in Bucharest who absolutely loved it. As this person was also computer savvy, it created a circumstance whereby he was able to facilitate a regular income for Roberto. Although it was not intended to be that way, the book essentially had an audience of one person. None of it, however, would have happened without Roberto's experiences with Sheckley. It completely changed Roberto's life. The moral of this story to any writer is pretty clear. Do not limit yourself and do not underestimate what your writing might do. Even if what you have to say is not going to be consumed by the masses, it might have a more potent effect if it reaches either one or only a few people.

When it was my turn to address the group during this seminar, I had not prepared anything to say; but it was clear to me that the only reason I was even at Atlantykron was a result of following my dream to be a writer. My dream had propelled me into Sorin's dream which was Atlantykron itself. Roberto was creating a further link, and he had already facilitated the filming of my story *My Kentucky Cousin*. Atlantykron is a place where dreams either come true or are facilitated. It was only after David (while he was in Germany) was invited to Atlantykron (as a last minute substitute for a German speaker who had cancelled) that he contacted me and brought me into his very unique world. Despite my recognition about pursuing my dream, however, I was overlooking *The White Bat* and how the dream that inspired that story was an underlying catalyst behind all of my involvement in Romania.

At the same time I tell you not to get discouraged, I want to repeat that most people write what they write for themselves. If you have a great message to teach people, you are most likely engaging in an act of self-discovery and personal exploration. Write for yourself and do not be ashamed of it. At the same time, be very aware of and respectful, at least as far as possible, to anyone who might pick up your book and read it. If you are writing about politics, religion or ethnicity, it is almost impossible not to offend someone. What you want to do, however, is state what you have to state in the most subtle and inoffensive manner as possible. People will still be offended, but such people are really more interested in squashing your freedom of speech than they are in tolerating or learning about views other than their own.

Once your writing is ready for publication, it has to be put into an acceptable format for being viewed. If it is a regular book, you would need typesetting software such as InDesign® by Adobe software. If it is an ebook, you can download a free epub (which stands for ebook publication) generator such as Sigil. Both of these programs have free tutorials. You can learn them with some patience. One can always hire someone to do such, but I do not recommend this if you do not have a generous budget. A good book that will guide you step-by-step from production to marketing is *The Complete Guide to Self-Publishing* by Tom and Marilyn Ross. There are other books, and it is recommended that you study up on such if you are going to produce something for actual publication. I am not going to cover this subject in any detail because extensive books have been written about it. Not only will they tell you whether or not you should be in the publishing business on any level, you will find out what to expect as an author. Such books are good to read in any event as you learn about the environment of publishing in general. I do not recommend that you attend any seminar on such subjects as you will pay far too much money for far too little information. Read the books.

As I have been in the publishing business for twenty years, I have accumulated a lot of knowledge. I also know a lot about the modus operandi of contemporary authors and publishers. After a few years in this industry, I was fully capable of setting up a side business as a publishing consultant. It would also be very easy for me to set up an additional imprint or name under which to publish other authors, particularly fledgling authors, and also charge them a fee for doing so. I have never done this for two reasons. First, it would take away from my current writing and getting the books I write into the public's hands. Second, this is a fundamentally dishonest operation for the most part. One can prey off the ignorance of people who want to get published. If the author does not have a presaturated market and no marketing campaign, the book will fail. The only way one can make a profit is to charge the author for your time, and you will likely be doing no one a favor. There are better ways to spend your time.

I entered the publishing arena in 1992 and was able to garnish just enough if not a lot of attention at the American Bookseller's Association (now called Book Expo America) in Anaheim, California. There were a number of reasons I was able to succeed, and a lot of it had to do with timing and good luck. What was even more important was that I had a quality book, *The Montauk Project: Experiments in Time*, that had intriguing content and an equally attractive cover that was rendered in a strategically commercial format that was recognizable and appealing to the industry. My ex-wife, who was a highly talented commercial artist, was an integral part of making this happen. Another important factor was that the topic had been seeded to a certain extent by various lectures of Preston Nichols and Al Bielek. In addition to this, everyone who had ever heard of the Philadelphia Experiment was a seeded audience. My contribution was not only having the patience and mental acumen to write the book with Preston, it was being able to recognize, understand, and put together all of the associated marketing angles.

Another point I will share with you from experience is that one person phoning a sizable book store every week and asking for your book is not going to create any meaningful impression on either the book store or a distributor. It will take numerous calls or in store requests PER DAY for it to register on their ordering and stocking meter. Further, you do not want one more book in a book store than will be sold. Why? If you are a publisher, you can expect unsold books to be returned. This can be a nightmare to a small publisher. A few years before I wrote *The Montauk Project*, I had a friend who used to work for science fiction publishers. He told me that if I was ever lucky enough to write and publish a book that would be accepted by the publishing industry that I could expect an order of maybe 30,000 books and then to have 25,000 of them returned. That sounds terrible, but it can happen, and many of those books will be in less than perfect condition. To deal in such levels, you need a warehouse.

None of this is meant to scare you away from the publishing industry, but it is the reality of the publishing industry. Most of the publishers and distributors I saw and did business with back in 1992 are now long gone. When they go broke and do not pay you, you also have to bear that burden.

On the other hand, ebooks and print-on-demand enable you to publish a book with very little capital investment whatsoever. You can also advertise your book on the internet. While this is not a pathway to riches, you can find your target market and also do internet radio shows to publicize your work. If the book has real potential in terms of a big market, this is not a bad place to start and test the waters. Go carefully and find your way. It is also important to point out that you will make far more money by selling 100 books that you self-publish in ebook or print-on-demand format that you would by selling 3,000 books with an already established publisher.

Books often serve best as a calling card or introduction to who you are and what you have to offer. Make sure that you have your purpose fully in mind when you write. Keep your dreams in mind, too, and never neglect them.

CHAPTER TWENTY-THREE

VALLEY OF THE GOLDEN THRONES

As previously indicated, I was very interested to get the *The Secret Parchment* translated before my trip to Romania with Jonette Crowley. I wanted both of us to read it so that we would have a full appreciation of the bigger picture as stated by Radu Cinamar. There were no particular expectations for the trip itself. My only disappointment was that the schedule did not provide us an opportunity to spend the prescribed three full days at Sarmizegetusa. As already stated, this is one of the most important criteria for a sacred journey to Sarmizegetusa.

In the second part of the English language version of *The Secret Parchment*, I gave a detailed account of the journey from my own perspective. I will not repeat it here, but it was quite an adventure. Much of it focused on sacred or prognostic dreams that I experienced. If anyone has any sort of spiritual aptitude or is a true seeker, one is going to forge some very deep connections on a journey to Sarmizegetusa. My dreams and various meetings with people were no exception. In this chapter, I will focus primarily on our journey to Fete Alba. This was the Dacians last stronghold against the invading Romans and there are still some ruins of it located high on a mountain. It is probably only a mile or two from Sarmizegetusa as the crow flies. We, however, were taking a circuitous path up the mountain so we would enjoy a minimum incline. It would take about an hour and a half from the paved road we departed from.

Through good fortune and spontaneity, we had met a guide at our local hotel, the Cotiso in Costesti, and he offered to take us to Fete Alba. He did not live far from the area. This was convenient as there was one point where we would pass through some private property that belonged to one of his neighbors. He said he had permission, and this was all very nice. When we got to the top of the mountain, we took a short break to take in the beautiful scenery. As we did, a local woman came out with a bushel of apples for us to enjoy. It was here that I learned for the first time about an ancient order of wizards with special knowledge and abilities. They are known as Solomonars and are often linked to the ancient Dacian priests. Also known as Zgri or Hultan, agenda driven literature will tell you that they were later name Solomonars by Christian priests who named them because they were comparable to the supernatural jinn in the legends of King Solomon. This is not true and is pure propaganda. The name Solomonari (plural) existed long before the legends of King Solomon. Both names refer to the sun (sol) and the moon (mon), and the whole concept is intertwined with the Lovers card in the Tarot. This equates to Gemini or Zalmoxis.

The Solomonars or Solomonari play a complex role in Romanian mythology and particularly within the psyche of Transylvanians. This has to with their interaction with the "other realm." Known to control the weather,

Solomonari live away from the world, often in caves where they access another realm. Sometimes the Solomonari will come into the common world in a particular guise. Sometimes it is as a beggar where they will test your heart in order to open gateways for you. It is also common for Solomonari to visit a human in the guise of a sheep or shepherd. In this role, they might show you a cave or entrance to the Inner Earth. They are always testing humans, and if they do not like your response, they can bring down hail or other ills. In human form, they traditionally often appear with red hair and white robes, sometimes accompanied by a dragon. They have the power to summon dragons and often ride them. The earlier versions of these legendary characters are much more pure than the later renditions which are deeply influenced by Christian agendas. The magical powers of such creatures was readily acknowledged by the first Christians and were even recognized as beneficial. As time went on, the Christian priests began to demonize them for their own benefit until the point where they were declared evil. This amalgamation of the original energy with latter day appellations has created a watered down synthetic myth in current times. It is, however, through interaction with such spirits that the Dacian priests of ancient history became initiated.

A very important part of this tradition is that children born with special signs, including those with the placenta on their head, might become a Hultan. Such children might be stolen by a Hultan and taken to a school in "Crugul Pamantului" where they are trained until the age of 20. "Crugul Pamantului" can be translated as "the middle of the Earth" and is sometimes expressed as being "raised in the middle of the wolves." This also alludes to Romulus and Remus, two twins of the virgin Vesta, courtesy of the god Mars, who were raised by wolves. It is not only ironic that Cezar Brad was born with a special sign, in his case a very large umbilical cord, but that his later life was in Department Zero under the tutelage of Dr. Xien. It further evolves into Cezar becoming an ambassador to the people of the Inner Earth. This gives us all cause to wonder if Dr. Xien is of the order of the Hultan himself. In any event, I find it fascinating that Cezar Brad's personal life story, whether intended to or not, parallels the legends of ancient Romanian mythology.

Although I had heard the legend about beggars in Romania, this was really my first introduction to the Solomonari. I would say that our guide was indeed a Solomonari, but he is also very much human. This is how the people who live in this area can be. It was as if he came down the mountain to guide us to our destination and teach us about the Solomonari. After his short talk, he took me aside and spoke through a translator.

Pointing down to a deep valley below, he said, "That is the Valley of the Golden Thrones."

I was rather dumbstruck. You mean it really exists? That was the question I asked myself. Not in a million years would I have expected to be guided anywhere near to the very area where Professor Constantin had discovered these remarkable golden tunnels, especially without trying to find them. I did not realize that my aptitude for synchronicity was in overdrive. Even if all of this is viewed only as a myth, it was now clear to me that the mythology of this area runs far deeper than what Radu has stated thus far. Radu alludes to a very deep mystery in *The Secret Parchment* but has not yet elaborated beyond what is said in that book, the summation of which you have already read. I was now learning that there are indeed more legs to this story but did not realize that a baton was literally being passed to me.

The Valley of the Golden Thrones is a beautiful valley that leads into pure wilderness. I was told that, within this valley, there is an entrance leading to the caves or tunnels described by Cezar. If you follow the tunnels long enough, they will eventually take you to the golden thrones mentioned in that same chamber. Those are the thrones that, according to Professor Constantin's account as relayed by Cezar, surround an elliptical vortex to another world.

Asking our guide if he knew about Professor Constantin, he said that he had known him. I privately wondered what the odds were of me serendipitously finding such a person. All of this was remarkable to me, and I knew right then that this was the climax of the entire trip, at least for me. I did not expect anything to be more spectacular than this revelation, and I was indeed correct on this point. It was crystal clear to me that my next step was to make a separate journey to explore this valley. I was warned, however, that one must ask permission of the spirits and not to expect to enter the tunnels themselves. The spirits will communicate through the caves. If they ever deem that you are worthy to visit the tunnels, you will be guided. As this tour with Jonette had all been planned in advance and there was a schedule to keep, there was no opportunity for me or anyone else to take such an excursion at this time.

As we made our way to Fete Alba, the citadel of the White Faces, our guide made a rather off-handed comment that he had once encountered Radu Cinamar in this area. This was also a surprise. Questioning him further, he said that Radu himself had been making a trip to Fete Alba — perhaps it was his own special pilgrimage of a sort — and that he saw him get out of a car. The guide said that he recognized Radu immediately, and that it was a spiritual identification. Radu did not admit to the recognition, but he did fit a proper description that I have for him. I am sure that he did meet the real person who is Radu. While this is not particularly important in terms of pragmatism, it has much more to do with quantum resonance and it suggested I was on the right track. When I detach myself from this experience with our guide and think about the actual circumstances, it is not at all unusual that he could have met Radu. As Radu has an interest in sacred Romania and has important esoteric business with such, it is likely that he would visit Fete Alba at some point. If he did, the area is so remote and as our guide lives on the easiest accessible path, it is likely that they would encounter each other, particularly if their psychic antennae were extended to any degree.

Fortunately for me, there was one other person who also heard what our guide had to say about the Valley of the Golden Thrones. While she had not yet read *The Secret Parchment*, she totally picked up on the energy of the valley as she was right there and could see and feel it. She also wanted to come back. Her name is Vanda Osman. Although she is the proprietor of Joy Travel and has organized and led sacred journeys since the early Eighties, Vanda was just a fellow journeyer on this trip. She wanted to come back and made a point of it. We agreed to talk about this upon our return.

There was more to our journey with Jonette, and I while I do not mean to minimize it, I will focus here on the Valley of the Golden Thrones. All I care to relay about what happened after that are my comments at our farewell dinner on the group's last night in Bucharest. After all the official acknowledgements and good-byes were done, Jonette thanked me publicly for my part in making this particular trip possible. Not having any prepared words to say, I reflected upon the moment and had a few interesting realizations. The trip to Sarmizegetusa, I said, would not have been possible if it were not for the earlier sacred journey I had taken with Nicole Vasilcovschi and Cristina Balan. I thought about the rough conditions we endured as we made our way on a train in the middle of the night. What had begun three years ago with the valiant effort of three people had now transmogrified into another journey with over forty people on it. I saw this as a dynamic spiral moving upwards and said I would return again and hoped to see everyone again on a higher spiral. My final words were that none of these journeys would have been possible if it were not for me being brought to Romania in the first place by a time travel scientist, Dr. David Anderson.

A few months after our return, Vanda and I began to have serious discussions about returning to Romania to see the Valley of the Golden Thrones and spend some time there. As Vanda is a professional in this area, I left her to make all of the arrangements. This was an excellent idea except for one thing. After she made initial inquiries with regards to costs, accommodations, and so on, no one would ever call her back with any meaningful dialogue. In other words, it was literally impossible for her to deal with any Romanian agencies or their derivatives. They would not follow up. Actually, this did not surprise me as I have experienced similar frustrations with Romanians, even when they are my friends. In about three decades of experience with international travel, Vanda had never experienced anything like this in her life. It was unfathomable. This is where my experience and contacts came into play. I had made the acquaintance of a translator who had attended one of Jonette's workshops on our last day in Bucharest. As she is a professional communicator in her work, she extended this courtesy to me, and we had many dialogues by email. Her name is Catalina, and she was very interested in learning more about sacred Romania as she was more used to taking sacred journeys to other locations outside of her own country. I put her in touch with Lenutz, the woman who I had met on my first trip to Sarmizegetusa, and she found another woman, Iulianna. This was all good fortune as Iulianna and Catalina were already familiar with each other. Vanda now had some people she could work with; and together, they all made our journey happen. Even so, there was much confusion as to schedules, availabilities, and it was a rugged experience for Vanda. In the end, Vanda probably worked harder to make this trip happen than for any other trip she had ever done. And for what? It was a spiritual mission, and she knew that. Although we secured enough people to make the trip happen, both Vanda and I had to cover certain expenses. This was not a disappointment, however, because we had both vowed to make the journey even if we went only by ourselves. We both recognized the trip as being that important. Our primary objective was to explore the Valley of the Golden Thrones. Many times though, we had to reiterate and insist upon this point. It always seemed that there was some force or predisposition at work to deter us from our appointed destination. What I would tell you is that the Solomonari are task masters when it comes to entering their territory. They test you. Vanda passed the test, and I am very grateful for all of her tireless work. In the end, we ended up with about eighteen people.

About a week before we left, I received an unexpected phone call from a man who I did not know. He said his name was Dimo, and he spoke in English with a thick accent that I immediately recognized was from Eastern Europe. He wanted to wish me good luck and offer his prayers that I might have a successful journey to Romania. It was public information that I was travelling, but he had a rather unusual if not abstract grasp of the importance of what I was doing. It was all very important to him. When I asked about his accent, he first said he was from Macedonia; but as he began to explain his life in a very summarized fashion, he told me that he had grown up as a young boy in Bulgaria and began to talk about the Strandzha Mountains. To his surprise, I told him that I had been there and also knew about the expedition to the Tomb of Bastet. He then went on to explain that he was raised by a woman named Vanga. He did not expect me to recognize or even react to the name Vanga either. As I said, most Americans are oblivious of her. At this point in the conversation, I stopped him and told him that I knew who Vanga was and also about her niece's involvement in the expedition. This was like opening a genie bottle with hundreds of colorful paper dragons streaming out of it. Dimo and I had several conversations before I left.

Dimo not only grew up with Vanga and knew her on an intimate basis, he was a part of the actual expedition to the Tomb of Bastet and personally knew all of the various players involved. This was a rather remarkable coincidence that was really not a coincidence. Now, I made a point of rapidly sending all of the information I had on the Bastet expedition to Vanda. At the same time, I was coordinating to have my Bulgarian publisher and translator meet us at Sarmizegetusa. I was hopeful that Vanda could some day expand her journeys with Joy Travel to extend to Bulgaria.

Dimo explained to me that he was lucky to have escaped from Bulgaria with his freedom and his life. Warning him, Vanga had instructed him to go to America and to be patient. Eventually, he would meet a man in America who would help him tell his story but only when the time was right. In the meantime, Dimo found himself a successful career in the technology sector. He keeps a low profile for the most part.

When I told my Bulgarian friends about Dimo, they had never heard of him nor of the existence of any such person. It would make sense that he would have escaped any mention in any publications, official or otherwise. Besides, my friends were rather tired of hearing about Vanga. There are probably more books in Bulgaria about Vanga than on any other topic. In addition to that, my translator's family had a bad experience with Vanga when her almost fully deaf and blind grandfather visited her and asked for help. Her bedside manner and advice were not too charming to say the least. What Dimo had to say, however, was data about Vanga that they had never heard about at all. It seems to me that the Bulgarian obsession with this lady had missed the forest for the trees.

I learned from Dimo that Vanga had worked extensively with the Communist Bloc government(s), and that she was extremely well paid for what she had done. We are talking in the millions of dollars, and this was all in a country that was extremely poor by Western standards. One of the projects she sponsored with her funds was the construction of a church. There is apparently far more to this woman than any of her adherents or followers might have imagined. It also fits into the paradigm of what might be called Bulgaria's own Department Zero. My publisher and I had long speculated that a "Bulgarian Radu" might surface. Now, here he was, surfacing in the personage of Dimo.

There was a peculiar feature of my conversations with Dimo, however. He wanted to talk a lot about his uncle's disappearance in conjunction with a UFO and also forwarded me a lot of information about secret projects. I, however, found nothing spectacular in this and certainly nothing that commanded my interest. It was rather more of the same sort of typical diatribe that circulates amongst UFO and paranormal investigators. To my astonishment, Dimo was surprised to think that anyone might want to hear about his personal story and the expedition to the Tomb of Bastet. Here he is, with arguably one of the best stories to surface from Eastern Europe, and he did not seem to recognize its relative importance. He did talk to me a little bit about the expedition, and from what I gathered, the experience had a profound effect upon him which was so astonishing that you might say it bordered on the traumatic. It was an incredible experience. What all of this suggests is that the experiences of those who participated in the expedition, along with what it turned up, is very closely guarded by powerful forces that we can call jinn, Solomonari or by whatever other name we choose.

Dimo also told me that at least part of his interest in my work was based upon a friendship he had acquired with a Romanian man by the name of Constantin Dragan. Before his death, Dragan was one of the wealthiest Romanians ever and had erected the famous statue of Decebel, the Dacian King, on the Danube. This is roughly Romania's equivalent of Mount Rushmore. Constantin Dragan had taught Dimo much about the ancient Dacians and how the history of Romania had been obscured. There was also another prophecy from Vanga that Dimo wanted to share with me. Vanga also told Dimo that, in the future, an American would reveal the truth about Romania to the world.

I had not even begun on my sacred journey and here I was communing with the seeds that had been planted from past sacred journeys. It seemed that destiny and fate were entering the mix as well and that Vanga had seen me coming from somewhere out of time. There are other Americans, not too many, who write about Romania; but I am writing about it at the deepest core level possible. It is from the mirror of time and all that the seven golden thrones and the parallelepiped represent. There are tomes of paradigm changing information available that can be either translated or written about the culture of Dacians, Thracians and proto-Thracians. I will leave that for others. All I choose to do is offer the core thread around which the academic orbit will eventually find itself.

I will also be quite frank with you. There have been several people who have approached me from Romania who can offer various leads and what not to further substantiate the claims of Radu Cinamar. If pursued, I could show you roads, military installations and other facts that would demonstrate a trail that would corroborate and make a case for his stories being accurate. None of this, however, would ultimately prove anything other than there is a secret department with secret facilities. For myself, and I would hope the same for you, I am more interested in the core psychological and transformative experience of what is being offered. If I access any of the highly secure locales, I want it to be by invitation from the likes of Cezar or Radu, not as an outsider trying to prove something for a sceptical public.

Earlier, I mentioned that I was scheduled to meet with Elinor, but it did not happen as of the writing of this book. While there might well have been security reasons that prevented this visitation, there was also another factor at work. For personal reasons, I was not ready to meet Elinor. I will not elaborate on this as it is personal, but I sent out a mental message that I did not want it to happen until a certain series of events would first take place in my own life. While I gladly would have met with him had the arrangement been offered as suggested, it seems that my own penetration of the subtle energies had done their trick. I still look forward to meeting Elinor, but he is no longer in Romania so I do not expect to meet him there, at least on my next journey.

Elinor originally appeared in Radu's narrative as an intermediary on behalf of Repa Sundhi. The lama also sometimes serves as an intermediary himself but on a broader and even more mysterious basis. He not only facilitated the finding of the parchment but also the unveiling of the Bucegi complex and its stewardship by Cezar Brad. When we consider that Vanga is in the mix as well, at least with regards to predicting my arrival and role in this scenario, it is important to point out to you that she lost her sight and received her gift after being struck by lightning. According to the tradition of the Solomonari that you have already read about, they are masters of lightning. It seems they had more than a little something to do with Vanga's gift.

When I first witnessed the Valley of the Golden Thrones from the mountains near Fete Alba, I was told that one simply goes to the tunnels and meditates or otherwise dialogues with the energies of the Inner Earth. Although I had seen the valley, I had not yet accessed or even been too close to these particular caves. The Solomonari, however, could not have helped but notice my presence. I had only learned about them on the last trip. My intention was to simply visit the Valley of the Golden Thrones in pursuit of the mystery presented by Radu in *The Secret Parchment*. I would not even have pursued that had it not been dropped into my lap by synchronicity. Perhaps this entire backdrop is an illusion created by the Solomonari to draw me into their fold.

It is obvious that there are many threads weaving their way into this scenario from many different perspectives. My personal pathway is simply one of these threads. It is unwieldy to think that all of Radu's books were written to serve my personal journey. One thing in this scenario, however, is clear. There is a great mystery behind the writing of all of Radu's books, and I was penetrating the mystery. As things would turn out, I would pursue and penetrate this mystery much further than I had ever even desired. The reason for this is that the mystery was also pursuing me.

CHAPTER TWENTY-FOUR

RETURN OF THE WHITE BAT

I met up with Vanda as we boarded the plane at JFK airport in New York. We visited Atlantykron for several days before meeting our fellow travellers in Bucharest and embarking on our journey. We arrived at our hotel in Transylvania, the Cotiso, on August 10th, the beginning of the annual biorhythm that runs from August 10-14 and when the star (system) Sirius is at its closest position to the earth. This biorhythm is also known for the dates of the Philadelphia Experiment (1943) and the Montauk Project (1983). Most of my trips to Romania have been during this period so as to coincide with Atlantykron's schedule which is purposely designed to avoid the flooding of the Danube River. While it is indeed a synchronicity that most of my magical moments in Romania have been during this period, it was always a matter of happenstance and never a result of specific planning.

The evening we arrived was a very suitable way to celebrate the beginning of the biorhythm. All sorts of people were gathering at the Cotiso Hotel, and it would far exceed the forty plus people from Jonette's trip. We had about eighteen on our bus and were joined by three of my Bulgarian friends. There were also at least a dozen Romanian friends who had followed us. To my great surprise, Nicole and her fiancee were there. This was another coincidence because they do not live in the area and it was now four years to the day Nicole and I had arrived in Transylvania to make our first pilgrimage to Sarmizegetusa. Besides the people following our group, there were others coming to hear a Romanian musician who was playing New Age music he had composed. It was a festive atmosphere, and I felt sheer joy to see so many of my friends from across the world and diverse cultures gather together as a result of my pilgrimage to this magical area. Unfortunately, I missed the highlight of this gathering when my Bulgarian translator was singing Bulgarian folk songs which would be followed by my friend Maria's singing of a Romanian folk song. This went on playfully, back and forth, but I did not get it on video as I was called away.

After our late arrival and dinner that evening, I was approached by two young men who wanted to talk to me. This created quite a stir within our group because they were very noticeable and no one knew who they were. They were students and friends of Tatiana Maassen, a woman of German extraction who is a General Colonel in the Romanian Army and was a quantum physics professor at the Aviation Army Unit. Of considerably more interest than this was that her teacher was Hermann Oberth, the mentor of German rocket scientist Werner von Braun. Oberth was a native Transylvanian who was recognized as the father of modern rocketry. After World War II, he was a prominent scientist in the American rocket program. Those who have pursued the mystique of repatriated Axis rocket scientists have often declared Oberth to be the most enigmatic and mysterious of them all. The most senior of all early rocket scientists in terms of age and experience, the enigmatic characterization of Oberth is due to his interest and participation in occultism. Although it is not well known to popular authors, I have learned from Tatiana that much of his occult associations had to do with Tibet.

Months before I departed for Romania, Tatiana had written several emails to me and had made friends with me online and had generously invited me to stay at a local hotel and speak to her friends. Unfortunately, I was not able to commit to any such excursions because I had obligations with the group Vanda and I had put together and also a tight schedule. Nevertheless, Tatiana stopped by the Cotiso Hotel upon the evening of my arrival and was hoping to meet me. When I spoke to her students, Teo and Danny, I told them that our agenda was to visit the Valley of the Golden Thrones the next day, and that our sights were set on doing nothing but that. Very familiar with the term I was using, they seemed a little puzzled and said that the Valley of the Golden Thrones is really a state of mind. It was not really a location as such. I was equally puzzled. Soon afterwards, they led me out to a very dark parking lot while my friends sang in the lounge. As there were no street lights, the environment was very dark. When I saw Tatiana, she greeted me with a big smile as I stood about ten feet in front of her. Oddly and quite unmistakably, I felt a pair of eyes staring at the back of my head. I turned around and saw nothing there.

"There is a spirit behind me," I said.

Tatiana nodded and walked to the exact spot where the spirit had occupied. It was exactly where I would have said the spirit had gotten my attention. She had either sensed it or seen it. Months later, I would deconstruct what had happened and only then was I able to visualize an angelic feminine spirit that had sort of passed a magical wand over me so as to welcome and acknowledge me in what could best be termed an initiatory process. I did not realize it at the time, but I was being greeted by the Solomonari, and this one had been assigned to me.

In the meantime, our hired guide did not show up, and this threw off all of our plans to visit the Valley of the Golden Thrones the very next day. He was getting drunk and partying with his girl friend. Our guide was the same man from the year before, but this time we were hiring him to take us to the valley. While this did not please anyone, I have come to expect such obstacles en route to a sacred journey in Transylvania. It is par for the course. Without our guide, we decided to utilize our time by visiting Sarmizegetusa the next morning. Before we left, however, our guide showed up. As he introduced me to several of his friends, I told them, through a translator, that I had realized that I was being pulled to their country long before I had ever gotten involved with the Montauk Project and then proceeded to tell them about my dream with the white bat. As soon as I told him about the white bat, our guide became very excited. He said that a girl had seen a white bat in Machandi's Cave just three days earlier. I had no idea there was such a place as Machandi's Cave. As surprising as this was to me, I was far more moved by the fact that this girl had witnessed a white bat. It was a great synchronicity, and I knew that I now had the ending to my book that was already being written. This made me very happy. Whatever else would happen on this trip, I had already achieved more than I could have expected. A white bat appearing in Machandi's Cave was pretty spectacular. My journey had come full circle; but as with all my experiences with synchronicity in the past, this experience prompted new questions to investigate. Where was Machandi's Cave? Was it named such before Radu's book came out? I then realized that it was only the morning of our first day of the journey. It was August 11th, and I was already riding the crest of the wave of the biorhythm.

We soon went to Sarmizegetusa. During a guided tour of the area, our guide said that the key to Sarmizegetusa is the Book of Zalmoxis, and you have to access it to learn all of its secrets. I had never heard this term before, but it was one more step of initiation into the Dacian tradition. After a meditation conducted by my Romanian friend, Dr. Teodore Vasili, everyone split up to explore the area. A Romanian woman who was not part of our group approached me privately and said that the Book of Zalmoxis is not a physical book. All you have to do to open it is to ask, but she warned that you must not misuse the power or you will have to pay for it. Wandering and looking around, I instantly made a decision to open the metaphorical Book of Zalmoxis. After making the decision, things began to be very placid and still. Although there were plenty of people around, I only noticed the trees and stones. I felt totally alone and had the "sure" feeling that nothing whatsoever would happen. The universe seemed empty and quiet.

The next thing I knew, the paper dragons were flying out of their box. It began when I saw my friend Cristina. She had driven my Bulgarian friends from the Cotiso Hotel. I was especially happy to be with her at this location, and I told her so. As I did, our guide strolled by, and I took this opportunity to ask him my questions about Machandi's Cave. It was extremely fortuitous that I was with Cristina as she could translate for me. Our guide told me that this cave was indeed known as Machandi's Cave and that the name was independent of Radu's book. I would later figure out, from rereading *Transylvanian Moonrise*, that it was the very same cave that Radu describes on his second visit with Machandi. The first was in Tibet but the second was in Transylvania near Gugu Peak when Radu had to persevere intimidating weather and strong energies with the help of the yidam. Machandi emerged so as to quell the bad weather and appeared before Radu's party. As I talked with my guide, however, I did not have all of these pieces of the puzzle clear in my head. Everything was happening very fast and it did indeed take me months to put everything together.

I then told our guide that I would like to meet the girl who saw the white bat in Machandi's Cave. To my surprise and delight, he said that she was right over there as he pointed to a circle of people twenty yards away. Her name is Lavinia, a young lady from Bucharest who is an actress. Lavinia is very unique, and I would describe her demeanor as cheery and chirpy. She speaks virtually no English however. As Lavinia was called over, my friend Nicole appeared out of nowhere. This was another amazing synchronicity as I did not know she would be with us again on this day, four years to the day of our first sojourn to Sarmizegetusa on August 11th, 2009.

Nicole translated for Lavinia, and it was like a dream to have her talking once again into my ear with her warm and very familiar voice. Lavinia told me about her encounter with the white bat and said that she was inside the cave and had seen it and that it was unmistakably white. It was not the result of a play of light and shadow. I then asked our guide about the logistics of getting to Machandi's Cave. He said it was a day's drive and a day's hike to get there. I was obviously not going to go on this trip on this journey, but I was already to make plans to return. He said I should come alone without all of these people, and I could then visit the cave.

Not long after noon, we returned to the Cotiso for lunch. Afterwards, there was an optional question and answer session with our guide in the lounge. Before long, someone asked our guide about the Valley of the Golden Thrones, and he began to look rather sad as he explained that many people come to this locale and look for this valley. He repeated what Tatiana's students had said to me the night before. It was a state of mind and not a physical location as such. This was in complete contradiction to what he had told me the year before on our journey to Fete Alba. After he finished speaking, I carefully reminded him about our conversation from the year before. I still did not get an adequate response. This sort of confusion is par for the course when dealing with jinn or Solomonari. I then narrowed down the parameters of our previous conversation. Instead of asking him about the valley, I asked him to point to where his house was. He pointed to a mountain. It was then easy for me to orient him to the conversation we had a year earlier and remind him that he had pointed to a valley which we all clearly saw and that he said was the Valley of the Golden Thrones. This was the keystone. He understood exactly what I was getting at and said that he was pointing to the valley we were now in. It soon became evident that we were already in the Valley of the Golden Thrones and that the Cotiso Hotel was as good as in the center of it. Although the valley he had pointed to looked mostly like raw nature, there were signs of civilization in the remote distance. It was only my assumption that the valley he had pointed to was more remote than it was. This area, with its population of about 3,000 people, is still very remote. I was now very pleased. Without even realizing it, we had arrived at the Valley of the Golden Thrones and had reached our planned destination. We had arrived physically the night before but the full mental realization did not occur until this revelation. I was very happy. I had experienced the white bat in the morning and now this. The Valley of the Golden Thrones had lived up to the magic that I had projected, and it was now easy to embrace the state of mind than I had been told about.

When our guide was done, Tatiana came in with four of her students and we sat down and had a long conversation. Telling her of my desire to return and to visit Machandi's Cave, she told me of a better entrance to the cave where I would have easier access and also see more. She also told me about Zalmoxis' Cave which has a direct link to Sarmizegetusa where it emerges through a tree. Her two male students, Teo and Danny, were accompanied by two ladies, Oana and Paula. Oana had lived in Brooklyn so we have a lot in common in terms of a New York connection. Paula and I met briefly at Sarmizegetusa, and we both recognized each other in a very strange way. Over ten years earlier, I experienced a dream within a dream wherein a beautiful friend of mine appeared in a business suit in the marriage corner (as per Feng Shui) of my house. Although this friend has a last name similar to the name Solomonari, my ex-wife addressed her in the dream as Paula. My brain, through the R.E.M. realm, was apparently recognizing Paula as well as the Solomonari themselves. Paula was only one year old at the time I had my original dream of the white bat, but as you will read, we have been brought together by destiny if not Machandi herself. Even so, I spent no time with Paula on this trip.

After I finished talking to Tatiana and her students, my old friends Lenutz and her husband came into the lounge. For me, it was almost like a Romanian version of the television program *This Is Your Life*. When I told Lenutz and her husband, through a translator, about the white bat, I was in for another surprise. Her husband, Mihai, had been with Lavinia when she witnessed the white bat in Machandi's Cave. He, however, insisted that the bat was black and that it only appeared gray or white because of the play of light and shadow.

By the time I was finished in the lounge, it was rather late. The New Age musician had returned and was playing on the lawn and there were many more people who had come to listen to him. There was also an inventor speaking in the conference room who had a device with a large crystal that would emit light to a person sitting in a chair. He was lecturing to many of our party. When I entered, I stood in the back and noticed Lavinia by the wall. I motioned her over. Even though she does not speak English, I was able to get across to her what my friend Mihai had said about the bat being black and not white.

Lavinia, who is a rather jolly person, understood me very clearly and then said vehemently in clear but strongly accented English, "That is because his heart is black!"

I was moved by her conviction that the bat was unequivocally white. There was no doubt in her mind. While I would not be so harsh about Mihai — he has been a wonderful friend — this divergence of opinion is symptomatic of so much phenomena that occurs in the spirit world. When you are dealing with the Solomonari and their influence on native Romanians, experiences can be loaded with contradictions and booby-traps. It is actually quite suitable to the phenomenon at hand that there would be dichotomous perceptions, particularly when it comes to such an important spiritual issue. The contradiction, regardless of who is right, is a sign that one is on the trail of the Solomonari.

The next day, August 12th, our group went to visit the grave of Father Arsenie Boca, the priest who had predicted the Bucegi discovery to Cezar Brad. I was asked to leave when a nun saw me doing Chi Gong in the vicinity of the grave. As I walked by hundreds of people who were coming to visit the grave, I saw many with limps and afflictions who were obviously seeking relief from their human suffering. I thought about how much I could help them with fifteen or twenty minutes of personal Chi Gong instruction tailored to their specific needs, but it would only happen if they would listen and apply.

That evening, it was arranged for me to speak to about seventeen of Tatiana's students. Her students were probably the most self-aware sentient beings I have ever spoken to. One of them was Sonia, but I do not know if it is proper to classify her as a student. She is a child of about four. Before I left for Romania, many of us had seen a youTube video where Tatiana did a healing on Sonia in an open field. As the healing came to its peak, an unmistakable ray of light emitted from the clouds above and went right into Sonia. It was so dramatic that it prompted some of my friends to wonder if it was video manipulation, but this was not the case. Tatiana, like Cezar Brad, has an extraordinary amount of natural chi energy. I can readily see this from my own Chi Gong training. Although I had not been introduced to Sonia before my lecture, I easily recognized her, and she took a separate chair and sat closer to me than anyone else. Sonia is a little young to understand my lecture, but she recognized me on some level and wanted to be near me. I would call her a very old soul.

I was very touched by Sonia but also by a primary question that Tatiana and her students asked about me as a writer. Very specifically, they wanted to know how I write what I write. In other words, they were specifically asking me about the process I use in writing the books I write. The book you are reading is a very specific answer to that question. I was, however, writing on this topic even before they asked me. These people from Transylvania, my dream of the white bat, and my writing are all on the same frequency. Later on, I would learn that they had gotten a copy of my book *Synchronicity and the Seventh Seal* and read it to the entire group with Teo translating it verbally into Romanian. I was highly amused over how they might convey the Tar Baby, a primary character in that book, into Romanian. Paula even told me that she took the time to look up all the bastardized English contractions that were a staple of the Tar Baby's speech. She wanted to understand the nuances of what was being said. This was a Roberto Quaglia-Robert Sheckley moment for me, and it demonstrates the powerful potential of writing. Here were people in a far off foreign country appreciating my writing in a way that most Americans are not likely to.

Their interest in *Synchronicity and the Seventh Seal* is not a coincidence, and it has to do with the bigger picture in Romania. That book focuses to a large degree on Solomonic magic, particularly as it was exercised through the Enochian calls given to John Dee. The angels who gave him his magic ring, which featured the letters PELE, said it was the very ring that King Solomon had used to rule or subjugate the jinn. In *The Secret Parchment*, I stated that the Romanian news media has encouraged reports that Prince Charles of England will succeed King Michael as the next King of Romania. Whether this happens or not, Prince Charles has been a constant presence in Transylvania and this fits hand-in-hand with the British Empire being an instrument of John Dee's Enochian magic which was, in turn, an instrument of Solomonic magic. Keep in mind that the same Freemasons who sought control of the Bucegi holographic chamber base their esotericism upon the template of Solomon's Temple. After all of my Romanian adventures, it is now apparent to me that the Solomonari are the underlying current of all of these traditions and is the template upon which they were based. Both black and white in their manifestations, the Solomonari are closely linked to the dualistic nature of the universe.

If you study the *Rider-Waite Tarot* and *Thoth Tarot*, you will find that duality originates or first emerges via the path of the High Priestess. This is the virtual or literal inception of black and white, Solomonari, jinn, or whatever name you want to give to these dualistic forces which eventually transmute into more complex manifestations such as the Goetia described in *Synchronicity and the Seventh Seal*. The ancient people of Romania were known as the Gettae which is phonetically no different than Goetia; and this is where the term *Goths* was derived from. Keep in mind, the history of the Goths was destroyed or hidden and admittedly so. History does say, however, that their god was Zalmoxis. The term *Solomonari*, an ancient designation that has not been properly acknowledged by historians, is a name based upon the sun (Apollo) and the moon (Diana) which flows (in the Tree of Life schematic) into Gemini (Zalmoxis or The Twins) via Tipareth, the crowning glory of manifestation. Tipareth, designated as beauty, is the realm assigned to Christ by Christian cabalists as it represents an interaction between the Creator and the "human." Tipareth is a little bit tricky because its inverse is the dualistic Baphomet which becomes the pathway of the Tarot card known as The Devil.

The Devil is the path between Hesod (Mercury or the realm of Hermetic wisdom) and Tipareth, the latter being where negative polarity is reconciled and transmuted into beauty. This is the station of the white bat and is symbolic of what I experienced in my dream. If you extrapolate the two-dimensional rendition of the Tree of Life into a three-dimensional rendition of two DNA strands, you will find that Tipareth exists within the shape of a Vesica Pisces, a symbol of the Age of Pisces which was designated as the Christ. This is where the white bat flies out of, and it represents the reconciliation of dark forces.

My last day in Transylvania was August 13th, and our guide took our group on a long hike where we would visit one of the many tunnels that lead to the Inner Earth. The objective was to simply go to the cave, meditate, and experience the energies that would manifest from the subtle planes. On the way of what was a rather long hike, I once again saw Lavinia, the girl who had witnessed the white bat in Machandi's Cave. She said that she had a message for me from Machandi but that it had been blocked by Tatiana. Asking her how she knew that Tatiana had blocked it, Lavinia told me that after she had been contacted by Machandi, all she saw was a picture of Tatiana. What had occurred here was complex and hard to figure out at the time. Tatiana had power, but who has the power to block Machandi? This did not make sense to me. Eventually, but only after I got home, would I figure out the situation and realize that Machandi was directing me to Tatiana.

Lavinia eventually went off with some others as I went with our core group to the cave and engaged in a guided meditation. The cave was inaccessible unless you had a rope and other spelunking equipment. After fifty feet, it leads to a narrow path over water and then to an ancient stone chair from the proto-Thracian days. It has been explored by others. As we did our meditation, Lavinia returned with some of our other friends but they all remained apart from us, about seventy yards away, as they did not want to interrupt our meditation. As we meditated, there was a true Solomonari experience. A shepherd came down to Lavinia and directed them to two more caves. This is exactly true to the legend of what Solomonari are known to do. I recognized immediately what was happening and would have gone off with them, but it would have been irresponsible as I was committed to staying with my group. In the final analysis, I could not complain as I had more than enough experiences for the last three days.

On the way back from the cave, we stopped once more at Sarmizegetusa. To my surprise, I ran into Nicole again. She was with a group from Suceava. I also saw Bogdan, a friend from Atlantykron who had replaced Bica, the resident astronomer. During our good-byes to each other over the years, Bica had said repeatedly to me that when my heart told me to return to Romania that I should listen to it. When I mentioned Bica to Bogdan, he told me that Bica was there, too. I was happy with this synchronicity but as our group was getting set to leave, I only got to have a few words with Bica. They were the last words we would ever share.

"We are going to take back Dacia!" he said with utter conviction and enthusiasm. His passion to revivify the knowledge and power of the ancient Dacians was infectious. I was happy for him and believed in his mission.

When I returned to New York, I received an email from Nicole who was by that time working at her new job as an economics professor in China. She told me the very sad news that Bica had died shortly after seeing me. He had gone to Zalmoxis's Cave, the same cave that Tatiana had told me about. Bica was standing on a steep incline and taking pictures of the cave from above. While doing this, he slipped and fell to his death. I could not help but think that Bica had become a sacrifice in the tradition of Zalmoxis. It occurred to me that perhaps his mission to take back Dacia might be more effectively performed outside of his human body. He will be missed by all of his friends at Atlantykron. The synchronicity of our last meeting and how it tied to his death at the Cave of Zalmoxis made me reflect on what he had said about following my heart. He was talking about me coming to live in Romania. While I do not know if that will happen, it is true that I have developed a stronger and stronger bond with that mysterious and very potent country. After all, I did open the Book of Zalmoxis and paper dragons were flying as never before.

There was a lot to digest upon my return. Opening the Book of Zalmoxis was not a casual thing. Right after I had performed this mental task at Sarmizegetusa, one of my friends noticed my auric field and said that I had definitely experienced a major activation, but it would take six months for me to integrate it all. He was very right as it turned out. I have only been able to write what you have read here after piecing it all together month after month.

Much of this revelation was enabled by my new friend, Paula, the lady I had recognized from a dream within a dream. I found out that Paula was not only a student of Tatiana's but is also her adopted daughter. She explained to me that Tatiana has lectured on Machandi for a long time, and this is completely independent of Radu Cinamar's reference to this goddess. This made it very clear to me that the transmission Lavinia had received from Machandi was directing me to Tatiana and to pay attention to her. The fact that it was transmitted in a confusing and convoluted manner is par for the course when you are dealing with the Solomonari or jinn. White means black and black means white — sometimes.

Paula is a very good looking lady, and I told her that she would have been perfectly cast as an elf when we did the production for *My Kentucky Cousin*. She then sent me a picture revealing that her left ear is actually pointed in a way that is reminiscent of an elf. I not only found this feature of hers adorable, but when we consider the concept of the alchemy of writing, it demonstrates that what I had written for Atlantykron was actually coming to life.

I also consider it significant that Paula was born in Piatra Neamt at the foot of a sacred mountain. Every August 6th two mountain peaks in this region form a shadow early in the morning that blends with the morning mist from the flora and creates a virtual hologram of a giant pyramid that is quite similar to the Great Pyramid of Giza. Many believe that the actual Great Pyramid was constructed based upon this phenomena in Romania. The Orthodox Church celebrates this occurrence every August as the Transfiguration of Jesus.

Paula had more magic in store for me that was, once again, symptomatic of working with the energy of the Solomonari. When I told her that I wanted to go back to the cave where the white bat had appeared to Lavinia, Paula made an off-handed comment that Machandi appears there every year between May 21-24 with a white bat which is her mascot. This was astonishing to me. It all seemed to come out of thin air, but Paula had said it with off-handed conviction. Why had she not said it before?

A couple of weeks later, I told Paula that I wanted to return the following May and go to the locale where Machandi is said to appear with the white bat. Paula, however, denied saying any such thing. We had an argument about it as I was sure I had not mistaken what I had heard. After all, I would not be so intent on making plans to go in May if I had not received such a strong message. It is far easier and less expensive for me to go in August when it is warmer and I am already in Romania for Atlantykron.

While Paula still denied that she had said anything about Machandi or the white bat appearing in May, she did say that May 21-24 is when the white lilac appears and that it is a symbol of Machandi. She further explained that *liliac* is the word for both lilac and bat in Romanian. I then said that she might have confused the two, but she said it was not the case. When informed of my disagreement with Paula, Tatiana said that human beings cannot always see or recognize the mysterious way that spirit works through them. Paula finally conceded that she might have been a medium in this regard. As for me, I know what I heard her say. Just like Lavinia, Paula had been utilized by Machandi to convey a message to me.

As I have repeatedly stated herein, it took me a long time to integrate all of my experiences from the Valley of the Golden Thrones. One important piece of the puzzle resolved itself when I recalled being very moved when I read in *Transylvanian Moonrise* about the young people who had dreams of Machandi and were instructed to report to a specific location in the Apuseni Mountains. When I originally read that, I wished that I had experienced one of those dreams, too. Only now did I realized that I did indeed have a dream that was sent by Machandi, but it was in 1989, just before the communist regime would fall in Romania. It was the dream of the white bat that you read at the beginning of this book. It eventually occurred to me that I had originally invoked her when I was studying the Tree of Life and realized the importance of seeking out or aligning myself with positive entities. It seemed as if Machandi had been guiding me on my path all along.

The result of all of this is that I am scheduled to return to Romania and visit Machandi's Cave during the May 21-24 period. Although I was specifically given this date through spiritual means, this is a time when neither tourists nor the local shepherds visit the area due to rainy weather and poor conditions of the mountain itself. It is dangerous and unpleasant. I have no expectations for what might happen, and this includes the possibility of either seeing Machandi or a white bat. All I know is that I have been in communication with a higher order that has directed me to this location. Instead of Radu, Cezar, Elinor or Repa Sundhi, I am being guided to the force that has guided them. All of this involves dialogue with the energies and mythos of the Inner Earth. After making my decision to return, this proposition was reinforced immediately.

The next thing I heard from Paula was that there had been a major earthquake in Transylvania on September 8th that was centered in the Valley of the Golden Thrones, right near Sarmizegetusa. This date marked the onset of Ganesh Chaturthi, the Hindu festival that celebrates the birth of the elephant god Ganesh by Parvati, another name for the Durga. Machandi, a goddess who is considered to be the composite of all goddesses, is also known as the Durga in the Hindu tradition as an exemplary archetype of a divine source of compassion. Durga means "invincible" or "inaccessible." The earthquake was said to be a response from Gaia herself in regards to the intent of Gabriel Resources, a Canadian Company, to use a cyanide extraction process in order to mine an area in Romania known as Rosia Montana. This will create horrific environmental degradation and also permanently block a major access point to the Inner Earth. Satellite surveys have revealed 75 conical holes of different sizes, some with diameters up to 70 meters, extending over a surface area of about four square kilometers. These conical tunnels lead to the nearby mountains, one of which extends under the sanctuaries of Sarmizegetusa. Besides gold, Gabriel Resources also plans to extract tellurium, a rare metalloid or semi-metal originally placed on the periodic table of elements after its discovery in Transylvania in 1782. Tellurium is abundant in the universe but not on earth, and it is more valuable than gold for its use in nuclear power and photovoltaic cells that power spacecraft.

As a result of these developments with Rosia Montana, I was informed that Tatiana had suddenly left Romania to go to her home, the City of Yellow Tea. The yellow tea flower is very rare and is the most sought after in Tibet. It was originally reserved only for royalty. I cannot explain more, but I am told that Romanian politicians at the highest level actually recognize Tatiana as coming from the City of Yellow Tea which is located in Agartha. Tatiana is considered to be an ambassador from Agartha, the ancient name for Transylvania which also refers to the realm of the Inner Earth.

What followed afterwards was the biggest environmental protest in the history of Eastern Europe as a human chain was formed around the parliament building in Bucharest. As a result, the Romanian Supreme Court blocked the effort to begin mining. Gabriel Resources, however, has vowed to find a way to get around this and toxify over 200 square kilometers of earth.

While some of you might relegate all of these happenings to tales of fantasy, it is far more than that. Others might think I have gone off the deep end, but this is not the case either. I have been in the deep end of the pool for a long time and am more of a lifeguard than a regular swimmer.

Tatiana and Paula have graciously offered to host me during my visit and will also accompany me on my journey to Machandi's Cave. While Tatiana is actually a spokesperson for Machandi, I am propelling her to return to Machandi's lair itself. Note the following quote from *Transylvania Moonrise*:

> "Goratri Mountain, which is mentioned in the prophecies of the great sage Padmasambhava (Rinpoche), is in fact Godeanu Mountain, the present name being a natural transformation of the initial one through the past millennia. This mountain is very important in the local energetic balance and also keeps some secrets that will astound the world. Machandi picked that place for a reason."

If Machandi picked this locale for a reason, it seems that she also picked me for a reason. What I will learn or experience, I cannot say. As per what I wrote at the end of the book *Synchronicity and the Seventh Seal*, any temptations for power will be turned down. Temporal power is misleading. Whatever I experience will be the *mis en abyme* reflection of the white bat. It will be a reflection of myself and my thoughts, just as was described in the second precept of the secret parchment (what you think is what you get).

So, as I write these final words, it is May of 2014; and I will soon be boarding a plane for Italy and then Romania as I literally send this book to the printer. Will there be a sequel? I would expect so, but it will take me at least a year to complete it.

I hope you have enjoyed this book, and I hope that you have learned how to write in a manner that will assist you in integrating both sides of your consciousness, the intuitive and the linear. While my personal journey might be interesting, it is not really so important with regards to yourself. What is important to you is whether or not you have been inspired. If so, I would once again invite you to write down your own inspirations and either begin or continue your own integration process.

The sky is the limit.

APPENDIX A — THE TREE OF LIFE

Scientifically, DNA is constructed upon a geometric pattern which includes the interfacing of pentagrams and hexagrams so as to form spirals, each known as a mobius strip. Although this data is relatively knew to scientists, who have only learned about it in the last century, this was recognized by the mystery schools who shared certain aspects of this information with their initiates. Pythagoras was one such initiate, and he is a name that even most mundane people will recognize. Accordingly, these mystery schools rendered this information in a two-dimensional model or template which was known as the Tree of Life and is associated with Cabala, Kabbalah, or Qabala. Note that Cabala with a C refers to an interpretative element for Christianity while Kabbalah with a K stands for the Jewish version and Q refers to the Islamic. There are also other versions which came long before any of these.

In its most fundamental emanations, life is a dynamic force that consists of motions that are repetitive and variant with yet further repetitions and variations of what has been already rendered. All of these, however, tend to conform to a certain orderliness, and this is what has been rendered by various cabalists into different forms known as the Tree of Life. How accurate these expositions are vary with the writers, but any of them are bound to give some insight into the hidden processes of life. What follows herein is only meant to serve as concise summary of the Tree of Life so that those who are unfamiliar with it can grasp the essential functioning. It should be noted that all archetypes, religions, and philosophies can be better understood by viewing them in a cabalistic context. That is because all such are emanations of life and the Tree of Life is a mirror or *mis en abyme* of life itself.

The Cabalistic Tree of Life includes ten sepiroth or sephiraat which is the Hebrew word for "sphere." These ten sepiroth are ten emanation points of life and flow from one to the other. To some degree, it is like a fountain or spring. Each one of these sepiroth conform to a numeral as well as a fundamental archetype of consciousness. As a single unit of life evolves into what it is eventually going to become, it passes through each one of these sepiroth and emphasizes some more than others. A male peacock, for example, stresses beauty while a more ferocious animal might draw more from the well of the martial energies in this so-called template. The philosophy of this template is such that it includes all aspects of potential life.

There is also a mysterious eleventh sepiroth which deals with all hidden or occult operations. It is postulated to be there because you can see its results or manifestations, but there is no visible evidence of it. It is known as Da'ath.

217

While not a part of this tree of life structure per se, there is another designated repository into which life also flows with regard to certain circumstances. It is, however, a darker side to life and is referred to as the q'lipoth. This is somewhat like a sewer because it is the repository into which flows all things that did not work out in the experience of regular life. In other words, the q'lipoth is the receptacle for that which has been rejected, for one reason or another, by the processes of the morphogenetic grid. For example, the memory of life organisms which did not succeed are relegated to this area of consciousness. This would include the memory of dinosaurs, mastodons, saber-tooth tigers, and a lot of other creatures that might be considered extinct. It is known from experience that this region includes monstrous type manifestations which can literally frighten the living daylights out of occult practitioners or naive explorers who penetrate this realm. I have personally noticed that those who either study or are preoccupied with the phenomena of the q'lipoth often become either obsessed or possessed by it without even realizing that it is consuming more of their attention than is healthy.

It should be noted that almost all Western versions of the Tree of Life have been interpreted through a patriarchal lens. Kenneth Grant, now deceased, would be an exception, and he has done some very interesting work on the Afrikan Q'abalah which deals with the feminine current underlying all such phenomena. In this book, I have kept mostly to conventional interpretations as this is what most readers are familiar with. The Tree of Life in any form is a life-long study. It is the ultimate *mis en abyme* and is inclusive of all.

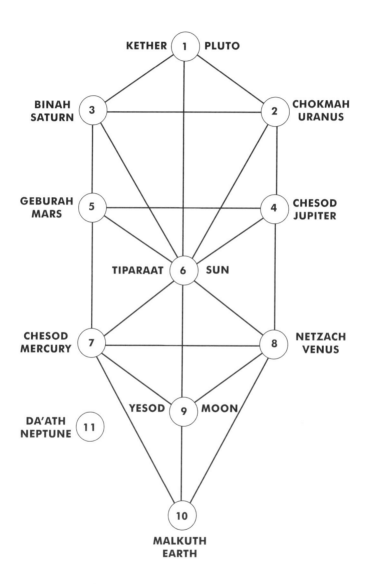

THE CABALISTIC TREE OF LIFE
Each sepiroth is designated by a number (also used in numerology),
the Hebrew letter used to describe it, and the planet which is
assigned as the primary influence of that sepiroth. Other
texts should be consulted for a more in-depth study.

APPENDIX B — THE BOOK OF THE LAW

The Book of the Law contains three chapters, each of which was allegedly written down in one hour, beginning at noon, on April 8, 9 and 10 in Cairo, Egypt in the year 1904. Crowley claimed that the author was an entity named Aiwass. Crowley, who never claimed to fully understand the book and stated he had spent his entire life trying to do so, wrote the following about it:

> "Certain very serious questions have arisen with regard to the method by which this Book was obtained. I do not refer to those doubts—real or pretended—which hostility engenders, for all such are dispelled by study of the text; no forger could have prepared so complex a set of numerical and literal puzzles..."

Crowley believed that *The Book of the Law* proclaimed the arrival of a new stage in the spiritual evolution of humanity, to be known as the "Æon of Horus." Unbeknownst to Crowley, the book actually demonstrates and predicts the characteristics of DNA long before it was ever understood in academic circles. It also directs our attention to the ancestry of the human race coming from the planet Mars. The book itself was transmitted and written during the zodiacal period of Aries which is ruled by Mars. Aries is a homonym for *Ares*, the Greek name for the god of war that the Romans called Mars.

This identification with the planet Mars should not be underestimated. Cairo, where the book was written, is derived from the Egyptian word for Mars which is *Al Kahira*. The archetype of Mars (Geburah in the Tree of Life) also has everything to do with the more horrific aspects of *The Book of the Law*, and it is these which sometimes prompt people to identify it with satanism or the like. The horror I am alluding to has to do with the mundane aspects or outer shell of the book which sometimes emphasizes the indiscriminate and rapacious forces of evolution. It is important to take stock of the fact that the evolutionary processes of nature are indiscriminate and sometimes down-right ruthless and cruel, at least from the perspective of our ordinary human mores. While it is humane to care for the feeble, aged and handicapped, it is a luxury when it comes down to issues of raw survival. The story of evolution is most definitely not a nice story of how those organisms who can't quite adapt are patted on the back and made to feel good about themselves. This strife or severity which occurs in the normal processes of life is designated as Geburah by the Hebrews. Out of this strife, life reinvents itself and adapts to the changing environment. Fortunately or unfortunately, it the hallmark of evolution, and this also includes the aspects of the mysterious radical or mutant gene. Evolution is the key to *The Book of the Law*.

When it is properly decoded, *The Book of the Law* reveals that The Key to It All is centered around the eleven lettered *Abrahadabra* which refers to the magical manifestation of life in the "Shape of a Beast." The fact that *Abrahadabra* has eleven letters is not a coincidence. Crowley named his system of magic as *magick* because the letter *k* is the eleventh letter of the alphabet. Taken a step further, this decoding explicitly reveals that eleven specifically refers to 5+6 which symbolizes the 5:6 magical or mystical ratio of the buildings blocks of life. This is a very important ratio and you will soon understand why it is considered magical or mystical. In biochemistry, inorganic compounds are six-sided or hexagonal while organic compounds are five-sided or pentagonal. While this is an observable laboratory fact of life, there is a much more esoteric aspect to 5+6 and this has to do with the pentagram and hexagram. When you place a pentagram upside down and beneath a hexagram (Star of David), you then have the basic template for the Cabalistic Tree of Life. When this template is twisted, it then represents a Mobius strip which is the pattern of a strand of DNA. 11-11 therefore represents two strands of DNA. Just as importantly, 11-11 also represents 22 or the Major Arcana of the Tree of Life. It is equally important to state here, if it is not already obvious to you, that the Tree of Life is actually an analogous map of DNA.

Keep in mind that when Crowley transmitted this information, it was 1903 and the academic world had no clue as to what DNA even was. Mystery Schools and Cabalists had templates for the Tree of Life, but its connection to DNA was known only by a select few if at all. This, however, is not where the mystery of the key ends. Of further importance is that the Great Pyramid itself is also constructed with specific reference to the 5:6 ratio. The capstone is 1/56th the size of the Great Pyramid which is 1/56th the size of the Giza Plateau which is 1/56th the size of Africa which is 1/56th the size of the earth. Whoever built the Great Pyramid built it in a manner and in a location that reflects the building blocks of life as expressed in DNA.

Although it was the focal point of his life, Crowley admittedly never fully or properly understood *The Book of the Law*. The book itself stated that someone would come after him who would. While it was no secret that the book was written in a code, no one could ever figure out the code. It puzzled occultists for over a century and no one was more puzzled than Crowley himself. Crowley was a virtual switchboard for different entities that interacted through him. You might say that lights were going on and off around him all the time, but he was overshadowed by a much greater force than he himself could understand.

The Montauk Pulse

If you would like to receive updates on the continued adventures of Radu Cinamar and Peter Moon, subscribe to the *Montauk Pulse* newsletter which will also features updates on Dr. David Anderson and other key developments, including the Montauk Project itself. The *Montauk Pulse* has remained in print and has been issued quarterly since 1993. The Pulse directly contributes to the efforts of the authors in writing more books and chronicling the effort to understand time and all of its components. Past support has been crucial to what has developed thus far. You will also read data that does not appear in the books. To subscribe, send $20.00 to Sky Books, PO Box 769, Westbury, NY 11590. If order is from outside the U.S., please add $12.00 for shipping. You can also subscribe via PayPal to skybooks@yahoo.com or visiting *www.skybooksusa.com.*

Transylvanian Wisdom School

If you would like to travel to Transylvania yourself and pursue some of the mysteries of Agartha, the Solomonari and explore some of the potentialities discussed in this book, Tatiana Maassen is the resident agent of a Wisdom School that is about knowledge beyond ordinary borders. "This knowledge has no laws. It does not have any laws because there are, in laws, borders that block freedom." *Note: Peter Moon is not affiliated with this school.*

LAMDA — The School of Wisdom
website: *http://www.enlamda.svit.ro/*
email: *shantideus@yahoo.com*

Cotiso Hotel in Transylvania

If you are traveling to Sarmizegetusa, Peter Moon recommends the Pensiunea "COTISO" which features modern accommodations including wireless internet. They serve excellent food and their hospitality is very friendly.

Pensiunea Cotiso
Located in Costeşti, Hunedoara in the Orăştie Mountains
website: *http://www.pensiuneacotiso.net*
email: *pensiuneacotiso@yahoo.com*
phone: 0722 919 886, 0753 511 527, 0254 246 676

If you are an English speaker, ask for Cristina or Alex

SkyBooks   ORDER FORM

We wait for ALL checks to clear before shipping. This includes Priority Mail orders. If you want to speed delivery time, please send a U.S. Money Order or use MasterCard or Visa. Those orders will be shipped right away. Complete this order form and send with payment or credit card information to: Sky Books, Box 769, Westbury, New York 11590-0104

Name	
Address	
City	
State / Country	Zip
Daytime Phone (In case we have a question) ( )	

☐ This is my first order ☐ I have ordered before ☐ This is a new address

Method of Payment: ☐ Visa ☐ MasterCard ☐ Money Order ☐ Check

\#   —   —   —

Expiration Date   Signature

TITLE	QTY	PRICE
The Montauk Pulse (1 year - no shipping US orders)...$20.00		
Transylvanian Sunrise (book 1)....................................$22.00		
Transylvanian Moonrise (book 2)..................................$22.00		
Mystery of Egypt — The First Tunnel (book 3)............$22.00		
Secret Parchment (book 4)...$22.00		
The White Bat (book 5)..$22.00		
The Montauk Project: Experiments in Time..................$15.95		
Note: There is no additonal shipping for the Montauk Pulse if you are in the United States. Subtotal		
For delivery in NY add 8.625% tax		
U.S. Shipping: $5.00 for 1st book plus $1.00 for 2nd, etc.		
Foreign shipping: $20 for 3 books		
Total		

Thank you for your order. We appreciate your business.